BALLET
AND DANCE

Linda Doeser

St. Martin's Press   New York

**Library of Congress Cataloging in
Publication Data**

Doeser, Linda.
    Ballet and dance.

    1. Ballet. 1. Title.
GV1787.D63   792.8'2   77–253
ISBN 0–312–06599–X

FOREWORD

A ballet company is a complex, organic unit and every member, from the youngest dancer in the corps de ballet to the most major international star, makes a personal and unique contribution to its success. *Ballet and Dance* describes the world's leading classical ballet and contemporary dance companies – choreographers, dancers, guest artists, repertoire, training and touring activities, past developments and future plans – and shows how these different elements and individuals intermingle to give each company its own distinctive quality.

A wide range of styles is included, as diverse as the Royal Danish Ballet and the Martha Graham Dance Company. Ballet spans the world from Canada to Israel, from Britain to Japan. Each company's work is illustrated; there are superb action photographs of the current repertoires and some fascinating glimpses into the formative past.

Ballet and Dance offers new insight into the world of dance companies themselves. It is a guide which any enthusiast will find indispensable.

CONTENTS

INTRODUCTION

It would be impossible for any two people to agree which dance companies rank as the most important in the world and so, inevitably, there will be inclusions and omissions in the following pages which will surprise and, perhaps, annoy. Clearly, some companies are so internationally famous that no-one could doubt their entitlement to the description 'major'. In the world of mainstream, classical ballet this category includes the New York City Ballet, American Ballet Theatre, the Royal Ballet, London, the Royal Danish Ballet, the Bolshoi Ballet and the Kirov Ballet. Equally, contemporary dance companies of similar stature include the Martha Graham Dance Company, the Twyla Tharp Dance Foundation, the Ballet Rambert, the Nederlands Dans Theater and Alvin Ailey City Center Dance Theater.

Beneath these in the hierarchy are companies which are generally agreed to be of an exceptionally high standard and which have exercised considerable influence on the development of dance, through the creativity of their choreography and the power of their performances. Relatively speaking, there are a considerable number of such companies, including the Stuttgart Ballet, the San Francisco Ballet, the Dance Theatre of Harlem, the London Festival Ballet, the National Ballet of Canada, the Louis Falco Dance Company, City Center Joffrey Ballet, Merce Cunningham and Dance Company and the Paul Taylor Dance Company.

Some companies are included because of the important role they have undertaken in the field of education, particularly with young people. Yet others provide an invaluable service to their art by constant travelling, frequently to towns and cities which rarely have an opportunity to see the bigger and more famous companies. Often these two functions are combined and here they are represented by such groups as Scapino Ballet.

There are also those companies which have not profoundly affected the direction of contemporary ballet and dance and which do not play a special part in informing and educating the public. This most controversial group includes many young companies which seem to promise a bright and exciting future, such as the Eliot Feld Ballet, the Irish Ballet and the Gothenburg Ballet. Furthermore, there are the pioneering companies which have established themselves in parts of the world not usually associated with either classical or contemporary ballet. Some have been in existence for a surprisingly long time, while others are much more recently established. Among these are the Ballet Folklorico de Mexico, the Tokyo Ballet and the Bat-Dor Dance Company of Israel. The opposite situation exists too, and some companies are included which are no longer major influences, although still highly professional, but which led the world of dance in the past, in some important way, towards the developments now taking place.

Finally, there are personal favourites. This is by far the smallest group, but, very occasionally, a private admiration and liking tipped the balance in favour of inclusion.

To explain omissions is a less straightforward task and serves little purpose. However, generally, companies which do not regularly perform abroad have not been included. This explains why some East European and Latin American companies are not mentioned.

It is not the aim of this book to trace the development of ballet throughout history and across the world if this were, in fact, possible. Nor is it intended to provide a documented history of the individual companies and biographies of the main figures associated with them. Rather, the intention is to describe the special qualities which make each company unique and to focus on its present activity. To do this, it is, of course, necessary to look at the influences and developments of the past which have led, by chance or design, to the present. Sometimes the direction in which a company has evolved is entirely due to the creative power of one individual. More often, it is the sum of many, varied personalities and the free interchange of dancers, choreographers, teachers, directors and, above all, ideas, which has led to a rich and heterogeneous dance heritage.

Dance is, perhaps, the most transitory of all the arts. Television and films can only record one particular performance and not even these can capture every shade and nuance. Still less can photographs and the written word adequately convey the quality and feel of a ballet. Neither, of course, are all the accounts which follow first-hand. Some are personal recollections, such as Galina Ulanova's interpretation of the title role in the Bolshoi Ballet's production of *Giselle*, Lucette Aldous' vibrant Kitri in the Ballet Rambert's *Don Quixote* and John Cranko's individual approach to *Swan Lake* for the Stuttgart Ballet. For the première of *The Sleeping Beauty* or *La Sylphide* and accounts of Maria Taglioni or Fanny Elssler, it was obviously necessary to rely on contemporary documents and newspapers.

These limitations accepted, a wide and representative selection of the world's major works and dancers are presented in the fields both of classical ballet and contemporary dance.

Kenneth MacMillan's Song of the Earth *is one of the most exciting items of the British Royal Ballet's contemporary repertoire.*

BEGINNINGS

Ballet has a long and varied history, dating back to the courts of Renaissance Italy, and beginning the process of formalization during the reign of Louis XIV of France. However, the birth of modern ballet can be dated far more accurately and is attributable to Serge Diaghilev.

He was born into a noble family at Perm in Russia, in 1872. In 1890 he went to study law at St Petersburg, where he quickly became involved in the cultural life of the capital. He had hoped to become a composer but was advised against it by Nicholas Rimsky-Korsakov. However, he remained part of a group of young musicians and painters, with whom he founded an arts magazine called *Mir Isskoustva*.

In 1889, he was appointed to an official post by Prince Volkonsky, Director of the Imperial Theatres. This involved editing the annual publication of the theatres and later led to the responsibility for the supervision of an opera. This proved highly successful and as a result he was entrusted with the supervision of the revival of the ballet *Sylvia*. Diaghilev's ultimate ambition was to become Director of the Imperial Theatres, but, in spite of a promising start to his career, his independence created enemies and, in 1901, he was compelled to resign.

Between 1904, when *Mir Isskoustva* ceased publication, and 1908, he organized a number of art exhibitions in St Petersburg and Paris. In 1908, he staged a production of *Boris Godounoff* at the Paris Opera and, as a result, he was commissioned to produce a season of Russian ballet at the Théâtre Châtelet, the following year.

For this project he assembled dancers from the Imperial Theatres. They included Adolph Bolm, Michel Fokine, Vera Karalli, Tamara Karsavina, Mikhail Mordkin, Anna Pavlova and Ida Rubinstein. The immensely successful repertoire consisted of four ballets by Michel Fokine, *Cléopâtre*, *Le Pavillon d'Armide*, *Les Sylphides* and *The Polovetsian Dances from Prince Igor*, also *Le Festin* and the opera, *Ivan the Terrible*.

The triumph of this season convinced Diaghilev that he should concentrate on ballet and the next year he returned to Paris and presented his company at the opera house. Three new works were added to the repertoire, *Shéhérazade*, *The Firebird* and *Giselle*, and Yekaterina Geltser made guest appearances.

The following year, he decided to form a permanent company, possibly prompted by Vaslav Nijinsky's resignation from the Imperial Theatres, after a quarrel with the management. Previously only summer seasons could be given because Diaghilev was dependent on the Imperial Theatres granting leave of absence to the dancers. In 1911, the Ballets Russes visited Rome, Monte Carlo, Paris and London twice. The repertoire included *Aurora and the Prince*, *Le Dieu Bleu*, *Le Spectre de la Rose*, *Narcisse*, *Petrouchka* and an abbreviated version of *Swan Lake*.

The phenomenal impact of the company was partly due to the superb choreography of Michel Fokine whose originality and vision staggered audiences quite unused to such innovation and imagination. The second factor was the extraordinary talent of Vaslav Nijinsky, the company's premier danseur. In 1912, he made his debut as a choreographer with *L'Après Midi d'un Faune*, more remarkable for the introduction of the element of sexuality into ballet, than for its creative force. The Ballets Russes presented seasons in Paris, London, Berlin, Venice and Budapest. Two new ballets by Michel Fokine were added to the repertoire, *Daphnis and Chloë* and *Thamar*. However, after this season, Michel Fokine returned to St Petersburg and in 1913, the Ballets Russes was without any new works by him for the first time.

Le Spectre de la Rose *was one of the most successful ballets of the early seasons of Diaghilev's touring company. It was created by Michel Fokine to music by Weber and the parts of the girl and the spectre remain permanently associated with their creators, the lovely Tamara Karsavina and the legendary Vaslav Nijinsky, photographed here in 1911.*

Artists of Diaghilev's Ballets Russes profoundly affected developments in ballet throughout Europe. Here Leonide Massine and Alexandra Danilova appear in Pas d'Acier *at His Majesty's Threatre, London in 1927.*

That season did bring the première of Nijinsky's controversial ballet *Le Sacre du Printemps* to an equally controversial score by Igor Stravinsky. It was booed throughout the première and the company performed it only six times in all. After visits to Monte Carlo, Paris and London, the Ballets Russes embarked on a tour of South America. Diaghilev had a phobia about the sea and so he did not accompany it. While on tour Nijinsky married a dancer from the corps de ballet whom he had met the previous year. As soon as the news reached Diaghilev, he dismissed him and the close association between the two men was never fully re-formed. Moreover his career as a dancer was virtually ended as a result of this episode.

Diaghilev returned to Russia to search for a replacement for Nijinsky and eventually settled on the young student, Leonide Massine. Michel Fokine also returned to the company for the 1914 season and created three new ballets, *Le Coq d'Or*, which was, in fact, a mixture of opera and ballet, *The Legend of Joseph*, in which Leonide Massine made his debut in the title role, and *Papillons*.

In 1914, Europe was plunged into war. Michel Fokine returned again to Russia and Diaghilev went first to Venice and then to Switzerland. In 1915, the company was invited to appear at the Metropolitan Opera House in New York. Under great difficulties, and with the assistance of Adolph Bolm, Diaghilev assembled the company for the American tour. After many problems he managed to secure the release of Vaslav Nijinsky who, as a Russian citizen, had been interned in Austro-Hungary. This was not achieved until the first season in New York was finished but he was able to join the company when it returned there for a second visit. Also during this eventful year, Leonide Massine's first ballet, *The Midnight Sun*, was presented.

The following years brought a succession of new works and new dancers, many of whom fled from Russia after the revolution. Additions to the repertoire included Nijinsky's *Til Eulenspiegel* in 1916, Massine's *Good Humoured Ladies* and *Parade* in 1917, his *La Boutique Fantasque* and *The Three-Cornered Hat* in 1919, a new version of *Le Sacre du Printemps* in 1920 and Nijinsky's *Le Renard* in 1922. The company visited Italy, Spain, France, South America, London and Paris several times and Belgium.

In 1923, Diaghilev signed a contract with the Principality of Monaco, making the company the official ballet of the Monte Carlo Opera. The name was changed to Les Ballets Russes de Monte Carlo. The steady flow of new and innovative ballets continued with Nijinska's *Les Noces* in 1923, *Les Biches* and *Le Train Bleu* in 1924, Massine's *Les Matelots* and Balanchine's *Barabau* and *La Pastorale* in 1925, Balanchine's *Jack-in-the-Box* in 1926, his *La Chatte* and Massine's *Pas d'Acier* in 1927, Massine's *Les Facheux* and Balanchine's *Apollon Musagète* in 1928 and his *Prodigal Son* in 1929. The association with Monte Carlo did not reduce the touring schedule and the company visited Turin, Milan, Germany, Austria, Budapest, Prague, Geneva, Brussels, Paris and London, many of them several times. Among the dancers who joined the Ballets Russes were Olga Spessivtzeva, Ninette de Valois, Anton Dolin, Serge Lifar, Alexandra Danilova, Alicia Markova and George Balanchine.

So phenomenal was the impact of the Ballets Russes that it was unthinkable to the public that any non-Russian dancer could be seriously considered. Consequently, it became common practice for the British dancers in the company to change their names to something which sounded un-English. In 1913, Hilda Munnings was transformed into Lydia Sokolova and she was followed by Sydney Francis Patrick Chippendall Healey-Kay (Anton Dolin), Lilian Alicia Marks (Alicia Markova) and Edris Stannus (Ninette de Valois). The great exception to this, was George Balanchine whose real name, Georgi Melitonovitch Balanchivadze, was so difficult for non-Russian speakers to

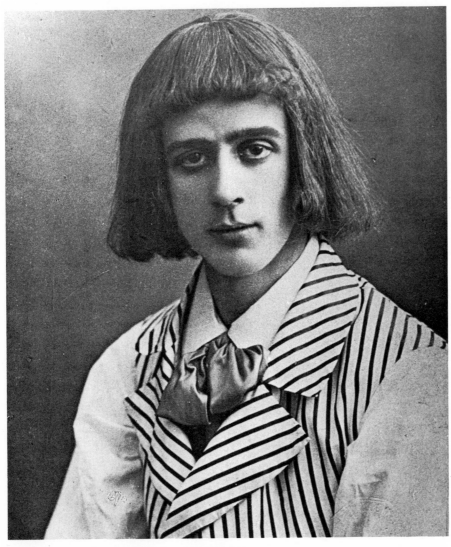

Above left *Michel Fokine was one of the major creative forces in Diaghilev's Ballets Russes. He was also closely associated with Anna Pavlova while she still danced in Imperial Russia and he remained there for a short while after the 1917 revolution. He later settled in the United States. He is pictured here in* Javotte, *with choreography by Pavel Gerdt, in 1906.*

Above *The influence of the Ballets Russes was very important on the development of Britain's Royal Ballet. Founder and, for many years, Artistic Director, Ninette de Valois is seen here on the left, with Henrietta Maicherska in* Narcisse.

pronounce and remember, he simplified it.

On August 19, 1929, Serge Diaghilev died in Venice. The company had given its last performance in London the previous July. After his death, various attempts were made to re-form the company – the René Blum and Colonel de Basil Ballets Russes de Monte Carlo, which later changed its name to the singular, Ballet Russe, and a rival Ballet Russe de Monte Carlo, set up when de Basil and Massine quarrelled in 1937. De Basil's company remained in existence under the title of the Original Ballet Russe until 1947 and many of the dancers were caught up in the 'ballet war', moving backwards and forwards between the two companies. In spite of the silliness and the bitter feelings brought about by this absurd situation, many worthwhile works were created and magnificent performances by some of the world's greatest dancers were given in places as far apart, perhaps fortunately, as New York and Australia.

However, none of this detracts from the achievements of the truly original Ballets Russes and its remarkable founder and guiding spirit, Serge Diaghilev. He was a man of extraordinary perception and possessed a fine intelligence which enabled him to recognize the major artistic talents of his time. His attractive personality and creative power equipped him to blend the talents of these dancers, choreographers, composers and painters into a harmonious unity. Diaghilev's Ballets Russes was the single most important factor in the development of twentieth century dance.

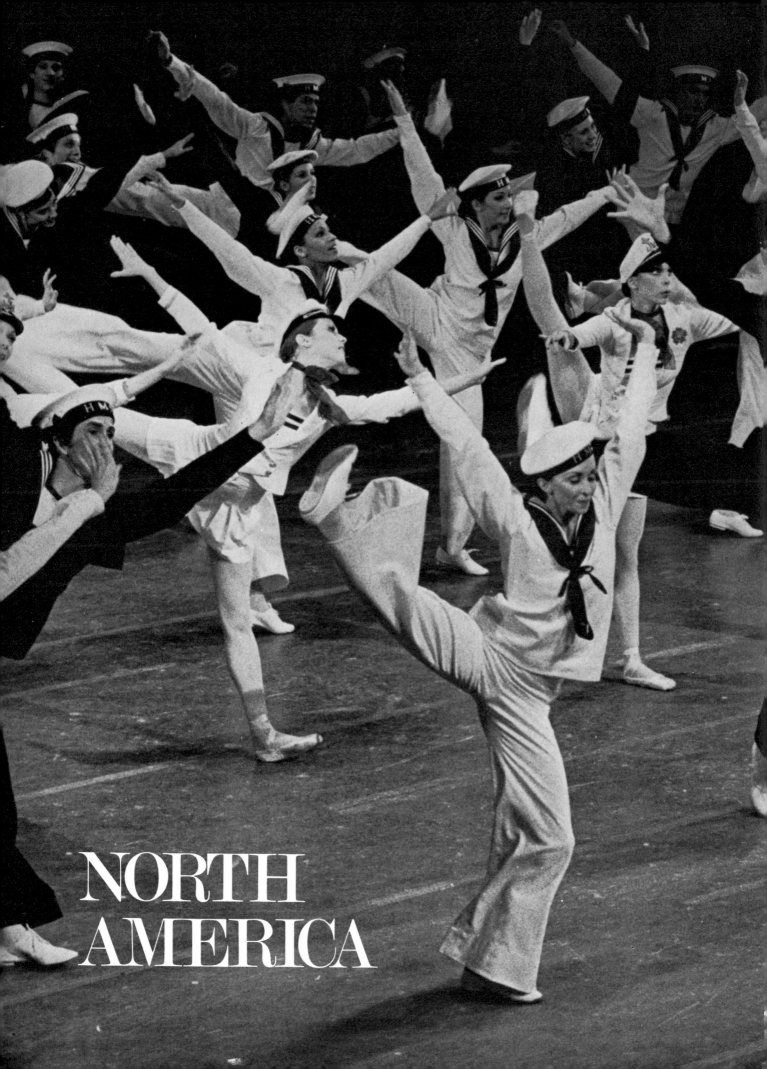

NORTH
AMERICA

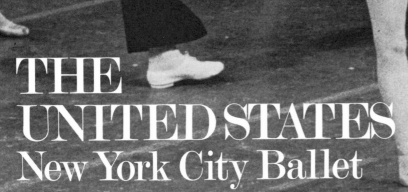

THE UNITED STATES
New York City Ballet

Not only is the New York City Ballet one of the foremost companies in the United States, but it is one of the most important in the world. The company owes its existence to the vision of Lincoln Kirstein and the genius of George Balanchine, whose collaboration has continued, with a number of interruptions, since 1933.

Never part of the European or Russian ballet traditions, the people of the United States, however, have a long history of receptiveness to dance activity. The introduction of ballet to the United States dates back to colonial days when a British dancer, Henry Holt, appeared in Charleston in 1735. His visit started a long series of tours of foreign artists who, to begin with, came mainly from the Paris Opera, the dance centre of Europe in the eighteenth and early nineteenth centuries. The great romantic ballets were introduced to the

Kay Mazzo, Jacques d'Amboise and Suzanne Farrell lead the New York City Ballet in George Balanchine's exuberant Union Jack. Created as part of the bicentennial celebrations in the United States, the ballet was premièred in May 1976.

United States and Fanny Elssler made a triumphant and extended tour from 1840 to 1842. Such visits inspired young Americans but they were severely limited by the lack of adequate schools and teachers.

It seemed as if this unfortunate situation might change with the opening of the Metropolitan Opera House in 1883. This, however, was not the case, as a school was not opened until 1909. Ballet did not feature in the repertoire in New York except as a minor part of the opera performances. In 1908, Adeline Genée, the Danish ballerina, visited New York and stimulated new interest in dance.

Her visit was soon followed by the triumphant appearance of Anna Pavlova and Mikhail Mordkin in 1910. Diaghilev's Ballets Russes presented *Petrouchka*, *Shéhérazade*, *Les Sylphides* and *L'Après-Midi d'un Faune* in 1916 to tremendous public acclaim. Anna Pavlova continued to make regular visits until 1925. During this period the Metropolitan Opera itself presented only four ballets.

Attempts were made to set up companies – Michel Fokine gave a few recitals and Adolphe Bolm founded the Ballet Intime in the late 1920s. Otherwise, there were very few professional performances until the visit of the Ballet Russe de Monte Carlo in 1933.

This, then, was the background to Lincoln Kirstein's vision of a truly American ballet company presenting the combined talents of the best American painters, musicians, poets, dancers and choreographers. To have such a dream, in the circumstances, is hardly surprising, but to have the drive and practicality to translate it into reality was an act of tremendous courage and determination. In spite of the vicissitudes of fortune over the years, Lincoln Kirstein has always been immensely practical in the way he tackled his plan, displaying that peculiarly American quality of combined far-sighted vision and a down-to-earth sense of reality.

In 1933, he met George Balanchine in Paris where he had formed his own company, working with artists such as Kurt Weill, Bertolt Brecht, Darius Milhaud and Henri Sauget. Lincoln Kirstein invited him to the United States and their long collaboration began. The first project was to open a ballet school intended to train professional dancers who would then provide the material for the future company. The School of American Ballet opened on January 1, 1934, and has since become one of the foremost schools in the United States.

The first performance in the United States, directed by Balanchine, was *Serenade* set to Tchaikovsky's *Serenade for Strings in C Major*. It was a workshop performance by the students of the School of American Ballet given in the open air and, inauspiciously, it rained. In 1935 Lincoln Kirstein and George Balanchine set up a touring company consisting of dancers from the school, calling it the American Ballet. During two weeks at the Adelphi Theatre, New York, seven works by George Balanchine were presented – *Alma Mater*, *Dreams*, *Reminiscences*, *Serenade*, *Transcendence*, *Mozartiana* and *Errante*. The following autumn the Metropolitan Opera invited the American. Ballet to become its permanent dance company with George Balanchine as Ballet Master.

There was, however, an almost immediate clash of artistic policy. Balanchine has always believed in the purity of dance and that nothing – story, costumes, scenery – should distract the attention from it. Moreover, although he always creates his works with the particular strengths and weaknesses of his principals in mind, he does not believe in virtuoso roles intended for international stars to show off their talents. Also, Balanchine is a phenomenally musical choreographer. In fact, when young he studied both ballet and music at St Petersburg and seriously contemplated a career as a composer. Consequently, his works are renowned for their musical abstraction and their subtle emotional approach. This, however, was not what the Metropolitan Opera wanted. Rather, it required the more traditional and spectacular works with which everyone – costume and scenery designers, musicians and the audience – was familiar. Only two pure dance programmes were presented between 1935 and 1938; a dance-drama version of Gluck's *Orfeo and Eurydice* and a programme of works by Stravinsky including a revival of *Apollon Musagète* and two new ballets, *Le Baiser de la Fée* and *Card Game*. Otherwise, ballets were performed as part of the evening's programmes combined with short operas.

Early in 1938, the Metropolitan Opera and the American Ballet separated on bad terms amidst considerable publicity. The American Ballet's financial situation was very serious. It had received a flat fee for its performances but had spent freely on guest artists. George Balanchine spent the next few years teaching at the School of American Ballet and working in theatre and films.

Dybbuk, later called Dybbuk Variations, *was created by Jerome Robbins to music by Leonard Bernstein. The immensely exciting combination of dance, drama and ritual is characteristic of the choreographer's work. A Dybbuk is a legendary spirit which takes over a living body and the ballet tells the story of a young man's tragic death after a foolhardy encounter with black magic and a ritual exorcism.*

In the spring of 1941, Nelson Rockefeller, head of the United States Offices for Co-ordination of Commercial and Cultural Relations between the American Republics, requested Lincoln Kirstein to assemble a ballet company for a goodwill tour of Latin America. With the assistance of George Balanchine, Lincoln Kirstein organized a company known as the American Ballet Caravan, with dancers and repertoire from the American Ballet and Ballet Caravan, an earlier enterprise of Lincoln Kirstein's. During this tour, which lasted from June to October, two, new, major works by George Balanchine were performed – *Concerto Barocco* and *Ballet Imperial*. The repertoire also included William Dollar's *Juke Box*, Lew Christensen's and José Fernandez' *Pastorela*, and Antony Tudor's *Time Table*. After the tour, the company disbanded.

During World War II, Lincoln Kirstein served in the army and from 1944 to 1946, George Balanchine was Artistic Director of the Ballet Russe de Monte Carlo. During this time he created *Raymonda Variations* and *La Sonnambula*, sometimes known as *Night Shadow*.

Once again, in 1946, Lincoln Kirstein and George Balanchine re-formed their remarkable partnership to create the company Ballet Society. This was a non-profit making society which gave performances to members only. George Balanchine created *Four Temperaments* (1946), *Renard* (1947) and *Orpheus* (1948) for Ballet Society. The repertoire also included the *Spellbound Child*, *Divertimento*, *Zodiac*, John Taras's *The Minotaur* and Merce Cunningham's *The Seasons*, as well as other works by George Balanchine.

On October 11, 1948, the company gave a performance, which included *Orpheus*, *Serenade* and *Symphony in C*, at the New York City Center for Music and Drama. Morton Baum, chairman of the City Center Finance Committee was so impressed by that evening, that he began negotiations which eventually resulted in an invitation to the company to join the City Center Municipal Complex and become the New York City Ballet. At that time, the New York City Drama and New York City Opera were also a part of the complex. Lincoln Kirstein had finally realized the dream he had worked for during the previous 14 years. Characteristically, he replaced one aim with another, promising Morton Baum that, in three years, the New York City Ballet would be the finest in the United States.

For nearly 30 years the New York City Ballet has been dominated by the unassuming figure of George Balanchine, considered a genius, not just by his own considerable following, nor just by the fans of the company, but by dance critics, teachers, the principals of the company and fellow artists like Igor Stravinsky. Igor Stravinsky and George Balanchine, both brilliant in their own areas of creativity, collaborated to produce some of the finest ballets of the twentieth century. The two men had much in common, particularly their quality of artistic detachment, seeing themselves as craftsmen rather than creators. They shared a native tradition and developed a very close relationship. George Balanchine found Stravinsky's music satisfying – a word he chose himself in preference to inspiring. Igor Stravinsky was impressed by Balanchine's remarkable musicality and his ability to translate the rhythm, melody, harmony and the intangible qualities of a musical score into the visual patterns of dance. The first ballet Balanchine created to music by Stravinsky was *Le Chant du Rossignol* in 1925. The impressive list which followed includes, *Apollon Musagète* (1928), *Le Baiser de la Fée* (1937), *Card Game* (1937), *Balustrade* (1941), *Danses Concertantes* (1944), *Elegie* (1945) *Renard* (1947), *Orpheus* (1947), *The Firebird* (1949), *Agon* (1957), *Monumentum Pro Gesualdo* (1960), *Jazz Concert: Ragtime* (1960), *Noah and the Flood* (1961), *Movements for Piano and Orchestra* (1963), *Variations* (1966) and *Requiem Canticles* (1968). In June 1972 a week-long festival was held at

Peter Martins and Suzanne Farrell are exceptionally lively and charming dancers, well-suited to George Balanchine's one-act ballet Allegro Brillante. The choreography demands masterly control and superb technique by its alternation between gentle lyricism and virtuoso brilliance. It has been a challenging ballet for many of the company's leading dancers, including Maria Tallchief for whom it was originally created in 1956. The vivid and forceful music is the only movement of Tchaikovsky's unfinished Third Piano Concerto.

the New York State Theater to celebrate what would have been Stravinsky's ninetieth birthday had he not died in April 1971. For the festival, Balanchine specially created nine works – *Sonata*, *Choral Variations on Bach's 'von Himmel Hoch'*, a revision of *Danses Concertantes*, *Divertimento from Le Baiser de la Fée*, *Duo Concertant*, *Pulcinella* (in conjunction with Jerome Robbins) *Scherzo à la Russe*, *Symphony in Three Movements* and *Stravinsky Violin Concerto*. In all, some 30 works were performed at the festival, including 14 by Balanchine.

Although the spirit of Balanchine has quietly dominated the New York City Ballet since its inception, the works of other notable and international choreographers have featured in the repertoire. Some of these are Sir Frederick Ashton, Todd Bolender, John Butler, John Clifford, Merce Cunningham, Lorca Massine, Richard Tanner, John Taras and Jerome Robbins.

These last two are George Balanchine's fellow Ballet Masters at the New York City Ballet. John Taras trained at the American Ballet School. After a tour with Catherine Littlefield's Philadelphia Ballet in 1939, he joined American Ballet Caravan for the Latin American tour. From 1940 to 1945 he danced with Ballet Theatre, which later became American Ballet Theatre. His wide dance and choreographic experience includes seasons with the Markova-Dolin Company, De Basil's Ballet Russe, Ballet Society, the San Francisco Ballet, the Metropolitan Ballet and the Grand Ballet du Marquis de Cuevas.

In 1960, he joined the New York City Ballet and has remained ever since, with the exception of two brief absences – once as Ballet Master for the Paris Opera Ballet and once as Artistic Director for the Ballet of the German Berlin Opera. Generally, his ballets are themeless, with a subtle, scarcely defined undercurrent of emotion. Among the works he has created for the New York City Ballet are *Ebony Concerto*, a re-staging of *Piège de Lumière*, originally created for the Grand Ballet du Marquis de Cuevas in 1952, *Concerto for Piano and Winds*, *The Song of the Nightingale* and *Daphnis and Chloë*. Probably his best known and most popular work is *Design for Strings*, and this has featured in the repertoires of several major European and American companies such as the London Festival Ballet, the Royal Danish Ballet, the Stuttgart Ballet and the Dance Theatre of Harlem.

Besides his work with the New York City Ballet, John Taras has also staged a number of George Balanchine's ballets for other companies – *Apollon Musagète* for the Dutch National Ballet, the Royal Ballet in London and the Vienna State Opera Ballet; *Prodigal Son* for the Dutch National Ballet, and the Vienna State Opera. *La Sonnambula* for the London Festival Ballet and the Royal Danish Ballet.

Jerome Robbins joined the New York City Ballet in 1950. He created a number of works for the company, including *The Cage, Fanfare, The Concert* and the famous *Afternoon of a Faun*. After leaving the company he became involved in a large number of theatrical activities including the organization of his own company, Ballets: USA, in 1958, for which he created *New York Export: Opus Jazz, Moves* and *Events*. He also worked as choreographer and director on many musical films and on Broadway. Among these were *On the Town, The King and I, Peter Pan, West Side Story, Gypsy* and *Fiddler on the Roof*. He rejoined the New York City Ballet in 1969, and has created numerous works for the company, – *Circus Polka, Scherzo Fantastique, In G Major, Ma Mère L'Oye* (*Fairy Tales for Dancers*) and *The Goldberg Variations*. Jerome Robbins has a very specific theatrical approach. His works are characterized by an almost ritualistic quality which extends from the work and the roles to the setting, music and dancers themselves. Nowhere can this be more clearly seen than in *Dances at a Gathering* which he created for the Royal Ballet, London, in 1970. Various pairs of dancers hint at themes and

Right above Jean-Pierre Bonnefous and Patricia McBride dance the roles of the traditional London figures of the Pearly King and Queen in Union Jack. *Patricia McBride is especially renowned for her vibrance and versatility and this is superbly matched by the supple grace and polished technique of her regular partner, the former Paris Opera étoile, Jean-Pierre Bonnefous, whom she married in 1973.*

Right below Jewels *is a characteristically abstract ballet by George Balanchine. He uses the music of three different composers — Gabriel Fauré, Igor Stravinsky and Peter Tchaikovsky — to capture the essential qualities of three different kinds of precious stones. His special view of the delicate shimmer of emeralds, the flamboyant brilliance of rubies and the elegant clarity of diamonds produces a unique visual opulence which has delighted audiences since the ballet's première in 1967. Pictured here are Anthony Blum and Violette Verdy, who, in 1978, will take over the Artistic Direction of the Paris Opera Ballet.*

A Midsummer Night's Dream is perhaps a little unusual for George Balanchine in that his works tend not to tell stories. Inspired both by Shakespeare's play and Felix Mendelssohn's music, this two-act ballet evokes a magical atmosphere. The first act is a dance drama and the second is a magnificent divertissement — a dance response to the 'play within a play'. Lavish costumes and sets and a superb blending of story and pure dance have made this a perennial favourite on the stage and a successful film.

relationships moving through a variety of emotions, all bound together by a scarcely articulated relationship with the earth. The very different, bold and bright *Goldberg Variations* has the same quality of ritual with the framing of the work by the eighteenth century duet at the beginning and end and the significant use of colours, costume and lighting. In this way Jerome Robbins acts as a magnificent foil to George Balanchine's impersonal and athletic approach so that the items of repertoire harmonize and contrast, demanding extremes of technique, dramatic ability and interpretation from the dancers.

The company has an arduous performing schedule each year. Two seasons are given at the company's New York home, the State Theater in Lincoln Center for the Performing Arts. In July it appears at the Performing Arts Center, Saratoga Springs and in August, at Wolftrap Farm near Washington, Ravinia near Chicago and, in alternating years, at Cleveland or Los Angeles. In addition, the company travels abroad and has visited most European countries and Australia and has made two visits to the USSR. New works are constantly added to the repertoire, involving extra study and rehearsing, particularly as George Balanchine tends not to begin his choreography until about three weeks before the date set for the première, and works exclusively with the dancers.

Many of the principals, including Jacques d'Amboise and Allegra Kent, have appeared as guest artists with leading European companies, and Edward Villella was the first American male dancer to appear with the Royal Danish Ballet. In 1978, Violette Verdy will return to her native country to become Artistic Director of the Paris Opera Ballet. Members of the company have also appeared on television and in films as well as giving performances at the White House before Presidents Kennedy, Johnson, Nixon and Ford as well as the Shah of Iran. Members of the company have received a number of individual awards and the French Government proclaimed George Balanchine a member of the Legion of Honour with the rank of Officer in 1975, in addition to the many other honours he has received.

Within forty years from its tentative inception, the New York City Ballet has become the realization of Lincoln Kirstein's ambitious dream and ranks with perhaps four or five other companies as the world leaders of ballet in the twentieth century and a major influence on the art.

The Company

Director:	Lincoln Kirstein	**Assistant Ballet**	
Ballet Masters:	George Balanchine	**Masters:**	Rosemary Dunleavy
	Jerome Robbins		Tom Abbott
	John Taras		David Richardson
Principal dancers:	Jacques d'Amboise	Sara Leland	Peter Schaufuss
	TV Karin von Aroldingen	Adam Luders	*TV* Helgi Tomasson
	Anthony Blum	*TV* Peter Martins	Violette Verdy
	Jean-Pierre Bonnefous	Kay Mazzo	(until 1978)
	TV Suzanne Farrell	*TV* Patricia McBride	Edward Villella
	Allegra Kent	Francisco Moncion	*TV Sean Lavery*

The Repertoire

X Afternoon of a Faun (Robbins)
Agon (Balanchine)
X Allegro Brillante (Balanchine)
A midsummer Night's Dream (Balanchine)
An Evening's Waltzes (Robbins)
Brahms-Schönberg Quartet (Balanchine)
Bugaku (Balanchine)

X Chaconne (Balanchine)
Chansons Madecasses (Robbins)
Concerto Barocco (Balanchine)
Coppélia (Balanchine)
Cortège Hongrois (Balanchine)
X Dances at a Gathering (Robbins)
Danse (d'Amboise)

20

Danses Concertantes (Balanchine)
Daphnis and Chloë (Taras)
Divertimento from Le Baiser de la Fée (Balanchine)
Divertimento Number 15 (Balanchine)
Donizetti Variations (Balanchine)
Duo Concertant (Balanchine)
Dybbuk Variations (Robbins)
Fanfare (Robbins)
Four Bagatelles (Robbins)
Four Temperaments (Balanchine)
Gaspard de la Nuit (Balanchine)
✗ *Harlequinade* (Balanchine)
In G Major (Robbins)
Irish Fantasy (d'Amboise)
Ivesiana (Balanchine)
✗ *Jewels* (Balanchine)
La Sonnambula (Balanchine)
La Source (Balanchine)
La Valse (Balanchine)
Le Tombeau de Couperin (Balanchine)
Liebeslieder Waltz (Balanchine)
Ma Mère L'Oye (*Fairy Tales for Dancers*)
(Robbins)
Meditation (Balanchine)
Monumentum Pro Gesualdo and Movements for Piano and Orchestra (Balanchine)
Orpheus (Balanchine)
✗ *Prodigal Son* (Balanchine)
Pulcinella (Balanchine/Robbins)
Rapsodie Espagnole (Balanchine)
Raymonda Variations (Balanchine)

Saltarelli (d'Amboise)
Scènes de Ballet (Taras)
Scherzo Fantastique (Robbins)
Scherzo à la Russe (Balanchine)
Scotch Symphony (Balanchine)
Serenade (Balanchine)
Sinfonietta (d'Amboise)
Sonatine (Balanchine)
Stars and Stripes (Balanchine)
Stravinsky Violin Concerto (Balanchine)
Square Dance (Balanchine)
Symphony in C (Balanchine)
Symphony in Three Movements (Balanchine)
✗ *Tarantella* (Balanchine)
Tchaikovsky Pas De Deux (Balanchine)
Tchaikovsky Piano Concerto No 2 (Balanchine)
Tchaikovsky Suite No 3 (Balanchine)
✗ *The Cage* (Robbins)
The Concert (Robbins)
The Firebird (Balanchine/Robbins)
The Goldberg Variations (Robbins)
✗ *The Nutcracker* (Balanchine)
The Steadfast Tin Soldier (Balanchine)
Tzigane (Balanchine)
Union Jack (Balanchine)
Valse Fantasie (Balanchine)
Variations Pour Une Porte et Une Soupir (Balanchine)
Watermill (Robbins)
Western Symphony (Balanchine)
Who cares? (Balanchine)

Touring   The company has toured extensively throughout Europe and visited Australia and the USSR.

American Ballet Theatre

It is ironic that a company which in its early days planned to be essentially American in character, should now be renowned as the leading international company in the United States, featuring stars from across the world. It was founded in the autumn of 1939 by Richard Pleasant and Lucia Chase and, although he left in 1941, she remains a Director still.

The nucleus of the company came from the Mordkin Ballet, which had been established by Mikhail Mordkin in 1937, as a performing outlet for his students. Richard Pleasant had been appointed general manager in 1938 and among the principal dancers were Patricia Bowman, Lucia Chase, Viola Essen, Dimitri Romanoff and Leon Varkas. By the summer of 1939 Lucia Chase and Richard Pleasant, feeling that the scope of the Mordkin Ballet was frustratingly limited, had formulated plans for a new company.

The company was called Ballet Theatre and Richard Pleasant was appointed Director. Its aim was to present a repertoire of the best classical ballets and to encourage young, talented choreographers to create new works. After considerable preparation the company launched its first season in 1940, presenting a remarkably varied and ambitious programme – Michel Fokine's *Les Sylphides* and *Carnaval*; Adolph Bolm's *Ballet Mécanique* and *Peter and the Wolf;* Mikhail Mordkin's *Voices of Spring*; Anton Dolin's *Quintet, Giselle* and *Swan Lake*; Antony Tudor's *Dark Elegies, Jardin Aux Lilas* and *Judgement of Paris*; Andrée Howard's *Lady into Fox* and *Death and the Maiden*; Agnes de Mille's *Black Ritual*; Eugene Loring's *The Great American Goof*; Jose Fernandez' *Goyescas*; Nijinska's *La Fille Mal Gardée* and Yurek Shabelevski's *Ode to Glory*. Many of the dancers were from the Mordkin Ballet and included Adolphe Bolm, Patricia Bowman, Lucia Chase, Karen Conrad, Anton Dolin, William Dollar, Viola Essen, Nora Kaye, Andrée Howard, Eugene Loring, Dimitri Romanoff and Antony Tudor. After a four week season in New York, the company visited other American cities and in November and December it acted as the official ballet company of the Chicago Opera.

Changes in organization took place in 1941. A new system of ranking was arranged, the dancers being grouped into only two classes – principals and the company. It is interesting to note that, among the 'company' of this time were Alicia Alonso, Nora Kaye and Jerome Robbins. The Ballet Theatre did not have a regisseur. Instead, the three resident choreographers acted as regisseur for each of the three divisions of the repertoire – Anton Dolin for the classical part, Eugene Loring for the American part and Antony Tudor for the new British part. In this year also, Richard Pleasant resigned as Director and there was general re-organization of the company's management. In addition, Alicia Markova and Irina Baronova were appointed ballerinas to the company and remained until 1942 and 1944 respectively. It was while

they were associated with Ballet Theatre that Alicia Markova and Anton Dolin organized the first International Dance Festival at Jacob's Pillow. The company spent most of the summer in 1941 living and working at Jacob's Pillow and appeared in many performances given there. The Festival has since become a major dance event and many distinguished international dancers and companies have appeared there.

Between 1941 and 1946 the Ballet Theatre functioned under the auspices of the impresario Sol Hurok. During this time the company visited Mexico City, toured the United States, and appeared at the Metropolitan Opera House. Dancers who joined the company or appeared as guest artists included Rosella Hightower, George Skibine, André Eglevsky, Tatiana Riabouchinska, Leonide Massine, Tamara Toumanova and David Lichine. A number of new works were created during this period. The most notable of these was Antony Tudor's *Pillar of Fire*, created in 1942, to Schönberg's *Verklärte Nacht*. This magnificently powerful and innovatory work was presented at the Metropolitan Opera House with Lucia Chase as the Eldest Sister, Annabella Lyon: Younger Sister, Antony Tudor: Friend, Hugh Laing: Young Man from the House Opposite and Nora Kaye as Hagar, a role which elevated her to the rank of ballerina, and which has been associated with her ever since.

Fokine re-staged *Petrouchka* and began work on *Helen of Troy* in 1942, but was unable to complete it before he died in New York on August 22. *Helen of Troy* was finally created by David Lichine. George Balanchine revived *Errante* and *Apollon Musagète* for Ballet Theatre in 1943 and Jerome Robbins created his first major work for the company, *Fancy Free*, in 1944. In addition to *Pillar of Fire*, Antony Tudor also created *Romeo and Juliet*, *Dim Lustre* and *Undertow*. Both *Pillar of Fire* and *Fancy Free* have featured in the company's repertoire since.

The contract with Sol Hurok was terminated early in 1946 and once again there were policy changes. Shortly before this, Lucia Chase and Oliver Smith became co-directors. Lucia Chase continued to dance leading roles in such works as *Petrouchka*, *Les Sylphides*, *Dark Elegies* and *Pillar of Fire* until 1960, although she undertook no new works. Generally, it was felt wise to return to the earlier aim of building up a company of a truly American character. It was also decided to draw on the strength of the company itself rather than import guest artists and stars from abroad.

In the summer, Ballet Theatre made a successful visit to Britain's Royal Opera House, Covent Garden. Whatever changes of administration and policy may have taken place, one aim of the company has remained consistent since its inception – the desire to present the best of classical and contemporary mainstream choreography. While Ballet Theatre was in London, Keith Lester's version of *Pas de Quatre* and Sir Frederick Ashton's *Les Patineurs* were added to the repertoire. The leading solosits on this visit were André Eglevsky, Nora Kaye and Alicia Alonso. Not long afterwards, Diana Adams, Melissa Hayden and Ruth Ann Koesun were appointed soloists and Antony Tudor became Artistic Administrator.

The visit to London was very successful but costly. The constant addition of new works, including George Balanchine's *Giselle* and Jerome Robbins *Facsimile* at the Broadway Theatre, in the autumn of that year, drained the company's finances. Fortunately, the strain on its resources was partially helped by the establishment of Ballet Theatre Foundation in 1947. Tax-exempt and non-profit making, it was intended to support Ballet Theatre, and is still carrying on its excellent work.

The company continued to stage new works – in 1947, George Balanchine's *Theme and Variations*, Antony Tudor's *Shadow of the Wind* and Agnes de Mille's *Fall River Legend*. The last of these provided Nora Kaye with another role, that of Lizzie Borden, which has remained permanently associated with her powerful performance. However, there was no autumn season that year and the company continued to suffer from the lack of a permanent home. Constant touring is not suited to a company of such a size which maintains a large and varied repertoire and regularly presents new works.

In 1950, Ballet Theatre made a tour of the United States in the early spring and then its first full European tour, sponsored by the State Department, at the end of the year. During this very successful four-month visit to Europe, the company was called the American National Ballet Theatre.

Few ballet companies have included so many famous names as American Ballet Theatre. Characteristically, it was determined to present not only the best works but the best dancers. The principal dancers on the European tour included the delightful Alicia Alonso, the wonderfully dramatic Nora Kaye, the versatile John Kriza, John Taras (now Ballet Master with the New York City Ballet with George Balanchine and Jerome Robbins), the lyrical Mary Ellen Moylan and the outstanding classical dancer Igor Youskevitch – an impressive list.

At the end of 1950, Ballet Theatre became the company of the Metropolitan Opera. It was not a successful association and lasted for only one season. At the end of the season, Diana Adams, Nora Kaye and Hugh Laing left the company to join the New York City Ballet. Antony Tudor also left the company to become Director of the Ballet Theatre and Metropolitan Opera Ballet School, where he remained when the Ballet Theatre withdrew from the project.

New guest artists appeared with Ballet Theatre in 1951 – Jean Babilée, Colette Marchand, Nathalie Philippart and Mia Slavenska. The flow of new works included the American premières of *Le Jeune Homme et la Mort*, *Les Demoiselles de la Nuit* and *L'Amour et son Amour* and *The Thief Who Loved a Ghost* by Herbert Ross, and Carmalita Maracci's *Circo de España*. In early summer, the company toured South America, followed by a season at the Metropolitan Opera and then a national tour.

The spate of new works decreased for quite a long time after this. The next few years marked a period of consolidation and extensive touring programmes. A second tour of Europe sponsored by the State Department took place from the beginning of May to the end of September in 1953. The next season was occupied in a major national tour and several television appearances. In 1955, Ballet Theatre celebrated its fifteenth birthday with a gala season at the Metropolitan Opera where many former stars returned to re-create the roles they had danced in original Ballet Theatre productions. Another tour of South America followed the festivities.

In 1956, the company established a workshop at the Phoenix Theatre in New York. This was created to give new and young choreographers a chance to experiment and present their works .The first of these workshops was moderately successful and the following year it certainly justified its existence with Kenneth MacMillan's *Journey* and Herbert Ross's *Paean*.

1957 also saw another European tour and a visit to the Middle East. During this tour, Erik Bruhn, the superb Danish danseur noble made the first of his many guest appearances with the company. After this, European tours followed and a visit to North Africa as well as a season at the Metropolitan Opera. However, in the late fifties, interest in ballet was at a low ebb and the financial problems which bedevil every company forced this one into temporary closure in 1959.

Fortunately, 1960 brought a revival of dance activity. A spring season at the Metropolitan Opera was followed by a visit to Europe, by now almost a second home to American Ballet Theatre. In September it became the first American company to visit the USSR. The company continued to add new works to the repertoire, but not at the rate it had in earlier years. 1960 brought the première of *Lady from the Sea* with Nora Kaye dancing the title role on her temporary return to the company. Another of Birgit Cullberg's works, *Moon Reindeer*, was presented in 1961 and Harald Lander's *Etudes*, which still features in the company's repertoire, was given with Toni Lander, Royes Fernandez and Bruce Marks dancing the principal roles.

At the end of 1962 the company moved to Washington where it was planned that it would perform under the auspices of the Washington Ballet Guild. However, by the spring of the following year, the arrangement was terminated because of the soaring expense and as a result the company was disbanded until the autumn of 1964, when it returned to New York. The Washington Ballet Guild later arranged to sponsor American Ballet Theatre's performances in Washington.

On its resumption of dance activity the company toured Latin America and then celebrated its twenty-fifth anniversary with a season at the Lincoln Center, which included an increased number of additions to the repertoire – Harald Lander's staging of *La Sylphide*, with his wife Toni in the title role, Agnes de Mille's *The Wind in the Mountains* and *The Four Marys*, Glen Tetley's *Sargasso*, created for the dramatic ballerina Sallie Wilson, Bentley Stone's *L'Inconnue*, and Jerome Robbin's distinguished version of *Les Noces*. At the end of the year the National Council on the Arts announced welcome financial grants to assist in support of a New York season and a national tour.

New major premières took place following the birthday celebrations. Glen Tetley's *Ricercare* was the most notable and Antony Tudor's *Pillar of Fire* was revived, with Sallie Wilson dancing the role of Hagar. It seemed almost impossible to follow Nora Kaye's original interpretation of the role without unfavourable comparison, but Sallie Wilson transformed the work into her own unique presentation which was acclaimed both in New York and in the USSR on the company's second tour there. She assured her reputation as a major dramatic ballerina, when she later danced the role of Lizzie Borden in *Fall River Legend*.

In 1971, American Ballet Theatre was named the official company of the John F. Kennedy Center for the Performing Arts in Washington and it gives regular performances there each year. The company is also going ahead with plans for a permanent home in New York. The Manhattan Center is being rennovated and Lucia Chase and Oliver Smith hope that it will eventually become the first great television dance theatre in the world. However, at the moment, the company appears at three major New York theatres – the Uris, Metropolitan Opera House and the New York State Theater. There are also plans to change and develop the American Ballet School to raise it to a truly professional standard. With this aim in mind, the management is studying the organization of the world's leading ballet schools.

American Ballet Theatre, within three decades of its foundation, and in spite of many changes in policy and fortune, has become one of the world's leading ballet companies. Present stars include such internationally renowned figures as Mikhail Baryshnikov and Natalia Makarova (ex-stars of the Kirov Ballet, Leningrad), Cynthia Gregory, Ivan Nagy and Gelsey Kirkland, while recent guest artists include Rudolf Nureyev, Erik Bruhn, Richard Cragun, Paolo Bortoluzzi, Marcia Haydée, Lynn Seymour and Carla Fracci. The repertoire perfectly reflects the desired blending of traditional and modern choreography and an excellent combination of recent acquisitions and earlier successes. Many of the modern additions to the repertoire were created specifically for American Ballet Theatre or re-staged for them by their choreographers – Eliot Feld's *At Midnight*, Erik Bruhn's *La Sylphide*, Alvin Ailey's *The River* and Rudolf Nureyev's *Raymonda*. The list of choreographers is as distinguished as the casts of dancers who perform the American Ballet Theatre's catholic and dynamic repertoire.

Mikhail Baryshnikov and Marianna Tcherkassky capture the haunting loveliness originally created by Vaslav Nijinsky and Tamara Karsavina, in Michel Fokine's one-act ballet, Le Spectre de la Rose. *The ballet has featured in the company's repertoire since 1941, when it was staged by the choreographer. Originally designed to provide a contrast between the phenomenal elevation of Nijinsky and the lyrical, dream-like quality of Karsavina's Young Girl, the ballet has been a daunting challenge to generations of dancers. With Marianna Tcherkassky's beautiful purity of line and Mikhail Baryshnikov's exemplary Russian technique, American Ballet Theatre has found the perfect re-creators of this small masterpiece.*

Right *A scene from Antony Tudor's dramatic ballet* Jardin aux Lilas, *which has featured in the company's repertoire since 1940. New scenery was designed by Tom Lingwood in 1970.*

Below *Natalia Makarova and Ivan Nagy dance* Swan Lake. *American Ballet Theatre includes all the Tchaikovsky classics in its repertoire, besides several other full-length ballets, such as* Giselle *and* Coppélia. *The current version of* Swan Lake *uses much of the original Petipa and Ivanov choreography with additions by the late David Blair.*

The Company

Directors:	Lucia Chase Oliver Smith	**Ballet Masters:**	Scott Douglas Michael Lland
Associate Director:	Antony Tudor	**Ballet Mistress:**	Fiorella Keane
Regisseur:	Dimitri Romanoff		

Principal Dancers:

Peter Breuer (handwritten)
Alexander Minz (handwritten)
TV ✱Kirk Peterson (handwritten)

TV Mikhail Baryshnikov TV Gelsey Kirkland TV Marianna Tcherkassky
TV Karena Brock TV Natalia Makarova TV Martine van Hamel
TV Fernando Bujones TV Ivan Nagy *Retired 1978* Sallie Wilson
William Carter Terry Orr Gayle Young
Eleanor d'Antuono TV Marcos Paredes *Patrick Bissell 1979* (handwritten)
TV Cynthia Gregory John Prinz TV *John Meehan* (handwritten)

Soloists:

Warren Conover TV Ruth Mayer Richard Schafer
Kristine Elliott TV Jolinda Menendez TV Frank Smith
Nanette Glushak Hilda Morales TV Rebecca Wright
Marie Johansson ✱Kirk Peterson *Victor Barbee 1979* (handwritten)
Kevin McKenzie 1979 (handwritten) *Gregory Osborne 1979* (handwritten)

The Repertoire

At Midnight (Feld) 1967
Awakening (Weiss) 1976
Brahms Quintet (Nahat) 1969
Billy the Kid (Loring) 1940
Carmen (Alonso) 1976
Concerto (MacMillan) 1967
Coppélia (Martinez) 1968
Dark Elegies (Tudor) 1940
Diana and Acteon (Vaganova) 1973
Don Quixote Pas de Deux (Petipa) 1944
Epilogue (Neumeier) 1975
Etudes (Lander) 1961
Fall River Legend (de Mille) 1948
Fancy Free (Robbins) 1944
Gemini (Tetley) 1975
✗ Giselle (Blair) 1968
Grand Pas Classique (Gsovsky) 1972
Hamlet Connotations (later, The Hamlet Case) (Neumeier) 1976
Jardin aux Lilas (Tudor) 1940
✗ La Bayadère (Markarova) (1974) *1980* (handwritten)
La Fille Mal Gardée (Romanoff) 1972
Las Hermanas (MacMillan) 1967
La Sylphide (Bruhn) 1972
La Ventana (Bruhn) 1975
Le Baiser de la Fée (Neumeier) 1974
Le Corsaire (Petipa) 1962
Le Jeune Homme et la Mort (Petit) 1975
Le Sacre du Printemps (Tetley) 1976

Le Spectre de la Rose (Fokine) 1941
Les Noces (Robbins) 1965
Les Patineurs (Ashton) 1946
Les Sylphides (Fokine) 1940
Medea (Butler) 1975
Moor's Pavane (Limon) 1970
Other Dances (Robbins) 1976
Petrouchka (Fokine) 1941
Pillar of Fire (Tudor) 1942
Push Comes to Shove (Tharp) 1976
Raymonda (Nureyev) 1975
Rodeo (de Mille) 1950
Romeo and Juliet (Tudor) 1943
Shadowplay (Tudor) 1975
✗ Swan Lake (Blair) 1967
Tales of Hoffman (Darrell) 1973
Texas IV (de Mille) 1976
The Leaves are Fading (Tudor) 1975
The Maids (Ross) 1957
✗ The Nutcracker (Baryshnikov) 1977
The River (Ailey) 1970
✗ The Sleeping Beauty (Skeaping after Petipa) 1976
Theme and Variations (Balanchine) 1947
Three Virgins and a Devil (de Mille) 1941
Undertow (Tudor) 1945
Vestris (Jacobson) 1975

Touring

Apart from regular national tours the company has been a frequent visitor to most European countries and has also appeared in Latin America, the Middle East and the USSR.

City Center Joffrey Ballet

In 1976 City Center Joffrey Ballet finally moved into the City Center 55th Street Theater premises in New York. The administrative offices had been located there for some years but studios and rehearsal rooms were in Greenwich Village in conditions that Robert Joffrey described as 'squalid'. The chief features of the old rehearsal rooms were two large pillars in the centre of the studio. Gerald Arpino, the company's resident choreographer, claims that a perceptive audience could tell the location of the pillars if they studied any of his works closely. Other choreographers, including Eliot Feld and Twyla Tharp, have refused to work in such trying conditions and John Hart, of London's Royal Ballet, found it almost impossible to rehearse the intricate and precise choreography of *The Dream* when he went to New York to stage Sir Frederick Ashton's ballet for the company.

It is difficult to understand, therefore, how this company has managed to overcome such circumstances to become one of New York's most popular and successful dance groups. The repertoire is unusual and varied and demands a wide range of techniques and abilities from the dancers. Robert Joffrey feels that the style of the company is not suited to the big classic 'set-pieces' like *Swan Lake* or *The Nutcracker* but smaller-scale mainstream works are ideal and they are adventurously interspersed with works by some of the world's leading exponents of modern dance. Choreographers whose works are featured in the repertoire of the City Center Joffrey Ballet include Leonide Massine, Michel Fokine, George Balanchine, Jerome Robbins, Frederick Ashton, Kurt Jooss, José Limon, Alvin Ailey, Twyla Tharp, Antony Tudor and John Cranko. The company's ability to respond to the classical purity of George Balanchine, the dramatic conceptions of Antony Tudor and the athletic unpredictability of Twyla Tharp, for example, make it tremendously versatile and means that there is no such thing as a typical Joffrey dancer.

Robert Joffrey trained at the School of American Ballet with Alexandra Fedorova and studied modern dance with May O'Donnell and Gertrude Shurr. He made his professional debut with Roland Petit's Ballet de Paris and later made frequent appearances with May O'Donnell's company in the early 1950s. He joined the New York High School of Performing Arts and some of his earliest works were performed by his students. In 1952, *Persephone* was staged as part of a choreographer's workshop programme and this was followed by *Scaramouche* and *Umpateedle* at the Jacob's Pillow Dance Festival in 1953.

The following year he formed his own company called the Robert Joffrey Ballet Concert. The company was attached to the American Ballet Center, its official school, and has remained so through the changes which took place in the years which followed. The company gave its first performance in 1954 presenting *Pas de Déesses* and *Le Bal Masqué*. Both works were by Robert Joffrey and the former delightful, gentle balletic satire on Lucile Grahn, Fanny Cerrito and Maria Taglioni, was revived for the City Center Joffrey Ballet in 1967. In the same year the Ballet Rambert invited Robert Joffrey to England where he staged *Pas de Déesses* and *Persephone*. In 1956, Robert Joffrey put his company on a more formal basis and re-named it Robert Joffrey's Theatre Dancers. Every season from then until 1964, the company made a national tour. Although it was officially based in New York, it never performed in the centre of the city owing to the prohibitive costs of theatres. The company consisted of six dancers with a repertoire of four ballets, all by Robert Joffrey, performing 'one-night stands' throughout the country. By 1958, two more dancers had been added and the company's name changed to the Robert Joffrey Theatre Ballet. The company continued to expand, in

Gary Chryst and Christian Holder pictured in a typically sculptural pose from Gerald Arpino's modern ballet The Clowns. *It is based on the idea that all men are, in some way, clowns and the architects of their own destruction. The 12 note score by Hershy Kay was commissioned specifically for the work.*

spite of a worrying financial instability. By 1960, it had become the Robert Joffrey Ballet and had added an orchestra as well as more dancers.

In 1962, the Robert Joffrey Ballet was invited to appear at the Spoleto Festival. Lack of money meant that the company would be unable to accept. However, Mrs Rebekah Harkness offered to pay the necessary expenses through the Rebekah Harkness Foundation, a philanthropic organization established to promote American cultural activity throughout the world. Robert Joffrey requested that the money should be spent instead on paying the dancers during a full rehearsal schedule before they toured the United States. Previously the company had been unable to afford this. Mrs Harkness and the Foundation not only agreed to this, but also offered to sponsor a summer workshop at Watch Hill. Choreographers were invited to this workshop to create new works which were then performed before an invited audience in September 1962. The Rebekah Harkness Foundation sponsored two foreign tours for the Robert Joffrey Ballet. In 1962 the company visited the Middle East, India and Pakistan and in 1963 it toured the USSR, under the auspices of the Department of State. A second workshop took place at Watch Hill in 1963.

At this time the company's repertoire consisted entirely of works by contemporary choreographers including Robert Joffrey, Gerald Arpino, Brian MacDonald and Alvin Ailey. In 1964 there was a dispute over artistic policy between Robert Joffrey and Mrs Harkness. As a result, the association between them came to an end. Mrs Harkness formed her own company, the Harkness Ballet, now defunct. In addition to withdrawing her financial support, she also kept the majority of the Robert Joffrey Ballet's dancers under contract. Consequently, after building up a reasonable sized company with relative financial stability, Robert Joffrey was left with few dancers and no support. However, he tenaciously set about re-building a company with the remaining dancers and students from his school and by holding auditions.

In this scene from The Clowns *the powerful, archetypal image of the clown is used as a striking means of revelation of the clownish quality of all men. This short, dramatic work was created in 1968 and has featured regularly in the repertoire.*

Later in 1964, the Ford Foundation donated a generous grant to the new Robert Joffrey Ballet, thus enabling it to resume a training and performing programme. A further grant followed in 1965 and the new company made its debut in August of that year at the Jacob's Pillow Dance Festival. The company also performed at the open-air Delacorte Theater in New York's Central Park and at the first Harper Theatre Dance Festival in Chicago.

The following spring the company gave seven performances at the New York City Center. Morton Baum, of the board of directors, who has been responsible for the financial stability of other performing arts companies including the New York City Ballet, was sufficiently impressed by the Robert Joffrey Ballet to invite it to become a resident company. The company accepted the invitation and its name was changed to City Center Joffrey Ballet.

Robert Joffrey retains a special affection for those people whose loyalty and co-operation enabled him to re-form his company after the break with Mrs Harkness. Naturally, choreographers were reluctant to create new works for a company with such an apparently insecure future. Consequently, when Anna Sokolow offered to create a new ballet for the company she earned lasting gratitude and affection. In recognition of this, City Center Joffrey Ballet staged a revival of her ballet *Opus '65* in 1976. Gerald Arpino, Associate Director and the company's resident choreographer, also remained a stalwart supporter. The current repertoire contains more than 10 of his works, including revivals of *Sea Shadow* and *Olympics* which gave the company its character in the early 1960s.

In 1976, City Center Joffrey Ballet presented a season of 30 works by American choreographers to celebrate the United States bicentenary, and as a tribute to the people who gave American ballet its national identity. The repertoire included Jerome Robbin's rarely performed *Interplay*, *Moves* and *New York Export: Opus Jazz*, Agnes de Mille's *Rodeo* and George Balanchine's *Square Dance* which the choreographer gave freely to Robert Joffrey as well as supervising the rehearsals, Twyla Tharp's *Deuce Coupe II*, a revised version of the work she created for her own company and City Center Joffrey Ballet, was also presented as well as her second creation for it, *As Time Goes By*.

The company is undoubtedly very popular and has a reputation for being 'trendy'. Yet this suggests a transitory quality which denies the unquestionable basis of talent and imagination which gave City Center Joffrey Ballet its strength. Robert Joffrey has a remarkably sensitive approach to the organization of the repertoire. Whilst encompassing a wide variety of styles the company never presents works outside the range of its size or personality. Revivals are well timed and a number of major works not commonly performed by other companies feature in City Center Joffrey Ballet's repertoire.

Plans for the future typically cover a wide spectrum. Robert Joffrey hopes to collaborate with a number of young American choreographers to develop new works for the company and to stage revivals of some major American works from the past, such as Eugene Loring's *Billy the Kid* and Lew Christensen's *Filling Station*. He also hopes to present a special season in 1980 to celebrate the one hundredth anniversary of Michel Fokine's birth. He plans

The company, its dancers and choreographers all display immense versatility. Confetti, *created by Gerald Arpino, is classically based and reminiscent of the tarantella. A light-hearted piece, it demands a dazzling virtuoso technique from the dancers, clearly demonstrated here by Francesca Corkle's spectacular leap.*

to continue and augment his policy of presenting major European ballets not regularly performed by other companies. Leonide Massine's *Parade* and Kurt Jooss' *The Green Table* already form a special part of the company's repertoire. The future of the City Center Joffrey Ballet promises to be as characteristically uncharacteristic as its present.

The Company

IP: In person

Artistic Director: Robert Joffrey

Associate Director: Gerald Arpino

Ballet Master: Basil Thompson

Assistant Ballet Master: Scott Barnard

Dancers:

Charthel Arthur	Carol Messmer	Larry Grenier
IP Lisa Bradley	Pamela Nearhoof	Jerel Hilding
Diana Cartier	Diane Orio	*TV* Christian Holder
IP Francesca Corkle*	Beatriz Rodriguez	*IP* Gregory Huffman
IP Donna Cowen	Trinette Singleton	Jeffrey Hughes
Starr Danias	Jodi Wintz	Chris Jensen
Ann Marie de Angelo	Rebecca Wright	Philip Jerry
Ingrid Fraley	Sara Yarborough	Kevin McKenzie—*ABT*
Erika Goodman	Dermot Burke	Russel Sultzbach
Jan Hanniford	Adix Carman	Paul Sutherland
Alaine Haubert	Gary Chryst	Burton Taylor
IP Denise Jackson	Richard Colton	Robert Thomas
Krystyna Jurkowski	Donn Edwards	Edward Verso
Miyoko Kato	Robert Estner	Glenn White
Jean McCabe	Tom Fowler	William Whitener

IP Cynthia Anderson
TV Glenn Dufford

IP Ursula Burke
IP Rachel Ganteaume
IP Susan Stewart
IP Carole Valleskey
IP Michael Bjerknes
IP Laurence Blake
IP Carl Corry
IP Gregory King
IP William Starret
IP Lisa Slagle

The Repertoire

Les Patineurs - Ford Aud. Feb. 24, 1979

Abyss (Stuart Hodes)
After Eden (Butler)
Astarte (Joffrey)
As Time Goes By (Tharp)
Ball in Old Vienna (Jooss)
X *Cakewalk* (Boris)
Confetti (Arpino)
Deuce Coupe II (Tharp)
Face Dancers (Sappington)
Feast of Ashes (Ailey)
Five Dances (Holder)
Interplay (Robbins)
Jeu de Cartes (Cranko, staged by Georgette Tsinguirides)
Kettentanz (Arpino)
Le Beau Danube (Massine)
Monotones I and II (Ashton)
Moves (Robbins)
N Y Export, Op. Jazz (Robbins)
Offenbach in the Underworld (Tudor, staged by Celia Franca)
Olympics (Arpino)
Opus I (Cranko, staged by Georgette Tsinguirides)

Opus 65 (Sokolow)
Orpheus Times Light (Arpino)
Parade (Massine)
Pas de Déesses (Joffrey)
Pavane on the Death of an Infanta (Jooss)
Petrouchka (Fokine, staged by Leonide Massine)
Pulcinella (Massine)
Reflections (Arpino)
Remembrances (Joffrey)
Rodeo (de Mille)
Sea Shadow (Arpino)
Secret Places (Arpino)
Square Dance (Balanchine)
Tchaikovsky Pas de Deux (Balanchine)
The Big City (Jooss, staged by Anna Markard)
The Clowns (Arpino)
The Dream (Ashton, staged by John Hart)
The Green Table (Jooss)
The Moor's Pavane (Limon)
The Relativity of Icarus (Arpino)
Trinity (Arpino)
X *Valentine* (Arpino)
Viva Vivaldi! (Arpino)
Weewis (Sappington)

Touring

Middle East, India, Pakistan, USSR (twice)

35

The San Francisco Ballet

The story of the San Francisco Ballet is like a fairy tale and like all good stories there is a happy ending, but not before the heroine, in this case the company itself, has suffered all sorts of torments and been snatched back, at the last minute, from total defeat. The company has gained the status of a major national group entirely through the efforts and determination of its members, especially the dancers themselves.

It was founded in 1933 as the San Francisco Opera Ballet, starting out as a wing of the established opera as so many European companies have. Its main function was to supply dancers for opera intermezzi but it was not long before it began to make an independent name for itself. At the same time as the company was founded, the San Francisco Ballet School was established to furnish a permanent supply of professionally trained dancers, and an exceptionally close association has continued between them since. The company's first choreographer and Ballet Master was Adolph Bolm, whose distinguished career began in St Petersburg, where he was a soloist at the Maryinsky Theatre. He later organized Anna Pavlova's first tours and danced with Diaghilev's Ballets Russes. In 1936 he was succeeded by Serge Oukrainsky who had also been associated with Anna Pavlova and was a soloist with her company and her partner for two years. Under his leadership William Christensen was appointed premier danseur and this began a long association with the Christensen family which was destined to become one of the most important relationships in the company's history.

Two years later William Christensen succeeded Serge Oukrainsky as choreographer and leader of the San Francisco Ballet. He immediately set about extending the range of the company and making it fully independent. He increased the repertoire to include full-length productions of *Coppélia*, *Swan Lake* and *The Nutcracker*. He also initiated the first tours, taking the company to many of the major cities in the Western States.

His brother Harold joined the company in 1940 and four years later, became Director of the San Francisco Ballet School. Under his guidance, until his retirement in June 1975, the School has grown in size and reputation and become one of the leading schools in the United States. The relationship between the company and the school has, consequently, been particularly close.

In 1951, William Christensen left the company to return to his home state of Utah where he took charge of America's first self-contained university dance department. His place at San Francisco was filled by a third brother – Lew Christensen, who remains one of the two Artistic Directors today. Michael Smuin is the other one.

When he became Artistic Director in 1951, Lew Christensen had already been a company member for some years and had previously gained experience, both as a dancer and choreographer, with companies in New York. He continued his brother's policy of building up the repertoire, adding many of his own creations. The company's financial resources were extremely limited and throughout the 1950s this created great difficulties for the mounting of new productions. As a result, Lew Christensen had to do almost all the choreography himself. Until recently, 75 per cent of the repertoire was his.

Lew Christensen was also a director of the New York City Ballet and organized an exchange agreement between the two companies in 1952. Under this agreement the companies could exchange dancers and perform works from each other's repertoire. The San Francisco Ballet was greatly enriched by guest appearances from the New York dancers and by a number of George Balanchine's creations, which considerably extended the repertoire

The massive financial problems which beset the San Francisco Ballet prevented Michael Smuin from staging his full-length version of Romeo and Juliet *until 1976. However, he presented a suite from the work in the previous year and now the complete ballet has been included in the repertoire with considerable success and critical acclaim.*

both in range and size. Such an arrangement encouraged larger audiences and the increasing success in San Francisco persuaded the company to make a tour to the eastern states. On this tour they danced at the Jacob's Pillow Festival and received much praise from the public and the press.

The company continued to develop throughout the late 1950s and early 1960s and was admired for its polished technique and unity of style. In 1957 the company manager, Leon Kalimos, organized the first international tour. The company embarked on a 10 week tour, travelling 35,000 miles, and appeared in Formosa, the Philippines, Hong Kong, Thailand, Burma, Cambodia, Singapore, Malaya, Sri Lanka, India, West Pakistan and Iran. Leon Kalimos organized further tours, until he left the company in 1969, to places including Latin America, the Middle East and Africa. He was also able to organize a number of substantial grants which gave the company relative financial stability for some time. By the mid 1960s, however, the company was suffering because many of its principal dancers were ambitious and anxious to further their careers with major national companies. Consequently they did not remain with the San Francisco Ballet and many went to companies in New York which could offer them more scope and opportunity as well as more money.

The loss of Leon Kalimos in 1969 was unfortunate for the administration of the San Francisco Ballet and the company was relatively inactive for the next three years. By 1973 it was clear that re-organization was the only alternative to disbanding the company. It became imperative that the company should achieve national rather than provincial status. Michael Smuin, who had left the San Francisco Ballet to become a soloist with American Ballet Theatre was invited to return as Associate Artistic Director. Several fellow soloists – Betsy Erickson, Dianna Weber, Paula Tracy and Vane Vest – joined him on the west coast.

Two spectacular new works were presented in June in the hope of arousing sufficient interest to keep the company going. The first of these was an elaborate production of *Cinderella*, started by Lew Christensen and finished by Michael Smuin because of lack of time. It was well received but the fact that it had not been fully worked out prevented it being the triumph they

Paula Tracy, Gary Wahl, Tina Santos and Michael Dwyer are shown in a scene from Michael Smuin's controversial work Shinju. *The music is by Paul Chihara and the sets and costumes were designed by Willa Kim. The ballet, based on stories by Chikamatsu, was premièred in 1975.*

hoped for. The second major new work was Lew Christensen's *Don Juan*. The sets and costumes were splendid and the choreographer had long planned to create a work on this theme. Consequently, the ballet was fully realized and expertly presented. This was much more successful than *Cinderella* and undoubtedly more representative of Lew Christensen's talents. The third programme of the season was unexpectedly the most successful. It presented Michael Smuin's *Harp Concerto* and *Eternal Idol*, Doris Humphrey's *The Shakers* and George Balanchine's *Symphony in C*. A varied and well-balanced programme, it showed off the virtuoso techniques of the company and was a major factor in the development of a permanent following for the San Francisco Ballet.

At Christmas the company presented the popular ballet *The Nutcracker* which had always featured in the winter repertoire since its introduction, and attracted large audiences. A short, successful tour of Hawaii followed and by January 1974 the company had planned a major season featuring 26 works, 11 choreographers and an impressive list of guest artists. *Cinderella* was re-worked and achieved the acclaim it rightfully deserved. *Don Juan* was presented again, with Alexander Filipov in the title role. Two George Balanchine ballets were added to the repertoire – *La Sonnambula* and *Four Temperaments*. Other new additions included Lester Horton's *The Beloved*, Michael Smuin's *Pulcinella Variations* and *Mother Blues*. Several very popular revivals, including *Les Sylphides* staged by Alexandra Danilova, completed the most successful season the San Francisco Ballet had ever had. Its popularity soared, not simply because audiences wished to see the array of guest artists, but because the company's true worth was being recognized.

It was, therefore, a particularly bitter blow in September 1974, when the directors announced that, if $500,000 was not raised within one month, the company and the school would be bankrupt and would have to close. Since its inception the San Francisco Ballet had relied on generous private donations. The economic climate of 1974 prevented this support continuing at its previous level. In order to qualify for official grants, the company had to prove it had sufficient public support to justify the spending of state money.

The San Francisco Ballet's repertoire includes several works by George Balanchine, whose abstract style adds vocabulary and range. Works by Balanchine include Four Temperaments, *shown here,* Symphony in C, Serenade *and* Agon.

39

It must have seemed wretchedly ironic to the dancers that this should happen when a sizeable regular following was just beginning to develop.

Shortly before rehearsals were due to begin, the dancers were informed that they would no longer be needed. Undaunted, Robert Gladstein and five other dancers assembled to see what they could do to help. First they collated all the names from lists of members of theatrical societies and contacted them. By the next board meeting, the six dancers had raised $3,000 and reckoned they could collect more. They persuaded the directors to carry on fighting to save the company and a campaign was launched. Help was sought from many sources and local press coverage assisted.

The most impressive part of the campaign was that undertaken by the dancers themselves, under the leadership of Robert Gladstein. They danced on street corners and in the windows of several main stores, collecting money in their ballet shoes. These unlikely activities aroused the interest of journalists and such a picturesque subject reached national television and newspapers. Publicity helped the cause and donations, large and small, poured in from every part of the country from adults and children alike. Hundreds of letters were written and many people volunteered to help with typing, answering telephone calls and going from house to house to collect money.

The board of directors tackled major corporations and associations and by the end of September the money to save the company had been raised. This preserved the San Francisco Ballet from immediate danger, but large debts still had to be paid off. They all continued to beg from every possible source, knowing that *The Nutcracker* programme at Christmas would also assist in their support.

At the beginning of October, the 'Marine World – Africa USA', a combined marine and wildlife park, offered help by lending the Marine World to the company for a day. It was decided to mount *Beauty and the Beast*, using real animals with the dancers. It was a completely crazy idea but one which caught the public imagination. The performing area was a concrete circus ring, covered with felt and Lew Christensen re-arranged the dances to suit it and the dancers, joined where possible by llamas, monkeys, birds, a tiger and an elephant. The exit of Beauty and the transformed Prince on top of an elephant must be one of the strangest and most sensational in ballet history. Again many artists and members of the public freely volunteered to help in the day's activities. Chamber orchestras, the Oakland Symphony Orchestra and a harpist all played in various parts of the park. Picnics, barbecues and cocktail parties were arranged and the day ended with a banquet attended by a number of film stars and at which a drawing by Picasso was auctioned.

The dancers were deeply touched by the public's generosity and the directors were impressed by the spontaneous efforts and devotion of the dancers. Financially viable, if not actually sound, the company returned to work. A tour of Hawaii was followed by *The Nutcracker* season which played to almost capacity audiences.

The 1975 season was a triumph, in spite of economic restraint. Guest artists included Valery and Galina Panov, Judith Jamison and Cynthia Gregory. Two new works by Michael Smuin were presented – *Shinju* and a suite from *Romeo and Juliet*. The campaign to raise money prevented him from staging a full-length version of *Romeo and Juliet* until the following year. Lack of money meant that a proper set could not be designed for the work and bits and pieces from other works had to be used instead.

Nevertheless, his sensitive interpretation of the story and the dynamic quality of the choreography suggests that it will rank with the versions of *Romeo and Juliet* by better-known international choreographers.

Michael Smuin is now co-director with Lew Christensen and he and Richard le Blond, the President, have taken over much of the day-to-day business so that Lew Christensen can have freedom to create new works. The company plans to extend its repertoire considerably to include works by a wider selection of choreographers. These plans included nine world premières and the addition of several works new to the company in the 1976/77 season. Michael Smuin also hopes to organize a tour of South America as well as a visit to New York. He is also determined to ensure that the press and the public recognize the stature of the San Francisco Ballet and no longer dismiss it as merely a provincial company. No other company has proved so conclusively its tenacity and determination and now these qualities can once again be directed towards the dance, instead of fund-raising, an interesting and successful future lies ahead.

The Company

Romeo and Juliet – Oct. 26, 1977 MSU *[handwritten]*
Diana Weber *[handwritten]*
Jim Sohm *[handwritten]*

Artistic Directors: Lew Christensen
Michael Smuin

Regisseurs: Richard Cammack
Virginia Johnson

Ballet Master: Robert Gladstein

Dancers:

IP Damara Bennett	J. Michael Dwyer	*IP* Lynda Meyer	*IP* Jim Sohm	
Sherron Black	*IP* Betsy Erickson	*IP* Cynthia Meyers	Michael Thomas	
IP Madeleine Bouchard	*IP* Attila Ficzere	*IP* Anton Ness	*IP* Elizabeth Tienken	
Maureen Broderick	Michael Graham	*IP* Gina Ness	*IP* Paula Tracy	
IP Val Caniparoli	Victoria Gyorfi	Anita Paciotti	*IP* Vane Vest	
Gardner Carlson	Stephanie Jones	Roberta Pfeil	Gary Wahl	
IP Laurie Cowden	Susan Magno	Laurie Ritter	*IP* Diana Weber	
IP Allyson Deane	Keith Martin	Tom Ruud	*IP* Jerome Weiss	
Nancy Dickson	John McFall	*IP* Tina Santos	*IP* Deborah Zdobinski	

[handwritten right margin:] IP-Dennis Marshall / IP-Robert Gladstein / IP-Robert Sund / IP-David McNaughton / IP-Don Schwenessen

The Repertoire

Agon (Balanchine)
Airs de Ballet (Christensen)
Cinderella (Christensen/Smuin)
Con Amore (Christensen)
Concerto Barocco (Balanchine)
Danses Concertantes (Christensen)
Don Juan (Christensen)
Eternal Idol (Smuin)
Fantasma (Christensen)
Filling Station (Christensen)
Firebird (Béjart)
Four Temperaments (Balanchine)
Garden of Love's Sleep (McFall)
Gershwin (McFall)
Harp Concerto (Smuin)
Jinx (Christensen)
Medea (Smuin)
Metamorphoses (Ruud)
Mobile (Ruud)
Mother Blues (Smuin)
Moves (Robbins)
N.R.A. (Gladstein)

Opus One (Cranko)
Peter and the Wolf (Weiss)
Pulcinella Variations (Smuin)
X *Romeo and Juliet* (Smuin) *In Person Oct. 26, 1977 MSU* *[handwritten]*
Scherzo (Smuin)
Schubertiade (Smuin)
Serenade (Balanchine)
Shinjú (Smuin)
Sinfonia (Christensen)
Songs of Mahler (Smuin)
Souvenirs (Bolender)
Stravinsky Pas de Deux (Christensen)
Symphony in C (Balanchine)
Tealia (McFall)
Tchaikovsky Pas de Deux (Balanchine)
The Ice Maiden (Christensen)
The Nutcracker (Christensen)
The Referee (Arenal)
Variations de Ballet (Christensen after Balanchine)
John Butler work created for Lynda Meyer

Touring

Far East, Middle East, Africa, Latin America, Hawaii (twice).

Dance Theatre of Harlem

Louis Johnson's Forces of Rhythm *is one of the most popular items in the Dance Theatre of Harlem's repertoire. Exuberant choreography, fusing classical ballet, ethnic and contemporary dance, has produced a work of rare charm, demanding the highest standards of technical expertise from the dancers.*

A little more than 20 years ago a young black dancer approached George Balanchine. He had studied dance at the School of Performing Arts in New York, winning an award in the year of his graduation. His physique was well suited to classical ballet and he was musical and undoubtedly talented. However, a classical black dancer in a white corps de ballet was unthinkable. He was given the option of training to be a soloist – quite a courageous decision in the 1950s and one which provoked a certain amount of unfavourable comment.

However, he trained at the School of American Ballet, joined the New York City Ballet in 1956 and was promoted to soloist three years later. The young man was Arthur Mitchell and he became one of the New York City Ballet's most exciting and interesting dancers. Among the roles he danced were Fourth Movement in *Western Symphony*, the male solo in *Interplay* and

Jason in *Medea*. He also created the Unicorn in John Butler's *The Unicorn, the Gorgon and the Manticore*, the pas de deux with Diana Adams in George Balanchine's *Agon* and the male lead in John Taras' *Ebony Concerto*, one of the four parts of *Jazz Concert*. He also created the role of Puck in George Balanchine's *Midsummer Night's Dream*, both on the stage and in the film of the ballet in 1962 and 1966.

When Arthur Mitchell decided to form a classically based, black, ballet company it was a political as well as a cultural decision. The Dance Theatre of Harlem was formed amidst considerable speculation and a certain amount of doubt. Arthur Mitchell was determined to create a classical company and not become diverted into traditional folk material or duplicate the kind of contemporary dance of Catherine Dunham or Alvin Ailey. Wisely he introduced some of the works of George Balanchine into the repertoire with their special blend of Russian tradition and American flavour. At present the company performs *Allegro Brillante*, *Concerto Barocco*, *Agon* and *Bugaku*.

The last two, in particular, are well suited to the company's style. It has developed a technical brilliance and smoothness very rapidly and the performances of George Balanchine's works are a fine showcase for these. In addition, the company has brought its own unique qualities of dynamism and warmth to the presentation of these ballets thus avoiding the danger of becoming a black imitation of the New York City Ballet. The extraordinary and pleasing effect of the Dance Theatre of Harlem performing the ingenious, combined Japanese and western celebration of *Bugaku* is delightful and defies description.

The repertoire also contains works by Arthur Mitchell himself. Both *Holberg Suite* and *Fête Noire* are clearly designed for the company which performs them with a distinctive agility and grace. *Holberg Suite*, particularly reflects Arthur Mitchell's association with the New York City Ballet but the influence of George Balanchine can hardly be considered anything but beneficial.

In a very short time the Dance Theatre of Harlem achieved public acclaim at home and abroad and was rapturously received when it visited London in 1974. It has, of course, continued to develop and is rapidly gaining a maturity and unity not dependent on its novelty value. However, it has reached that point in its career which comes to all companies, when it is necessary to make firm policy decisions about its future direction.

The current repertoire is indicative of this stage of the company's development. Works like *Forces of Rhythm* and *Dougla*, by Louis Johnson and Geoffrey Holder, are enormously popular with audiences in the United States and abroad. The entire company participates in these exciting celebrations of ethnic and classical dance with a rhythmic fluency which has become characteristic of it. Unquestionably, such works have a place in the permanent repertoire, but not necessarily a major one. Only the most pedantic of purists could object to their inclusion.

However, there are a number of works which are not so well suited to the company's character. William Dollar's *The Combat*, originally created for Roland Petit's Ballet de Paris, tells the tragic story of the fight between Tancredi and Clorinda ending with her death and his realization that he has killed the woman he loves. It is a heavily dramatic work and, although it has been most successfully received, the Dance Theatre of Harlem is better suited to ballets requiring a more subtle emotional approach. The three classical pas de deux from *Le Corsair*, *Don Quixote* and *Romeo and Juliet* also show an uneasiness. The first two lack really mature arrangement and do not yet bear comparison with the brilliant virtuoso performances and emotional depth of other major companies. Doubtless, as the dancers gain experience and increase their range, such criticisms will not be levelled. However, Gabriella Taub-Davash's choreography for *Romeo and Juliet* does not really give the principals the scope they require. It is a rather weak creation and inevitably suffers from comparison with the several excellent versions by some of the world's leading choreographers.

Equally, the repertoire includes works which demonstrate the company's strengths and the special qualities of the principal dancers. John Taras' gentle, graceful abstract ballet *Design for Strings* is an ideal vehicle to display the subtlety and fluidity of the company and Lydia Abarca, in particular, gives an extraordinary, beautiful and precise performance of the leading female role. Lester Horton's *The Beloved* provides an opportunity for powerful dramatic interpretation and James Truitte's revival is totally successful. It seems quite possible, that the Dance Theatre of Harlem will explore further the potentialities of dramatic works in the future. Certainly it is a direction that would suit the talents of such dancers as Gayle McKinney and Roman Brocks.

This pose from George Balanchine's Agon *clearly demonstrates the wonderful purity of line of Lydia Abarca and the rhythmic fluidity of Derek Williams.* Agon *is one of several George Balanchine ballets featured in the company's repertoire. Created to specially commissioned music by Igor Stravinsky, the ballet consists of an introduction and three parts. It is an intricate intermingling of short dances for the company and two, three or four dancers.*

44

Joseph Wyatt's and Elena Carter's vibrant technique is especially well suited to the dynamic Don Quixote Pas de Deux.

The real strength of the company lies in the works created specially for it – a very healthy situation for its future development. William Scott's *Every Now and Then* has received public and critical acclaim and Arthur Mitchell promises to become one of the major choreographers of the twentieth century. Besides his lyrical *Holberg Suite* and the purity of *Fête Noire*, he has also created *Manifestations*, based on the Biblical story of the Garden of

Eden. The dramatic situation and expressive movement of the ballet are superbly suited to the company. Mel Tomlinson's creation of the Snake, from his dramatic slow entrance, head-first from above, to his final serpentine coiling and undulating exit, is a magnificent example of the polished technique and powerful interpretation of which the company is capable. The serious dedication of the dancers to their art can be seen from the fact that Mel Tomlinson, who does not really like snakes, bought one while rehearsing this role in order to study the way it moved. Certainly such extreme devotion to his art has proved its value in his most remarkable performance. The classical purity of the dance created for Adam and Eve complements and counter-balances the athletic portrayal of the Snake.

The Dance Theatre of Harlem is a young company and, although perhaps harsh, it is to its credit that critics judge it by the same standards as they apply to the world's established, major companies. It has been much praised both in the United States and in Europe and is especially popular in Britain, where it has twice appeared at the Royal Variety Performance, the most spectacular theatrical event of the year and one, which many people, who would not normally see ballet, watch on television. Unique in the field of ballet, not just because it is the world's only classical black company, but because of its particular qualities of rhythmic fluidity, grace and elegance, the Dance Theatre of Harlem promises to have a bright and exciting future.

The Company

Directors and Producers:	Arthur Mitchell Karel Shook	**Co-Producer:**	Hal de Windt
		Ballet Master:	William Scott

Dancers:	Lydia Abarca	Susan Lovelle	Ronald Perry
	Karen Brown	Gayle McKinney	Walter Raines
	Laura Brown	Melva Murray-White	Paul Russell
	Stephanie Dabney	Sheila Rohan	Allan Sampson
	Elena Carter	Roslyn Sampson	William Scott
	Brenda Garratt	Karen Wright	Samuel Smalls
	Yvonne Hall	Gerald Banks	Mel Tomlinson
	Joyce Handy	Roman Brooks	Derek Williams
	Virginia Johnson	Homer Bryant	Joseph Wyatt

The Repertoire

After Corinth (Raines)
Afternoon of a Faun (Robbins)
Agon (Balanchine)
Allegro Brillante (Balanchine)
Ancient Voices of Children (Sparemblek)
Biosfera (Mitchell)
X *Bugaku* (Balanchine)
Caravansarai (Beatty)
Carmen and Jose (Page)
Concerto Barocco (Balanchine)
Design for Strings (Taras)
Don Quixote Pas de Deux (Shook)
Dougla (Holder)
Every Now and Then (Scott)
Fête Noire (Mitchell)

X *Forces of Rhythm* (Johnson)
Fun and Games (Mitchell)
Haiku (Raines)
Holberg Suite (Mitchell)
Le Corsaire Pas de Deux (Chabukiani, staged by Karel Shook)
Manifestations (Mitchell)
Mendelssohn Concerto (Dollar)
Ode (Mitchell)
Rhythmetron (Mitchell)
Romeo and Juliet (Taub-Darvash)
The Beloved (Horton)
The Combat (Dollar)
Tones (Mitchell)
Wings (Johnson)

Touring

1971 Spoleto Festival, Mexico.
Several European tours.

The Eliot Feld Ballet

Probably the smallest major classical company in the United States, the Eliot Feld Ballet was founded in 1973. At that time Eliot Feld was 30 years old and already had the reputation of being one of the finest young choreographers in the United States, based firmly on those of his works featured in the repertoires of such discerning companies as the American Ballet Theatre, the Royal Swedish Ballet, the Royal Winnipeg Ballet, City Center Joffrey Ballet, the National Ballet of Canada and the Royal Danish Ballet.

He is a native of New York and studied at the School of American Ballet as well as with the New Dance Group and the High School of Performing Arts. He has been called the *enfant terrible* of the dance world and this is not without some justification. He made his first public appearance at the age of 12 in the Phoenix Theater's musical, *Sandhog*. He joined the Broadway cast of *West Side Story* when he was 16 and appeared in the film as Baby-John.

He joined American Ballet Theatre when he was 21 and created his first work, *Harbinger*, for it in 1967. The impact of his debut as a choreographer evoked comparisons between him and the young Jerome Robbins, whose presentation of *Fancy Free* for Ballet Theatre (now American Ballet Theatre) took place in 1944. Later the same year, Eliot Feld created his second work, a haunting and poetic ballet called *At Midnight*, set to Mahler's Ruckert songs. His association with American Ballet Theatre was stormy. Although he wanted to be a dancer from a very early age, he attended only the minimum of classes and shocked the rest of the company by his apparent lack of dedication. The critical success of his first two original ballets made him decide that he wanted the greater artistic freedom of his own company. Against the advice of his colleagues and amidst a bitter argument about the artistic policy of American Ballet Theatre, he left to establish the American Ballet Company.

American Ballet Company was an ambitious project. It became the resident company of the Brooklyn Academy of Music and Eliot Feld insisted on the use of a live orchestra. He created a number of works for the company, including *Intermezzo*, *Cortège Burlesque*, *Pagan Spring*, *Early Songs*, *Cortège Parisien*, *Romance* and *The Gods Amused*. Sadly, such a major enterprise is expensive and the company simply could not rely on large audiences in a big city with so many leading companies competing for the attention of the public. Two and a half years after its inception, the American Ballet Company had to be disbanded. Quite rightly, Eliot Feld resents the suggestion that this venture was a failure. Artistically it was enormously successful and that is what is really important. Financially, it was disastrous because of the impracticality of a young, small company trying to maintain itself in a theatre with over 2000 seats.

After the closure of his own company, Eliot Feld recommenced his rather tempestuous association with American Ballet Theatre. During this time he created several works for it and was also in demand as a freelance choreographer. Ballets he created at this period were *A Soldier's Tale* and *Eccentrique* for American Ballet Theatre, *Winter's Court* for the Royal Danish Ballet and *Jive* for the City Center Joffrey Ballet. He also staged earlier works for other companies.

In 1973, Howard Klein, Director of Arts for the Rockefeller Foundation, took the unprecedented step of suggesting that Eliot Feld should establish a new company of his own, if a grant could be arranged. After some thought Eliot Feld decided that he did need to work with his own dancers and that he was unable to fulfil his real potential working with a variety of different companies. The Rockefeller Foundation assisted financially and other grants were also offered. In addition, Joseph Papp, producer of the New York Shakespeare Festival, offered rent-free rehearsal rooms and the use of the

Eliot Feld, Richard Gilmore and John Sowinski pictured in Tzaddik, *a work rooted in the Jewish tradition of the significance of learning. Undoubtedly a deep, personal statement, the ballet has, nevertheless, a universal appeal, not least because of the vivid character dancing, the pathos and the humour. Despair, satire and comedy are portrayed by exaggerated, almost grotesque movements. The music is Aaron Copland's Vitebak and is played by a trio of piano, violin and cello.*

The Gods Amused, *created in 1971, is a splendid vehicle for displaying the talents of the company's dancers — here Helen Douglas, Linda Miller and Edmund Lafosse. It is a fine example of Eliot Feld's most fluid choreography.*

Newman Theater. Consequently, the company would only have to pay the cost of running itself. The size of the theatre is ideally suited to a small company, having only 300 seats. So much co-operation and encouragement from so many sources is a measure of Eliot Feld's stature as a choreographer.

The Eliot Feld Ballet gave its first public performance on May 28, 1974. Christine Sarry, a gifted principal with American Ballet Theatre, had joined Eliot Feld's first company and rejoined him on his second venture. John Sowinski and Elizabeth Lee also returned and other dancers were harvested from many parts of the country making a total of 18. A three-week season was planned, the programme consisting mainly of revivals including *Theatre*, *Intermezzo* and *The Gods Amused*. Two new works, *Sephardic Song* and *Tzaddik*, were also presented. Naturally the dance world watched the new company with great interest and considerable speculation. All those who had manifested their faith in Eliot Feld in practical ways were not disappointed. The season was so popular it was extended for a further two weeks and the theatre was packed throughout.

A second season followed in November and December. Eliot Feld presented a new work, *The Real McCoy* to music by George Gershwin. *The Consort* was revived and the company presented its first work by another choreographer, Glen Tetley's *Embrace Tiger and Return to Mountain*, originally created for the Ballet Rambert.

As well as regular seasons in New York with a programme of revivals and new works, the Eliot Feld Ballet has also appeared at Wolf Trap, Artpark, Meadowbrook and Detroit. The company has also made two tours of the mid-west and has visited the north-east and west coast of the United States. In the summer of 1976, it made a nine-week tour of Latin America under the auspices of the State Department. March 1977 saw the company's first appearance at an uptown New York theatre when it gave a two-week season at City Center 55th Street Dance Theater.

The secret of success for the Eliot Feld Ballet lies in the fact that he is a very sensitive choreographer with an enormous dance vocabulary and the polished technique of the dancers enables them to respond closely to his work. The dancers always seem very young and full of youthful enthusiasm and enjoyment, although, in fact, several are experienced, mature and at the peak of their technique.

Eliot Feld's work has a delicate fluid quality, firmly rooted in classicism, although he approaches it in a way usually associated with contemporary dance groups. He is a very musical choreographer and there is never any sense of conflict between the separate elements of his works. His ballets are sparse and uncluttered but never harsh or ungentle. Generally abstract, they nevertheless have a rich emotional texture. The trio from *The Gods Amused*, for example, is a subtle blend of dignity and playfulness. *Mazurka*, created in 1975, moves at an extraordinary pace and, within the framework of the traditional dance, rapid shifts of emotion and movement take place.

He makes enormous demands on his dancers, expecting and getting a response to his broad range of technique. He is a splendid and intensely dramatic dancer himself, frequently dancing leading roles. No single work demonstrates his power as well as the intense and hypnotic *Tzaddik*, in which he danced the title role.

Eliot Feld continues to extend his scope as a choreographer and the range of the company. His more practical approach to running his own company has meant that he has had a more stable situation in which to create some of the most beautiful new ballets of our time.

(all IP)
Catherine E. Ulissey
Nancy Thuesen
Traci Owens
Megan Murphy
Kay Johnson

The Company

Artistic Director: Eliot Feld

The Dancers:			
	Arturo Azito	*IP Johanna Baer*	*Timothy Cronin*
	Helen Douglas	*IP Gloria Brisbin*	*Richard Fein*
	Mona Elgh	*IP Patrick Lea*	*Judith Garfinkel*
IP Eliot Feld	*IP James Cohen*	*Kenneth Hughes*
	Richard Gilmore	*IP* Charles Kennedy	Jennifer Palo
	Michaela K. Hughes	*IP* Emund Lafosse	*IP* Mary Randolph
	Cynthia Irion	*IP* Remus Marcu	Shirley Reevie
		IP Linda Miller	*IP* Christine Sarry
		IP Gregory Mitchell	*IP* Jeff Satinoff
		George Montalbano	Paul D. Stewart
		Mark Morris	Gwynn Taylor

The Repertoire

IP Jan.30, 1980 MSU ✱*A Soldier's Tale* (Feld)
A Poem Forgotten (Feld)
At Midnight (Feld)
Cortège Parisien (Feld)
Excursions (Feld)
IP Jan.30, 1980 MSU ✱*Harbinger* (Feld)
Impromptu (Feld)
Intermezzo (Feld) – *IP Jan.31, 1980 MSU*
Mazurka (Feld)
Sephardic Song (Feld)
The Consort (Feld)
The Real McCoy (Feld)
Tzaddik (Feld)
Waves (Posin)

Touring

1976 Latin America   *A Footstep of Air – IP Jan. 30, 1980 MSU*
Half Time – IP Jan. 31, 1980 MSU

The Martha Graham Dance Company

The company cannot be separated from the remarkable and iconoclastic figure of Martha Graham herself. Unbelievably she is over eighty years old but remains a dynamic creative force behind the company and is still the most influential figure in contemporary dance, not only in the United States, but across the world. In fact, so powerful is her influence that a question mark must hover over the company's future possibilities when she is no longer with it.

Martha Graham was born in 1893 at Pittsburgh into a typical New England family. Her work with dance has been compared to Emily Dickinson's with poetry and there is certainly a common characteristic in the subtle blending of the mystical and the real. She was brought up in California and had determined on a career as a dancer while still at High School. When she graduated in 1916 she persuaded her family to send her to the famous Denishawn School in Los Angeles, a year after it had opened. The school was the idea of the dancers Ruth St Denis and Ted Shawn who had both established major reputations as dancers and choreographers before they began teaching. Dance was taught in an open-minded, eclectic way and a multiplicity of techniques and styles was offered to the student – oriental dance, primitive dance, ballet and a system of movement techniques calculated for the specific needs of the individual. Although she later grew discontented with her association with Denishawn, Martha Graham was undoubtedly deeply influenced and affected by the broad dance background and imaginative approach the school offered during her early years as a dancer.

Takako Asakawa has been a leading soloist with the Martha Graham Dance Company for some years and has won special acclaim for her interpretation of the Girl in Red in Diversion of Angels. *It is a lyrical ballet about the nature of being in love for the first time. The title is taken from a poem by Ben Bellitt.*

Three years after joining the school, Martha Graham was given the leading female role in Ted Shawn's Aztec ballet *Xochitl*. She remained at Denishawn for seven years, studying with both Ruth St Denis and Ted Shawn. It is, perhaps, significant that she trained more with Ted Shawn than with his wife and so was probably more affected by his interest in essentially American themes – folk tradition, American Indians, American negroes, ordinary labourers, farmworkers and seamen – rather than by Ruth St Denis's fascination with the oriental and Indian.

By 1923, Martha Graham had grown dissatisfied with the Denishawn School and Company and left. For two years she danced as a soloist with the *Greenwich Village Follies* but she found revue frustrating. In 1925 she joined the Eastman School of Music as a teacher. While she was there she found the opportunity to experiment and explore new possibilities. This was apparent when she made her New York debut in 1926 although she was still clearly directly affected by her experiences at Denishawn in works like *Three Gopi Maidens* and *A Study in Lacquer*.

However, it was not long afterwards that what eventually was known as the Graham technique began to emerge with such works as *Revolt* and *Four Insincerities*. In the 1930s she turned to American Indian themes with works like *Primitive Mysteries* and *Ceremonials* and also to contemporary American life, creating *American Provincials* and *American Document*. Although undoubtedly she owed an obvious debt to Ted Shawn's vision, she transcended her earlier training to create something genuinely original and truly revolutionary.

With the establishment of her company, Martha Graham increased the scope of her creativity and began to develop more extended and dramatic works. The first of these new dramatic creations was *Letter to the World* based on the inner life and some of the poems of Emily Dickinson. Lines selected by Martha Graham were spoken; the music was by Hunter Johnson. The first performance was given in 1940 at Bennington College. Martha Graham took the part of The One Who Dances and others who appeared were Margaret Meredith as The One Who Speaks, Jane Dudley as The Ancestress, Eric Hawkins as The Lover and Merce Cunningham as March. Merce Cunningham was a soloist with the company until 1945 creating a number of remarkable roles – Acrobat in *Every Soul is a Circus*, Revivalist in *Appalachian Spring* and the Christ Figure in *El Penitente* – and is perhaps one of the most important figures associated with the early days of Martha Graham's company. Another dancer who was a student with Martha Graham was a young woman named Betty Bloomer, who later married ex-president Gerald Ford.

Letter to the World was followed by *Deaths and Entrances* in 1943, again based on the inner mind of the artist. The title, in fact, is derived from a poem by Dylan Thomas, but the artists concerned are the three Bronte Sisters. *Deaths and Entrances* was Martha Graham's first use of objects as symbols – each one evoking recollections when touched, which temporarily possessed a greater reality than the present.

Not all her works of this period were solemn, intense and inward-turned, *Every Soul is a Circus* (1939) and *Punch and the Judy* (1941) were both comedies. *Appalachian Spring* (1944) was a simple and sweet tale of a young American pioneer couple and is considered by many to be one of the greatest pieces of American choreography.

All her life Martha Graham has never allowed herself to become rigidly committed to one style or technique and has constantly developed and evolved, not discarding what she had already learned and created but building on from it. In the mid-1940s she created the first of her dance-dramas based on classical Greek mythology – *Cave of the Heart*. This is derived from the story of Medea's desertion by Jason and her subsequent hatred and revenge. Like all Martha Graham's works, this is not a straightforward dance-narrative but an exploration and revelation of human behaviour using the legend as a starting point. Similarly, in *Errand into the Maze*, she explores the inner psychological labrynth of a woman's emotional nature and the process of conquering fear, using the myth of Theseus and the Minotaur. *Night Journey*, from the Oedipus legend, begins at the moment of Jocasta's awful realization of her incestuous relationship and explores the way she recognizes the past. Other dance-dramas of this genre include *Clytemnestra*, *Alcestis*, *Phaedra* and *Circe*.

Although the origins of these works were in literature and mythology, Martha Graham remained unequivocally an American artist with American concerns. Her work has been an unmistakable part of an essentially American artistic paradox, partially derived from the conflict between the Old World and the New and partially from a Puritan consciousness. After *Appalachian Spring* in 1944 however, she created no more works on specifically American themes until *The Scarlet Letter* in 1975, based on Nathaniel Hawthorne's novel of Puritan New England.

Martha Graham is not just a revolutionary choreographer, she also changed the whole presentation of dance performances. The pianist, composer, writer and teacher Louis Horst was the musical director at Denishawn when Martha Graham was there. He left at the same time as she did to become her musical director. Little development in music for dance took place during the late 1920s and 1930s in spite of Louis Horst's particular sensitivity to the needs of dance but changes gradually began to happen. Previously, dance compositions were generally created without any music and when they were completed the choreographer presented the composer with the metrical requirements and he eventually produced a score.

Louis Horst and Martha Graham introduced a new and vital element into

this process. He would observe the choreographic sessions from quite an early stage. Consequently, the score he eventually produced grew out of the total creative process. Since Louis Horst, Martha Graham has collaborated with some of the most exciting composers of the twentieth century – Gian-Carlo Menotti, Dr William Schuman, Robert Starer, Paul Hindemith, Caros Chavez, Aaron Copland, Samuel Barber and Carlos Surinach.

Martha Graham has shown a similar originality in the way she treats scenery and costumes. Settings, costumes, materials, colours and fabrics are linked inextricably into the total work in just the same way as the music. In conjunction with such artists as Isamu Noguchi she has contrived to dress her dancers and herself so that they are as striking motionless as they are in movement. Her talent is undoubtedly dramatic and her creative energy is directed towards a cohesive theatrical unity.

Appalachian Spring has been described as one of the greatest creations of American choreography. The music was commissioned from Aaron Copland and the ballet was designed by Isamu Noguchi. It was premièred in 1944, during Martha Graham's 'first American period' and represents one of her finest achievements in this field.

Ballets based on themes of classical mythology used as a means for exploring the human psyche have formed a major part of Martha Graham's creative concerns. She, in fact, retired from the stage in 1969, but she is shown here in Clytemnestra *created in 1958.*

Martha Graham displays an unflagging commitment to dance, constantly exploring new possibilities and pushing forward the frontiers of her art. It is perhaps not surprising that so many of her works explore emotional, physical and psychological boundaries when she has spent most of her life as a pioneer. Her phenomenal drive has sometimes meant that she was not always clear where she was aiming and this has led on occasions to disaster, but equally, it has been the force which has enabled her to overcome her failures. It is typical that *Clytemnestra*, considered by many authorities as the supreme achievement of her career and undoubtedly a major work of the twentieth century, should have been created in 1958 after one of the longest and blackest periods of her life. Similarly, after a serious illness in the early 1970s, she resumed work with the company reviving 16 earlier works, creating new ones and staging a special programme, *An Evening with Martha Graham*.

She has always avoided formalizing her techniques and vigilantly searches out new movements to correspond with her developing ideas of emotion and personality. Even in her teaching she is continually concerned with creative freshness. Yet there is a characteristic Graham style, apparent in her own dancing particularly, and noticeable to a lesser extent in that of her company. Graham trained dancers are unmistakable even when they have matured as choreographers, often with their own companies; for example Paul Taylor and, to a lesser extent, Merce Cunningham. Her own performances were characterized by recurrent movements and gestures and her own special style permeates the work of her company whether it is performing her earlier more dynamic works or the softer more gentle modern ones. She is especially famous for the fluidity of her movements and her use of fall and recovery.

She achieved her greatest success as a performer and choreographer during the 1960s, approaching the age of 80. She did not retire as a dancer until April 1969. For many years she was reluctant to re-stage past success, but has done so more regularly since the American Dance Festival in 1964, when she revived *Frontier*, *El Penitente* and *Primitive Mysteries*. Honours, awards and grants have been showered on her and her company has been acclaimed in many parts of the world. The 'Graham technique' is taught in almost all the major ballet schools. No other single figure in the world of contemporary dance has maintained such a dominant and important position for so long. Once she was a controversial figure but now the Martha Graham company has become established and a certain glamour is associated with it. Classical stars have appeared as guest artists including Margot Fonteyn and Rudolf Nureyev, who appeared with the Martha Graham Dance Company in *Lucifer* in 1975. Martha Graham has also been invited to create works for some of the world's major dancers.

In 1976 the company was invited to dance at the Royal Opera House, Covent Garden, surely a measure of its stature in Britain. Naturally, Martha Graham's sense of the theatrical and the dramatic enabled her to make magnificent use of this opportunity. She has always tended to create for the proscenium stage and her dramatic style was well suited to the Royal Opera House. The sheer size of her concepts and concerns and her desire to create an encompassing moral and aesthetic unity gave the season a ritualistic quality. Besides a summer season in London the company toured Europe, performing at many important dance festivals as well as giving regular Broadway seasons.

Martha Graham made her debut as a choreographer over 50 years ago. Her style has developed, matured and mellowed during that time but it has always reflected her search for a dramatic medium to depict universal human concerns through dance.

The Company

Artistic Director:	Martha Graham

Rehearsal Directors:	Ross Parkes	Robert Powell
	Patricia Birch	Diane Gray
	Carol Fried	

Dancers:	Takako Asakawa	Tim Wengerd	Elisa Monte
	Phyllis Gutelius	Mario Delamo	Susan McGuire
	Yuriko Kimura	Daniel Maloney	Shelly Washington
	Ross Parkes	Peter Sparling	Henry Yu
	David Hatch Walker	Lucinda Mitchell	Judith Hogan
	Diane Gray	Diana Hart	David Chase
	Janet Eilber	Bonnie Oda Homsey	Carl Paris
	Peggy Lyman	Eric Newton	

The Repertoire

Appalachian Spring (1944)
Cave of the Heart (1946)
Chronique (1973)
Circe (1963)
Clytemnestra (1958)
Dark Meadow (1946)
Deaths and Entrances (1943)
Diversion of Angels (1948)
El Penitente (1940)
Embattled Garden (1958)
Errand into the Maze (1947)

Frontier (1935)
Herodiade (1944)
Holy Jungle (1974)
Lamentation (1930)
Letter to the World (1940)
Lucifer (1975)
Night Journey (1947)
Plain of Prayer
Point of Crossing
Seraphic Dialogue (1955)
The Scarlet Letter

Touring	Great Britain, Greece, Germany, Yugoslavia, Belgium, Austria, Holland, France.

Alvin Ailey City Center Dance Theater

All art is a process of combining individual experience and cultural heritage and then selecting and organizing it within a framework to create something of timeless universality. Contemporary dance has tended to do only half this. It has kept itself a little apart and, in spite of claims to the contrary, it has deliberately confined itself to a rather rarefied, intellectual world. Even Martha Graham, high priestess of contemporary dance, whilst creating and developing the most beautiful and exciting technique, was inclined towards the deliberately abstruse in her early choreography. Not so Alvin Ailey, whose activities in dance are comparable with the blues in music.

He was born in the small town of Rogers, Texas in 1931 – the days before Martin Luther King and the popular civil rights movement. Being black and living in the South at that time has left him with deep rooted memories of segregation and a profound consciousness of black American culture from revivalist religion to the blues and jazz. He lived in Texas until he was 12 when he moved with his mother to Los Angeles. His background can all be seen clearly in *Revelations*, generally accepted as his masterpiece and created in 1960.

Traditional black music is used throughout and the work is divided into three parts. The first part involves nine dancers drawn together in an affirmation of shared strength and ends in a deeply moving pas de deux of emotional commitment delicately worked around a tender responsiveness between the two dancers. The second part is a bright and joyous baptism. A spectacular piece of theatre, it closes with a male solo – *I Want to Be Ready* – of stunning sinousness and tensile precision. The third part – *Move Members Move* – is a magnificent evocation of a revivalist meeting ending climactically with *Rock My Soul in the Bosom of Abraham*.

It must not be thought, however, that Alvin Ailey's work is limited or insular. His training and personality would never permit this. His first introduction to dance was a school trip to see the Ballet Russe de Monte Carlo. Having discovered the theatres of Los Angeles, he returned and was deeply impressed by Katherine Dunham and staggered to realize that there were black dancers. Stimulated by this and by a school friend's demonstration of something he had learned in a dancing class, Alvin Ailey began attending the Lester Horton School in 1949. He gave this up when he began to study Romance languages at UCLA. Later he returned to the Lester Horton School where he delighted in the atmosphere. All kinds of topics were discussed – literature, painting, music and politics. Moreover, Lester Horton had a lifelong interest in ethnic dance and had become an authority on the dances of American Indians.

In November 1953 Lester Horton died and Alvin Ailey took over the direction and choreography of the company. A year later he travelled to New York where he appeared in the Broadway musical *House of Flowers*. Whilst in New York he embarked upon an exhausting training schedule, studying contemporary dance with Martha Graham, Hanya Holm and Charles Weidman, composition with Doris Humphrey, ballet with Karel Shook and acting with Stella Adler and Milton Katselas. He appeared in a number of Broadway and off-Broadway shows as both a dancer and an actor at this

Alvin Ailey created Hidden Rites *in 1973. His typical use of the extended line and stretched limbs can be seen clearly in this pose.*

Judith Jamison is undoubtedly one of the most exciting dancers on the current dance scene. Her extraordinary strength, control and suppleness, combined with an air of relaxation and ease, have inspired a number of choreographers, besides Alvin Ailey himself, to create works specially for her. Here she is seen in Louis Falco's Caravan.

time. In 1958 he formed the American Dance Theater which made its debut at the YMHA's Kauffman Auditorium.

Ten years of spasmodic performances in the United States followed. A few performances were given in New York and a few more in different parts of the country throughout the year. Meanwhile, the company's tours abroad were triumphant. Over 60 curtain calls were recorded in Hamburg and the company extended its visit to London by six weeks. In January 1969 this hopelessly ironic situation seemed to change. A week's programme at the Billy Rose Theater received massive public and press acclaim. The following spring, the Brooklyn Academy of Music invited the company to become resident.

This arrangement was never satisfactory and came to an end in the spring of 1970. A visit to the USSR had been arranged for the autumn of that year and in a delightfully direct way, Alvin Ailey called a press conference which 'blackmailed' the State Department into arranging a tour of North Africa to keep the company together until the Russian cultural exchange should take place. The six week visit to the USSR was triumphant. The company received a standing ovation after the last performance of the visit, given at Leningrad. The audience refused to leave and pressed Alvin Ailey to sign his autograph on programmes, pieces of paper and even their arms. The reception was equally tumultuous at Moscow with 30 curtain calls. The company was the first American group to appear on Moscow television and it was seen by 22 million viewers.

Such a successful reception in so demanding a country as the USSR could not fail to stimulate new interest in the United States. The company's first engagement on its return to the United States was a two week booking at the ANTA Theater. By the beginning of the second week the tickets were completely sold out. As the popular saying goes – the rest is history.

Although the company came into existence and managed to survive 13 years of undeserved relative anonymity in the United States, because of Alvin Ailey's spirit and determination to 'celebrate the beauty of mankind', he does not insist on the kind of 'absolute rule' so common in contemporary dance groups. Perhaps this has come about because individual choreographers had such a harsh lone struggle for the recognition of their art. Alvin Ailey, however, is a revolutionary of a different sort. He has directed his energies towards building up a balanced repertoire of works by an assortment of choreographers. Besides Alvin Ailey himself, the works of nine choreographers are featured. The size of the company has expanded too, from seven to thirty. Until 1964 it was an all-black company. Alvin Ailey became aware that a kind of inverted racism was being practised. He also objected to the comments of some critics who claimed, mistakenly he believed, that only black dancers are suited to jazz. Not only does he feel that this is false but that it places unreasonable limitations on black dancers. Since then, he has aimed at presenting an integrated multi-racial company truly reflecting the best of American art.

In addition to the works he has created for his own company, Alvin Ailey has also been associated with other companies. Among these are *Mingus Dances* for the City Center Joffrey Ballet, *Sea Change* for American Ballet Theater, a long ballet for the world première of Virail Thomson's *Lord Byron* and the dances for the Metropolitan Opera's *Carmen*. He has also been invited to create ballets abroad.

In 1972 the company changed its name from the American Dance Theater to the Alvin Ailey City Center Dance Theater and moved to the City Center of Music and Drama. Now the company is renowned nationally and internationally and performs frequently on television. It has also extended to develop a school and the Alvin Ailey Repertory Workshop, a young company

An overwhelming impression created by Alvin Ailey's works, whatever the mood or theme presented, is that dance itself is physically pleasurable and delightful. He has done much to break down the myth that contemporary dance is somehow ponderously intellectual. Hector Mercado makes this exciting leap from Kinetic Molpai *seem completely effortless and as much joy to perform as it is to watch.*

which explores areas that the main company is unable to.

In 1975 the Alvin Ailey City Center Dance Theater again made history by being the first American dance company to tour Hungary under a Department of State arrangement. Dancers of the Budapest Opera Ballet rushed on stage after the final performance to congratulate the dancers. Like the last night in Leningrad, the audience continued cheering and applauding for 40 minutes after the time planned for the final curtain.

Such success is due to the tenacity and vision of Alvin Ailey. The immense popular appeal and critical acclaim of the company are fitting tributes to his endeavours towards universality, humanity and control. More than anything the Alvin Ailey City Center Dance Theater has proved anew that dance is a joyous and enchanting thing.

The Company

Artistic Director: Alvin Ailey

Ballet Master: Ali Pourfarrokh

Principal Dancers:

Ulysses Dove	Mari Kajiwara	Estelle Spurlock
Judith Jamison	Hector Mercado	Clive Thompson
Melvin Jones	Kenneth Pearl	Dudley Williams

The Repertoire

A Song for You (Ailey) 1972
Blues Suite (Ailey) 1948
Cry (Ailey) 1971
Hermit Songs (Ailey) 1961
Hidden Rites (Ailey) 1973
The Lark Ascending (Ailey) 1972
Love Songs (Ailey) 1972
The Mooche (Ailey) 1975
Night Creature (Ailey) 1974/5
Pas de 'Duke' (Ailey) 1976
Reflections in D (Ailey) 1976
Revelations (Ailey) 1962
Three Black Kings (Ailey) 1976

Streams (Ailey) 1970
According to Eve (Butler) 1972
After Eden (Butler) 1966
Carmina Burana (Butler) 1959
Portrait of Billie (Butler) 1959
Caravan (Falco) 1976
Echoes in Blue (Myers) 1975
Kinetic Molpai (Shawn) 1935
Liberian Suite (Truitte /Horton) 1952
Missa Brevis (Limon) 1958
Rainbow 'Round My Shoulder (McKayle) 1959
The Road of Phoebe Snow (Beatty) 1959

Touring

Seven European tours, Hungary, USSR.

Twyla Tharp
Dance Foundation

The company undoubtedly enjoys its rehearsals. The members at this time (January 1976) were, from left to right, Rose Marie Wright, Larry Grenier, Kenneth Rinker, Jenifer Way, Shelley Washington and Tom Rawe.

To be exact, the Twyla Tharp Dance Foundation is not the real name of the company. Twyla Tharp has reverted to her earlier system of calling the company by the names of the members beginning with her oldest associates, so rightfully it should be called Twyla Tharp/Rose Marie Wright/Kenneth Rinker/Tom Rawe/Jenifer Way/Shelley Washington.

Revolutionary and avant-garde undoubtedly, but Twyla Tharp has a classical purity of style which separates her from the simply iconoclastic contemporary choreographer. An extensive dance and musical background – tap, ballet, jazz, contemporary dance, baton twirling, piano, violin, viola, drums, musical theory, harmony and composition – have provided an enormous dance vocabulary and fluency making her as capable of working with the City Center Joffrey Ballet and the American Ballet Theatre as with her own group of dancers.

She was born in Portland, Indiana and began music lessons when two years

old. Her mother's educational theory was that it was worth learning everything possible because it might prove useful later. Apart from her dance and musical studies, Twyla Tharp also learnt shorthand and typing. She moved to California at the age of ten and then to New York City where she studied for and achieved a degree in art history. She continued her dance studies in New York, although she had no intention of becoming a professional dancer. Following her mother's principles she investigated every kind of dance including classical ballet classes with Igor Schwetzoff, Pereyaslavec, William Griffith and Margaret Craske and modern dance with Martha Graham, Eric Hawkins, Alwin Nikolais and with Merce Cunningham for whom she has enormous respect and liking.

Shortly before she graduated from Barnard, she joined the Paul Taylor Dance Company. She performed with this company for about a year. Although she admired Paul Taylor's work and personal style very much, she found she was unable to explore her own ideas and was becoming frustrated. So often modern dance companies, with the notable exception of Alvin Ailey's, are vehicles for the work of one specific choreographer and this makes enormous demands of discipline on the dancers. Consequently, aspiring choreographers usually leave such companies to found groups of their own. There are, of course, advantages to this kind of arrangement. Not all dancers are capable of or want to be choreographers and so respond well to a clearly defined framework. An intimate rapport can also be built up between a choreographer and company which only performs his or her work.

Eight Jelly Rolls is a suite of dances created in 1971 to the music of the jazz master Jelly Roll Morton. It marked the beginning of a new phase in Twyla Tharp's creative development and has proved immensely popular both at home and abroad. She can be seen on the extreme right of the picture.

Twyla Tharp left the Paul Taylor company and produced her first original work in 1965. It was called *Tank Dive*, lasted less than four minutes and was designed for one dancer and four non-dancers. Characteristically, she still maintains that it was a perfect piece, feeling that she was unable at that time to create a longer, sustained work and that it was better to create a short, good work than a long, bad one.

The mid-1960s were times of cultural change and New York audiences and critics were responsive to revolution in art. Twyla Tharp was not accepted without criticism but she certainly aroused a lot of interest. Her first dances had a self-conscious, aggressive quality. A semi-formulated artistic policy suggested that it did not matter whether the audience liked the works or not, although it would be more pleasant for everyone if they did. The dancers all had unsmiling, belligerent expressions almost as if they resented dancing, the work and the audience. *Re-Moves*, created in 1966, is typical of this period. It is a work for three dancers in four parts and is indicative of Twyla Tharp's interest in spatial relationships which later found more successful expression in meticulously plotted movement. The first part of *Re-Moves* is in the open, the second is half-hidden, only one third is visible in the third section and the fourth is entirely hidden. Later, Twyla Tharp found ways of exploring space less frustrating for the audience.

1968 brought about a movement away from the rather static, conceptual approach of previous years. Dance began to feature centrally in her work as opposed to the earlier combinations of fixed poses, abrupt movement and a lot of walking about. The size of the company increased and with this came a new inter-relationship between the dancers, who were all female. Facial expressions and a deceptively easy fluidity of movement replaced the earlier style. Music had never been prominent in Twyla Tharp's works and now she eliminated it completely, along with scenery and lighting. Apart from the movement itself, all that existed in the dances were the costumes, designed by her husband Robert Huot, and the sounds of the dancers' feet, gasps of effort and, sometimes, someone counting the rhythms out loud.

She continued to explore space and the uses of it. *After-Suite*, presented at the Billy Rose Theatre in 1969, was performed by seven dancers in three adjoining squares. As each section of the dance was completed it was immediately repeated in the square next to it. *Group Activities* was a double quintet, each group occupying a space of 20 feet by 40 feet and duplicating accurately each other's movements. *Medley*, scheduled as one hour long, is performed outdoors, beginning one hour before sunset. There are six soloists and a chorus of 60 who perform the last three minutes of the work individually, the work ending when the last dancer has finished. Apparently, the present record is two hours 37 minutes. Another exploration into the possibilities of visibility was *Dancing in the Streets of London and Paris, Continued in Stockholm and Sometimes Madrid*. Sections of the work are performed in different rooms, on different levels and on staircases, the whole piece being held together by a closed-circuit television system. A catastrophic performance was given at the Metropolitan Museum of Art, New York, because the television system had not been supplied and chaos resulted. It has been performed successfully elsewhere.

In 1970 Twyla Tharp moved to a farm which quickly became a kind of dance workshop. A period of intense activity resulted in a number of changes in company policy. It was decided to abandon the rather negative approach to dance as a performance. Dance is essentially a performing art and to isolate it from audience response and pare it down purely to a series of actions is pretentious and self-defeating.

Another major change was the decision to incorporate music. Rather than being a compromise of her principles these developments marked a new maturity in Twyla Tharp's work and a remarkable collection of new creations emerged from the farm workshop.

One of the most exciting of these was *Eight Jelly Rolls*, a suite of dances to the music of the famous jazz band, Jelly Roll Morton and the Red Hot Peppers. This was her first work set to music and led to *The Bix Pieces* to music by Bix Biederbecke and Paul Whiteman's Orchestra, also in 1971, and *The Raggedy Dances* – to the unlikely combination of Scott Joplin piano rags and Mozart variations – in 1972.

One of the most attractive features of these later works is that they look so easy. The free flowing movement and informal style make them seem as if anyone could join in if he or she wanted to. Just as the classical ballet dancer must make lifts, beats and jumps seem completely effortless, the Twyla Tharp dancer conceals the meticulous planning and complex technique which support the air of casualness and general impression of fun. She has been accused of not working out the choreography of her works completely. Nothing could be more inaccurate for her planning is as detailed as a battle campaign. When she was pregnant – her son, Jesse, was born in the spring of 1971 – each week she made a 30 minute video-tape of herself dancing to a Willie Smith record. This gave her a unique opportunity to observe changes in her style and the influence of other factors on the dancer. In fact, she incorporated a dance she was working on as an exploration of her unstable condition the day she went into labour, into the drunken dance in *Eight Jelly Rolls* – a remarkable demonstration of a choreographer's single-minded determination.

There are numerous other instances of her controlled, structured approach to choreography. *The One Hundreds*, for example, is divided into three parts. In the first part, two dancers perform 100 11-second dance phrases simultaneously, each phrase separated by an interval of four seconds. In the second

From left to right, Tom Rawe, Twyla Tharp, Rose Marie Wright and Kenneth Rinker demonstrate the carefully planned moves of Sue's Leg, *a work dedicated to Suzanne Weil.*

part, five dancers simultaneously perform 20 of the phrases each, and in the third part, 100 dancers dance simultaneously, one phrase each, completing the full set in 11 seconds.

Equally, if the choreography of the 'Tea for Two' section in *Sue's Leg*, were not absolutely planned and rehearsed, the outcome could be disastrous. The three dancers in turn spin around and with the appearance of no preliminary movement fall suddenly and are caught by each other. If the timing were not perfect there would have been some unfortunate accidents.

In 1972, Kenneth Rinker joined the company, the first male dancer. Since then, other men have joined the company, introducing a new element into the works. Twyla Tharp re-staged *The Fugue* to include male dancers. It was originally created in 1970 for a trio of female dancers and this apparently slight change caused quite a major and interesting shift of emphasis in the work.

Twyla Tharp is one of the rare creators in whose works it is possible to trace a clear line of development and at the same time, recognize an underlying continuity. In 1973, a further development occurred when Twyla Tharp was invited to create a co-production for her own company and the City Center Joffrey Ballet. It was set to a selection of music by the pop group, the Beach Boys. Previously, the music she had used was the popular dance music of an earlier era or was by classical composers – Jelly Roll Morton, Mozart, Guiseppe Torelli, Bix Biederbecke or Scott Joplin.

The scenery for *Deuce Coupe*, a title derived from one of the Beach Boys' songs, consisted of a long paper sheet winding across the back of the stage on which graffiti was sprayed during the performance. Throughout the work, Erika Goodman worked her way systematically through a dictionary of ballet steps, regardless of the antics of the other dancers. The work is a confrontation between rock and ballet dancing but reveals the similarities as well as the differences between the two styles. In this new venture Twyla Tharp's work was inevitably uneven in quality. Sometimes it was remarkably subtle, as in the quartet danced to a rather sentimental and banal love song. The four dance closely together but constantly move their heads so that their eyes never meet. In contrast, some of the work captures the high-spirited quality of the music, evoking the 1960s image of happy-go-lucky youth in perpetual summertime and is pure fun. Occasionally, the dances do not work quite so well, as in the lively counterpoint to *Little Deuce Coupe*, which does not have enough sharpness to avoid looking untidy and *Alley Oop* seems to drag during Erika Goodman's continuation through the ballet glossary.

Nevertheless, it was an exciting venture into new realms for Twyla Tharp and proved to be the triumphant success of that season for the City Center Joffrey Ballet. It was certainly typically entertaining and fun. In 1975 Twyla Tharp created *Deuce Coupe II* at the request of the City Center Joffrey Ballet which wanted to include the work in the repertoire. The second version was fundamentally the same. The changes were partly adaptations as Twyla Tharp's company obviously could not be included in a work intended for a permanent repertoire. The remodelled version also shows a revision of some of the less satisfactory parts of the original. The graffiti was replaced by a huge pop painting and the sequence of the songs has changed. More fundamentally, the contrast of styles has almost disappeared and only their similarities remain giving the work a greater unity. She also created *As Time Goes By* for the City Center Joffrey Ballet.

Between the two versions and after *Deuce Coupe II*, Twyla Tharp continued to create works for her own company including *Sue's Leg* to music by Fats Waller, once again demonstrating her wonderful ability with jazz. She does not seem so much at ease with pop music, although *Ocean's Motion* to music by Chuck Berry was very successful on the company's debut at the Spoleto Festival in 1975.

In 1976 the American Ballet Theatre commissioned a work from her. *Push Comes to Shove* was a magnificent meeting of talents – Twyla Tharp and one of the major classical ballet companies in the United States. More personally it was a splendid meeting of the remarkable talents of Twyla Tharp and Mikhail Baryshnikov.

Push Comes to Shove was very successful and immensely surprising, incongruous and funny. The wonderful technical expertise of Mihail Baryshnikov was exploited fully for the element of surprise with typical Twyla Tharp movements which have no apparent preparation. Elements of American vaudeville, baton twirling (involving a hat which appears and disappears throughout the performance, becoming at one point, two hats), subtle and amusing references to well-known classical ballets and the dynamic energetic dancing characteristic of Twyla Tharp combine in a delightful and essential witty way.

The element of parody in *Push Comes to Shove* is indicative of a further maturity in Twyla Tharp's work. The posters which advertised the 1976 season poked gentle, friendly fun at George Balanchine and *Give and Take*, created by Twyla Tharp, used Sousa marches which had featured in George Balanchine's *Stars and Stripes*. It is probably typical that Twyla Tharp should have the effrontery to make fun of George Balanchine but it is also typical that she should have the imagination to do so in a subtle, delightful, entertaining and thoroughly inoffensive way.

The Company
Founder: Twyla Tharp

Dancers: Twyla Tharp   Tom Rawe
Rose Marie Wright   Jennifer Way
Kenneth Rinker   Shelley Washington

The Repertoire

Tank Dive (1965)
Stage Show (1965)
Stride (1965)
Cede Blue Lake (1965)
Unprocessed (1965)
Re-Moves (1966)
Yancey Dance (1966)
One Two Three (1967)
Jam (1967)
Disperse (1967)
Three Page Sonata for Four (1967
Forevermore (1967)
Generation (1968)
One Way (1968)
Excess, Idle, Surplus (1968)
After-Suite (1969)
Group Activities (1969)
Medley (1969)
Dancing in the Streets of London and Paris, Continued in Stockholm and Sometimes Madrid (1969)

Pymfyppmtynn Ypf (1970)
The Fugue (1970)
Rose's Cross Country (1970)
The One Hundreds (1970)
Up and Down I and II (1971)
Eight Jelly Rolls (1971)
Mozart Sonata, K. 545 (1971)
The Willie Smith Series (1971) – videotape
Torelli (1971)
The Bix Pieces (1971)
The Raggedy Dances (1972)
Deuce Coupe (1973) – for City Center Joffrey Ballet. Co-production.
The Bach Duet (1973)
In the Beginnings (1974)
Sue's Leg (1975)
The Double Cross (1975)
Ocean's Motion (1975)
Give and Take (1976)

Touring   Germany, Holland, Britain, Italy.

The Paul Taylor Dance Company

On September 21, 1976, 21 years after its inception, the Paul Taylor Dance Company was disbanded as a result of the cancellation of a tour of Latin America planned for the winter. It seemed most unlikely that such a leading contemporary dance group would be allowed to disappear so easily after a long and successful career in the forefront of dance developments, not only in the United States but also in Europe.

From left to right, Victoria Uris, Elie Chaib and Linda Kent appear in Paul Taylor's Runes. *The ballet has a ritualistic, almost Druidic quality and the choreography evokes a mysterious and mystic world. It is set to a plangent piano solo by Gerald Busby and the primary motivation is musical, impelling the dance through subtle shifts of mood.*

Paul Taylor has been a major force in contemporary dance for many years. He was born in Pennsylvania, grew up in Washington and attended Syracuse University where he had a scholarship to study painting. Later he studied dance at the Julliard School of Music, the Martha Graham School and the Metropolitan Opera Ballet School. His teachers included Margaret Craske, Martha Graham and Antony Tudor and the particular qualities of each of these helped shape Paul Taylor's unique style. He was a soloist with the Martha Graham Dance Company for some years and a guest artist with the New York City Ballet in 1959, when George Balanchine created a special variation in *Episodes* for him. This solo has not been danced by anyone else since.

He founded his own company when only 25 years old and attracted public attention with *Three Epitaphs*, one of his earliest works. Since then he has consolidated his reputation as one of the most exciting and original choreographers in the world of contemporary dance. He has received many honours and awards including two Guggenheim Fellowships and the Capezio Dance Award, and was elected Chevalier de l'Ordre des Artes et des Lettres by the French Government.

The company has toured extensively since its European debut at the Festival of Two Worlds in Spoleto, Italy in 1960. Nine of the company's 22 foreign tours were sponsored by the Department of State and it has represented the United States in Arts festivals in 35 differents countries.

Since he formed his own company, Paul Taylor has created over 70 original works for it. It is ironic that in 1976 three of his most exciting and powerful works were premièred. His individual style is an unusual and informed blend of humour and seriousness with an extraordinary range of depth and texture. There is an element of consistency throughout his work, which enables him to present a programme containing works from different periods of his life without any strain, such as *Polaris* (1976), *Aureole* (1962) and *Three Epitaphs* (1954). Nevertheless, he always manages to surprise and delight his audience. *Polaris*, for example, consists of two parts. The second part is an accurate repetition of the choreography of the first but using different dancers, music and lighting, shifting the emphasis, feel and appearance in a curiously complete and incomplete way. *Three Epitaphs* is full of humour, rarely found in contemporary choreography. *Runes* is a strange blend of mysterious ritual and acrobatic trickery. *Esplanade* has a beautiful formal elegance excellently suited to the Bach violin concertos to which it is set, and *From Sea to Shining Sea* is bitingly satirical.

The dancers too have recently developed from strength to strength. They respond magnificently to the blend of individual virtuosity and total unity demanded of them by Paul Taylor's choreography. They have an exceptionally graceful quality which can, perhaps, be traced back to the influence of Martha Graham with whom half the dancers, as well as Paul Taylor himself, trained. He, in fact, no longer dances, but concentrates exclusively on choreography. Moreover, the dancers give the general impression that they

are actually enjoying themselves and like to dance, an effect which adds enormously to the audience's pleasure and which is another uncommon feature among contemporary dance groups, with the notable exception of Alvin Ailey's.

Before the company's abrupt termination of activities in 1976, it had many plans for the immediate future. Besides the cancelled tour to Latin America, it had planned to visit the Far East and to make a further tour of Europe. The company has achieved huge public and critical acclaim in the many European cities it has visited, including London, Paris, Madrid, Barcelona and Copenhagen, where it taught *Aureole* to the Royal Danish Ballet in 1968.

Aureole is one of Paul Taylor's most popular works and has become something of a signature piece for the company. It was particularly delighted when, in 1974, Rudolf Nureyev appeared as guest artist in the role originally created by Paul Taylor. *Aureole* also featured in the programme *Nureyev and Friends*, with members of the Paul Taylor Dance Company as guests. The company has also appeared at Dame Margot Fonteyn's Royal Gala Matinée in London – the first contemporary dance group to do so.

Other plans for the future included a national tour, a Broadway season in Spring 1977 and the fourth annual seven-week residency at Lake Placid. Financial troubles are the curse of every dance company, large or small, classic or contemporary. However, the cancellation of a major tour when it is too late to organize alternative appearances, is a damaging blow to a small, contemporary group. However, with a background of international fame and the promise of future seasons, the Paul Taylor Dance Company was re-formed early in 1977, to continue to surprise and delight its many fans.

Esplanade to two violin concerti by J. S. Bach, has a formal elegance and light-hearted beauty. The dancers move with ease and fluidity from sculpture-like poses to the demanding, but delightful, final movement.

The Company

Artistic Director;   Paul Taylor

Dancers;

TV *Thomas Event,*
TV *Susan McGuire*
TV *David Parsons*

TV	Carolyn Adams	TV Bettie de Jong
TV	Ruth Andrien	Linda Kent
TV	Elie Chaib	TV Robert Kahn
	Eileen Cropley	TV Monica Morris *TV Monica Byron*
TV	Christopher Gillis	TV Victoria Uris
TV	Nicholas Gunn	Lila York

The Repertoire   *World Premier – "Profiles" July 1979 on TV*

Agathe's Tale 1967
American Genesis 1973
Aureole 1962
X *Big Bertha* 1970
X *Book of Beasts* 1971
Churchyard 1969
Cloven Kingdom 1976
Duet 1964
X *Esplanade* 1975
Fetes 1971
Foreign Exchange 1970
From Sea to Shining Sea 1965
Guests of May 1972
Insects and Heroes 1961
Junction 1961

Lento 1967
Noah's Minstrels 1973
Orbs 1966
Piece Period 1962
Polaris 1976
Post Meridian 1966
Private Domain 1969
Public Domain 1968
X *Runes* 1975
Scudorama 1963
So Long Eden 1972
Sports and Follies 1974
Three Epitaphs 1954
Tablet 1960
Untitled Quartet 1974

Touring   22 foreign tours including Europe, North Africa, Latin America, Asia, Middle East, Far East.

Merce Cunningham and Dance Company

Merce Cunningham's activities in the field of contemporary dance have been compared with those of Sir Frederick Ashton in the world of mainstream ballet. Perhaps an even more striking parallel could be drawn between Merce Cunningham and George Balanchine. Within their different techniques both choreographers preserve an impersonal approach and each believes in the expressiveness of a single movement unimpeded by the obtrusion of other elements, such as plot or scenery, and with no feeling of compulsion towards or away from a climax. There are, of course, fundamental differences between the two men. George Balanchine is the most musical of choreographers while Merce Cunningham is committed to the physicality of dance independent of sound. Individual works also suggest comparison with other choreographers. The patterns and movements of the dancers in *Tread* are reminiscent of *Dances at a Gathering* by that other luminary of the New York City Ballet, Jerome Robbins.

However, comparisons with other choreographers can only reveal half the story. Merce Cunningham is one of the major figures participating, not only in the revolution taking place in dance, but in the upheavals occurring in the

wider spectrum of the arts in general. This is indicated by the list of distinguished contemporary artists who have worked with him – Robert Rauschenberg, Andy Warhol, Robert Morris and Frank Stella.

Merce Cunningham was trained in a variety of dance styles including tap, folk and exhibition ballroom dancing. He danced with the Martha Graham company as a soloist from 1940 to 1945 creating a number of roles – Acrobat in *Every Soul is a Circus*, Christ figure in *El Penitente* and March in *Letter to the World*. He also taught contemporary dance at the School of American Ballet.

Out of this diverse background he began creating his own works. To begin with, these were mainly solos for himself – *The Wind Remains, Totem Ancestor, Root of Unfocus, Dream, 16 Dances for Soloist and Company of Three*.

In 1953 he formed his own company and began the kind of work that is characteristic of him today, if anything can ever be called characteristic of a man so wholly committed to chance and change and whose works vary in size, content and presentation from one performance to the next. The first of these works was *Symphonie Pour Un Homme Seul*, later renamed *Collage*. The keynote of these works is the element of chance. Continuity is supplied by the movement of the dancers but the interpretation of the expression is left exclusively to the individuals of the audience. This haphazard quality does not mean, however, that the work lacks control. In fact, the opposite is

Generally, Merce Cunningham's works are not easily adapted for other companies familiar with a more formalized approach to dance. Summerspace, however, has been successfully performed by such companies as the New York City Ballet, the Cullberg Ballet, Stockholm and the Boston Ballet. Here it is danced by Robert Kovich and Chris Komar, whose fluid movements evoke perfectly feelings of both light and spatial freedom.

Merce Cunningham's own Solo *is a particularly graceful piece. Much of the movement is close to the ground with strong emphasis on hands, feet and head. It is often used as a kind of interweaving thread of continuity among the other items of an Event.*

true, in that the dance must be self-supporting. There is nothing left to chance in the actual movement. If Martha Graham is renowned for her falls and recoveries and Alvin Ailey for his masterly sense of timed delay, then Merce Cunningham may be remembered for the way he extends the bodies and arms of his dancers.

The idea of the 'Event', for which Merce Cunningham is now so well-known, originated in 1964. The company was faced with an unusual performing area in the Museum of the Twentieth Century in Vienna. There was no stage, and audience, musicians, curtains and so on could not be arranged in a conventional manner. It also seemed to Merce Cunningham that an interval in the performance would have been inappropriate and uncomfortable. Typically, he accepted the situation as a *fait accompli* and proceeded in a characteristically direct manner. The result of this was Event Number One. Since then, there have been about 200 Events, the idea having been extended to enable the company to give performances in college buildings, indoor sports centres and other such places unsuited to a conventional approach.

Each Event is staged for the particular place where it will be performed. The content is flexible, consisting of complete dances, excerpts from the repertoire and new sequences designed for the occasion. There is no intermission and frequently several dance activities take place simultaneously creating a collage effect.

Merce Cunningham has a marked preference for Events rather than separate, discrete works and they are performed on conventional stages as well as at non-theatrical locations. In this way, existing material never becomes stagnant but is constantly given new vitality. Inevitably such Events are uneven in quality and make taxing demands on the dancers. Audience reactions tend to be extreme and noisy, grumbling exits from the auditorium are not unusual. Enthusiasm for the company is usually just as extreme but indifference or boredom are rare.

Merce Cunningham and John Cage have a long history of collaboration. Merce Cunningham never creates a work to a particular score and sometimes the dancers have never heard the music until the first performance. This can be very amusing or extremely tiresome and the chance element in all the works means that it is impossible to predict which it is to be. John Cage's interest in the inherent possibilities of sounds as music and his aleatory style is well suited to Merce Cunningham's technique of random selection of movement. John Cage has developed a composing technique based upon the Chinese philosophy of *I Ching* – the most formalized kind of chance. Other composers who have been associated with Merce Cunningham include David Behrman, Earle Brown, Morton Feldman, Toshi Ichiyanagi, David Tudor and Christian Wolff.

A similar random technique is applied to design. For example, Andy Warhol filled the stage with large rectangular, silver balloons for *Rainforest*. They were placed at different heights and those at floor level bounced across the stage as the dancers moved past them or pushed them with their feet, creating a fascinating contrast of rapid and ponderous movement, once again wholly dependent on chance.

Although Events tend to predominate, the company also performs individual works with the decor and music that rightly belongs to them. Besides *Rainforest*, *Canfield*, *Solo* and *Sound Dance* are very popular. *Canfield* is based on a kind of patience and the full work has 52 dance sequences, one for each card. The full series is not always given and the abbreviated versions have the quality of a truncated game which has not worked out. It may be that an individual series represents a particular hand of cards and a specific game. The audience can, as always, interpret the work in its own way. The music for this work is Pauline Olivero's *In Memoriam: Nikola Tesla, Cosmic*

Engineer and it is one of the occasions where strategically placed microphones eavesdrop on the audience. The random quality is further encouraged by haphazard movement of the lighting.

Recently Merce Cunningham has begun experimenting with videotapes. In 1973 he disbanded the company for six months to give him time to study the use of videotapes in dance. CBS Television have broadcast some of his work with video and he continues to experiment with these projects.

Merce Cunningham is one of the few creative artists who can be described as genuinely avant-garde. He dispenses with pre-conceived ideas and theatrical expectations, constantly surprising and challenging his audiences by means of his own relaxed approach, combined with controlled technique. What he presents is not an expression of life but a piece of it which can never be repeated and changes as life changes, developing and evolving into a new experience.

The Repertoire

Minutiae (1954)
Springweather and People (1955)
Galaxy (1956)
Lavish Escapade (1956)
Suite for Five in Space and Time (1956)
Nocturnes (1956)
Labyrinthian Dances (1957)
Changeling (1957)
Picnic Polka (1957)
Suite for Two (1958)
Antic Meet (1958)
Summerspace (1958)
Night Wandering (1958)
From the Poems of White Stone (1959)
Gambit for Dancers and Orchestra (1959)
Rune (1959)
Crises (1960)
Hands Birds (1960)
Waka (1960)
Music Walk with Dancers (1960)
Suite de Danses (1961)
Aeon (1961)
Field Dances (1963)
Story (1963)
Open Session (1964)

Paired (1964)
Winterbranch (1964)
Cross Currents (1964)
Variations V (1965)
How to Pass, Kick, Fall and Run (1965)
Place (1966)
Scramble (1967)
Rainforest (1968)
Walkaround Time (1968)
Canfield (1969)
Tread (1970)
Second Hand (1970)
Signals (1970)
Objects (1970)
Landrover (1972)
TV Rerun (1972)
Borst Park (1972)
Solo (1973)
Sounddance (1974)
Westbeth (1974)
Rebus (1975)
Changing Steps (1975)
Loops (1975)
Torse (1976)
Squaregame (1976)

Touring

1958	Stockholm	1969	Rome
1960	Venice, Berlin, Munich, Cologne	1970	France, Holland, Italy
		1972	Iran, Italy, Poland, Yugoslavia, Britain, Germany, France, Yugoslavia
1964	France, Italy, Austria, Germany, Britain, Sweden, Finland, Czechoslovakia, Poland, Belgium, Holland, India, Thailand, Japan		
		1973	Rome
		1976	Caracas, Australia, Japan, France, Israel, Greece, Yugoslavia
1966	Paris		
1968	Mexico, Venezuela, Brazil, Argentina		

The Nikolais Dance Theatre

The work of Alwin Nikolais does not really fit into the category of dance. In fact, conventional labels – choreographer, designer, composer – are quite inadequate as descriptions of this extraordinary and versatile man, who is all these things and many others besides.

Like its founder and director, the Nikolais Dance Theatre defies traditional classification. Many artists, especially modern dance groups, have aimed at a totality of theatrical experience in their presentations. This takes many forms in the world of dance. Most commonly and, generally, most successfully, it is the result of close collaboration between designer, composer and choreographer, as in the Louis Falco Dance Company, for example. Alwin Nikolais has extended this idea to its logical conclusion and instead of collaboration with others, he creates the entire work himself – dance, music, lighting, costumes, stage design. Moreover, each of these elements is an integral part of the total creation, having equal importance.

The second major feature of Alwin Nikolais's work is the way he uses his

dancers, although this is really another aspect of his 'total theatre'. Again, Alwin Nikolais extends a fairly common concept to an extreme, but quite logical, conclusion. His works are abstract, but not in the same sense as those of George Balanchine, Twyla Tharp, Merce Cunningham or Jerome Robbins. He uses his dancers as a dynamic function of the entire creation, so that although they are part of the work, they are not necessarily featured. The result is a kind of kinetic 'op art' sculpture. For example, in the recent work *Triad*, the whole impression is kaleidoscopic. Triangular mirrors within triangular mirrors reflect a multiplicity of images as the dancers move and the complex lighting arrangements change. The magnifying effect of the mirrors is expoited, enlarging whole bodies of parts of them to create strange patterns, sometimes not even recognizable as human. The dancers are dressed so that half their bodies are covered in black and juxtaposed with mirrors so that they seem suspended in mid-air. In *Temple*, the dancers are attached to long elastic streamers offstage. As they dance, geometric patterns form, even a cat's cradle. In the *Suite from Sanctum*, an extract from an earlier work which often introduces the programme, the dancers are enclosed in bands of material which stretch, move, pulsate and form weird unearthly patterns. *Cross-Fade* uses lighting effects for illusion. The dancers move against a dazzling array of projected images, sometimes becoming indistinguishable

In the Group Dance from Sanctum, the dancers are encased in bands of material, creating a strange, non-human, sculptural effect. Lines and patterns pulsate rhythmically to a background of electronic music, creating a primaeval mood.

from their background. An enlarged abstract appears behind the dancers and a life-size image of the same thing appears on their bodies. They mimic the poses of huge naked pictures of themselves, appearing to be naked at the same time because the lighting affects their costumes. The effect is almost like a cartoon. All these are examples of Alwin Nikolais's philosophy that man is inseparable from his environment. When the elastic streamers in *Temple* collapse, so too, do the dancers.

Creations like these have provoked charges that Alwin Nikolais dehumanizes his dancers in his works. Certainly the works are abstract to an advanced degree – no plots, no emotions, no pretence at anything but illusion. At the same time, there is comment and a kind of impressionism. Moreover there is dance contact, and, in some cases, humour. *Tribe*, for example, presents the dancers as a group, assembling and re-assembling into large and small units. The title of the work is significant and there is an impression of a community forming, growing and banding together, although such an impression is never forceful enough to be called symbolic. *Foreplay*, however the invidual watcher chooses to interpret the significance, is immensely funny. The dancers treat each other as puppets, manipulating limbs and heads into extraordinarily complex patterns, illuminated by a series of fantastic and exciting dances. A particularly humorous episode involves the attempted manipulation of a seemingly huge mannequin by a small and pretty girl.

A further accusation levelled at Alwin Nikolais is that he is 'gimmicky'. It is true that a vast array of technical paraphernalia is essential to his productions. *Scenario*, for example, requires the simultaneous use of 12 machines, using 50 slides each and with 200 cues. The manipulation of the control panel, which apparently resembles a piano keyboard, requires a degree of technical expertise not usually associated with anything as transitory as a gimmick.

This kind of production demands tremendous accuracy from the dancers. Not only do they need the ordinary physical discipline that every dancer requires for complete mastery of his or her body, but they must have split second timing and great spatial precision. A fraction too late or too far and the spectacular effects of light projected on to their bodies is lost. In *Cross-Fade*, for example, the light and slides projected on to the dancers make them appear to be wearing all kinds of different costumes. Apart from these rather static and sculptural effects, the dancers also participate in startling, dynamic visual effects as well as performing solos and duets in an apparently effortless way.

Such surreal and plastic theatre seems a very modern phenomenon and it is difficult to believe that Alwin Nikolais founded his company in 1948. He was born in 1912 and attended sessions at the Bennington School of Dance from 1937 to 1939. Later he studied in New York with Martha Graham, Doris Humphrey, Charles Weidman, Louis Horst and, particularly, with Hanya Holm. His theatrical career began as a musician and, in 1936, he became a puppeteer. His dance studies also began in this year. His experiences with puppets were clearly influential and puppets, mannequins and so on have remained a major fascination. (Besides *Foreplay*, which features puppet-like movements, he created a work for British television which required 20 display mannequins). In 1939, he staged his first full-length production, *Eight Column Line*, and this led eventually to a national tour. In 1948 he was appointed director of the Henry Street Playhouse and he set about assembling a group of dancers to present his unique theatrical productions. The first of these 'total theatre' pieces was *Masks, Props and Mobiles* in 1953. Extracts from this – *Tensile Involvement* and *Noumenou* – are still performed by the company as introductory works both to the performance and to the more recent works. *Masks, Props and Mobiles* was followed at irregular intervals

with further works developing Alwin Nikolais' ideas about environment, theatre and illusion, including *Forest of Three* (1953), *Kaleidoscope* (1956), *Mirrors* (1958), *Allegory* (1959), *Totem* (1960), *Vaudeville of the Elements* (1965), and the more recent works like *Scenario*, *Styx* and *Triad*.

In addition to the many live performances in the United States, the company has frequently performed on television both at home and abroad. Since his first television appearance in the Steve Allen Show in 1959, Alwin Nikolais has explored the possibilities offered to him by the use of such a medium and has received a number of awards for his television productions.

The company first travelled abroad to the Spoleto Festival in Italy in 1963. However, his ideas did not really receive publicity outside the United States until the first European tour in 1968. Since then the company has visited major cities in Latin America, Europe, North Africa and the Far East and likes to joke that the date of its first performance on the moon at the 'Lunar Base Theatre' will take place at a 'date to be announced'. Certainly, should such a theatre ever be built, no company would be more suited to appear there. As well as performing in many of the world's major cities, Alwin Nikolais has set up centres for teaching dance and his theatrical technique in several countries. His own school in New York has over 200 students.

Alwin Nikolais is undoubtedly one of the most remarkable figures in the world of theatre as well as dance. However difficult it may be for critics to categorize and classify his work, audiences everywhere find his productions startling, surprising, entertaining and never boring.

The Company

Founder-Director: Alwin Nikolais

Projection and.
Rigging Technician: David Williams

Electrician and
Sound Engineer: John Philip Luckacovic

Dancers:

Lisbeth Bagnold	Gerald Otte	James Teeters
Rob Esposito	Chris Reisner	Fred Timm
Bill Groves	Jessica Sayre	
Suzanne McDermaid	Karen Sing	

The Repertoire

Allegory (1959)
Alphabet (1959)
Cross-Fade (1974)
Foreplay (1972)
Grotto (1973)
Imago (1963)
Masks, Props and Mobiles (1953)
Sanctum (1964)

Scenario (1971)
Somniloquy (1967)
Styx (1976)
Temple (1974)
Triad (1976)
Tribe (1975)
Vaudeville of the Elements (1965)

Touring

1963   Spoleto Festival

1968   Nice, Paris, Milan, Parma, Rome, Venice, Geneva, Lausanne, Berlin, Belgrade, Dubrovnik, Lublajana, Sarajevo, Skopje

1969   Vienna, Brussels, Aix les Bains, Chatillons-sous-Bagneaux, Toulouse, London, Athens, Amsterdam, Arnhem, Groningen, Rotterdam, The Hague, Budapest, Nervi, Turin, Baalbek, Warsaw, Geneva, Hamburg, Munich, Stuttgart.

1971   Vienna, Paris, London, Southampton, Amsterdam, Eindhoven Nijmegen, Rotterdam, The Hague, Monte Carlo, Coimbra, Lisbon, Oporto, Carthage, Hammamet, Weisbaden, Dubrovnik, Split.

1972   Vancouver, Angers, Rennes, Sochaux, Strasbourg, Ber Sheva, Ein Gev, Haifa, Jerusalem, Tel Aviv, Casablanca, Rabat, Bucharest, Bilbao, Madrid, Geneva, Lausanne, Zurich.

1973   Buenos Aires, Brasilia, Curtiba, Rio de Janeiro, Sao Paulo, Santiago, Lima, Caracas.

1974   Hamilton, Ottawa, Vancouver, Angers, Paris, Sochaux, Guadalajara, Mexico City, Barcelona, Berlin, Frankfurt, Leverkusen, Stuttgart.

1975   Buenos Aires, La Plata, Brussels, Ghent, Leuven, Brasilia, Curtiba, Port Allegre, Rio de Janeiro, Sao Paulo, Bogota, Cali, San Jose, Edinburgh, Persepolis, Teheran, Monte Carlo, Guadalajara, Mexico City, Panama City, Lima, Barcelona, Caracas, Santiago.

1976   Hong Kong, Nagoya, Osaka, Sapporo, Tokyo, Manila, Singapore, Seoul, Taichung, Tainan, Taipei, Bangkok.

Louis Falco
Dance Company

A company founded by such an extraordinary and revolutionary figure as Louis Falco is certain to surprise and excite. So much creative energy is concentrated in this small group, almost anything said or written about it is out of date before it is finished.

A native of New York City, Louis Falco studied drama and then dance at the High School of Performing Arts and this early training has been a great influence in his work. He was taught by Alwin Nikolais, Murray Louis and Charles Weidmann. In his final year he was invited to join the José Limon Dance Company and toured with it in South and Central America in 1960. He remained with the José Limon company for 10 years, touring extensively and encountering and absorbing all kinds of influences from the world of contemporary dance.

In 1967, his interest in choreography and his desire to create his own works, led him to leave the José Limon Dance Company. The first full evening of his works, including *Argot* which continues to feature in the company's repertoire, was given at the Kauffman Auditorium, New York in December 1967. As a result of this he was invited to appear at the 1968 Jacob's Pillow Dance Festival, for which he created *Huescape*. This established his reputation as a choreographer and, at the same time, convinced him of the need to form his own company.

Louis Falco, in a scene from Twopenny Portrait, *shows a uniquely personal blend of dance and theatre. He is an exceptionally fluid dancer, with a deep emotional commitment. His choreography is rich both in content and form and he is capable of immense humour and wit which delight audiences at home and abroad.*

The company has always been small, usually seven or eight dancers, because Falco creates his works around the individuals and their interaction. The members of the company work very closely together and have established an exceptional dance relationship with each other and with Louis Falco as a choreographer as well as a dancer. Consequently, it is virtually impossible to transfer one of Louis Falco's works to another company.

Recently he has worked with other groups including the Boston Ballet, the Ballet Rambert, the Nederlands Dans Theater and a season in New York with Rudolph Nureyev and Merle Park in *The Moor's Pavane*.

The essence of Louis Falco's work is his concern with human relationships. He does not believe in the concept of 'abstract' dance. He believes that the mere presence of dancers, before they even begin to move, establishes a relationship between them and their surroundings. All Louis Falco's works display a cohesiveness and he demands a remarkable sense of space and timing from his dancers.

Louis Falco has worked very closely with the painter William Katz and the composer and musician Burt Alcantara. Very close collaboration between choreographer, designer, composer, musicians and dancers has resulted in a theatrical unit which typified the work of the company. Recently, Louis Falco has moved away from this very close association to explore new ideas. However, William Katz remains the company's artistic adviser and Burt Alcantara continues to lead the company's accompanying group of musicians, Vertical Burn.

The Sleepers created in 1971, is a fine example of both the total theatrical experience created by Falco and his company and his concern with human relationships. Normally, when a choreographer introduces dialogue into dance it tends to be intrusive, stilted, awkward and interrupts the flow and tempo of the movement. In *The Sleepers*, however, the members of the company succeed in being both actors and dancers with apparent ease with neither aspect of the performance dominating the other. From the beginning of the work, the dancers establish their relationships. The first couple move

into a rapid and brilliant dance combined with fast and pithy conversation. The second couple bicker in dance and in repartee. The effect is one of complete integration of forms and, incidentally, is very funny.

Fun is as central to Louis Falco's work as innovation. Eight large, white, fake sturgeons are used as properties in the circus-like *Caviar* and the whole performance seems to be as much pleasure to dance as it is to watch. Louis Falco is very concerned to present dance as accessible to everyone and is determined that his work, however innovative in choreography, has an immediacy which can be readily appreciated by the general public. At the same time, the works he presents are not merely entertaining but challenging both to the public and to other creative artists.

The Louis Falco Dance Company has a firm basis in a strong technique from which it develops its apparently easy, natural, free-flowing looseness or energetic, brilliant almost frantic pace. Unconventional and uninhibited the company may be, but it is always creatively, not destructively, revolutionary.

The Company

Artistic Director: Louis Falco

Associate Director: Juan Antonio

Principal Dancers: Juan Antonio
Louis Falco
Georgiana Holmes

Dancers: Tony Constantine   Lisa Nalven
John Cwiakala   Ranko Yokoyama
Jane Lowe

The Repertoire

Argot (Falco) 1967   *I Remember* (Antonio) 1974
Avenue (Falco) 1963   *Pulp* (Falco) 1975
B-Mine (Antonio) 1976   *Soap Opera* (Falco) 1973
Caviar (Falco) 1970   *Storeroom* (Falco) 1974
Dreamers (Holmes) 1974   *Timewright* (Falco) 1969
First Base (Antonio) 1971   *The Sleepers* (Falco) 1971
Huescape (Falco) 1968   *Twopenny Portrait* (Falco) 1973
Ibid (Falco) 1970

Touring

As well as touring in the United States, frequently
appearing at universities, the Louis Falco Dance
Company has also visited France, Holland and
Britain and appeared on Dutch and German
television.

CANADA

National Ballet of Canada

In 1949 the only professional Canadian ballet company was the recently established Winnipeg Ballet – it was not granted the title 'Royal' until 1953. In that year, the Sadler's Wells Ballet (later, the Royal Ballet, London) visited Toronto on the first of its many North American tours. These two things combined to inspire a group of ballet enthusiasts to begin to set up a classical company in Eastern Canada.

Dame Ninette de Valois, director of the Sadler's Wells Ballet, was asked for advice and, at her suggestion, Celia Franca, a young British dancer, choreographer and teacher was invited to Canada for consultations. In spite of formidable obstacles – lack of money, of facilities and even of fully trained dancers – she agreed to direct the new company. The National Ballet of Canada, made its debut on 12 November 1951, at the Eaton Auditorium, Toronto. The programme included *Les Sylphides* and the *Polovetsian Dances from Prince Igor*.

The repertoire of the new company was, at first, closely modelled on that

Guest artist Rudolf Nureyev and Karen Kain dance the roles of Siegfried and Odette in Swan Lake. *The major nineteenth century classics have formed an important part of the National Ballet of Canada's repertoire since it was founded. During his season as guest artist, Rudolf Nureyev appeared in* The Sleeping Beauty, Don Juan, Giselle, Les Sylphides *and* The Moor's Pavane.

of the Sadler's Wells Ballet. It was decided that the National Ballet of Canada would be a classical company with a repertoire of both traditional and contemporary works and the company has not deviated from this policy throughout its history. Another important early policy decision was that the company would take care to foster and develop Canadian talent.

A period of rapid growth and development followed soon after the 1951 debut. In 1953 the company appeared at the Jacob's Pillow Dance Festival – the first foreign company ever invited. Shortly afterwards it embarked on a tour of Canada and the United States and also visited Mexico City. During the next five years the company expanded and its repertoire extended to include full-length productions of *Swan Lake*, *The Nutcracker* and *Giselle*. New works by contemporary choreographers were gradually included and by the end of the first decade, 12 of these had been acquired.

In line with Celia Franca's early statement of policy, the company encouraged and developed its own choreographers. Grant State, who joined the company at its inception and who was appointed Assistant to the Artistic Director in 1958, has created many ballets for it. Early works include *The Fisherman and his Soul* (1956), *The Willow* (1957), *Ballad* (1959) and *Antic Spring* (1960). Similarly, David Adams who also joined the company in 1951 and who was, for many years, the premier danseur, created a number of ballets – *Ballet Composite* (1951), *Ballet Behind Us* (1952), *Pas de Chance* (1956) and *Barbara Allen* (1960).

During these years Celia Franca herself was one of the company's ballerinas and assumed many of the leading roles until she retired in 1959. In spite of an arduous schedule as Director and dancer, she also found time to present her own ballets, including *The Dance of Salome*, *Le Pommier* and her own versions of *The Nutcracker*, *L'Après-midi d'un Faune* and *Dances from the Sleeping Beauty*.

At this time the repertoire also included *Coppélia, Act II*; Frederick Ashton's *Les Rendezvous*, Kay Armstrong's *Etudes*, four Antony Tudor ballets – *Jardin aux Lilas*, *Gala Performance*, *Offenbach in the Underworld* (première by the National Ballet of Canada in 1955) and *Dark Elegies*, and John Cranko's *Pineapple Poll*.

As the company grew and the demand for dancers who had attained the high standards required by Celia Franca increased, it became apparent that a school must be established. In the late 1950s the National Ballet School was founded. The Company's first Ballet Mistress, Betty Oliphant, was appointed Director. The taxing standards she demanded and her unceasing care have built up the school's fine reputation and it is now the company's principal source of dancers.

By the 1960s, the National Ballet of Canada had established firm foundations on which to build, and it lost no time in doing so, expanding and developing enormously in the next decade. Its growth coincided with the expansion of general arts facilities throughout Canada, which enabled the company to tour extensively with its major productions.

In 1962, the National Ballet staged its first ballet by George Balanchine – *Concerto Barocco*, and in 1964 a new era in the company's development was heralded by John Cranko's staging of his own *Romeo and Juliet*. A year later the Danish dancer Erik Bruhn, internationally recognized as one of the most outstanding dancers of his generation, began his association with the National Ballet by presenting *La Sylphide*. In 1966 he presented his new *Swan Lake* and a new production of *Coppélia* in 1975. He is now Resident Producer with the company.

In 1969 the National Ballet was invited to inaugurate the new National Arts Centre in Ottawa and commissioned a new work, *Kraanerg* by Roland Petit, for the occasion. A shorter Roland Petit work, *Le Loup*, was presented the following year. The company's quickly growing reputation resulted in a unique invitation to perform at Expo '70 in Osaka. Also in 1970, Peter Wright, Associate Director of the British Royal Ballet, produced a new *Giselle* for the company and presented his own work, *Mirror Walkers*, the following season.

1972 was a momentous year for the National Ballet. For the first time the company made a European tour commencing in London. The success of the visit, particularly to London, must have confirmed for Celia Franca how right her decision 21 years previously had been. Also in 1972 the company signed a contract with the American impresario Sol Hurok. Perhaps the single most significant outcome of this association was the invitation to Rudolf Nureyev to appear as guest artist with the National Ballet.

The company, with Rudolf Nureyev, made two extended tours of the United States, including five engagements at the Metropolitan Opera House, New York. For its New York debut in 1973 the company presented Nureyev's own spectacular version of *The Sleeping Beauty* to great public and critical acclaim.

During the second New York season in 1974 John Neumeier, the celebrated American choreographer, presented his *Don Juan*. In the same year Mikhail Baryshnikov, former Kirov dancer, made his debut in the West, appearing in *La Sylphide* with the National Ballet. He also danced with the company in 1975 and 1976 and has danced with it for a special television programme.

The National Ballet has always felt an obligation to Canadian audiences and so ensures that it makes regular tours to all parts of the country. It also has a long history of successful association with the Canadian Broadcasting Corporation. Several of the 22 major television productions have won awards,

Tomas Schramek, Veronica Tennant and Charles Kirby appear in a scene from Erik Bruhn's Coppélia. *This colourful and charming ballet has been very popular both in Canada and on the company's tours abroad.*

89

notably Norman Campbell's productions of John Cranko's *Romeo and Juliet*, Celia Franca's 1968 version of *Cinderella*, Nureyev's *The Sleeping Beauty* and Erik Bruhn's *Swan Lake*. A film of *Giselle* was made especially for the Canadian Broadcasting Corporation to celebrate the National Ballet's twenty-fifth anniversary in November 1976.

In 1975 Alexander Grant, a character principal of the Royal Ballet, London, for many years, was appointed Artistic Director. He began work in 1976 by arranging the celebratory season which featured a revival of *Romeo and Juliet* and the Canadian première of Sir Frederick Ashton's *La Fille Mal Gardée*. It is interesting to note that the part of Alain in the British Royal Ballet's original production in 1960 was one of Alexander Grant's most triumphant creations.

The choice of anniversary programme is indicative of the character of the National Ballet of Canada – an imaginative and ambitious blending of the best elements of traditional and contemporary classical ballet.

The company

Founder:	Celia Franca	**Ballet Master:**	David Scott
Artistic Director:	Alexander Grant	**Resident Ballet Master:**	Daniel Seillier
Resident Producer:	Erik Bruhn		
		Choreologist:	Susa Menck
Ballet Mistress:	Joanne Nisbet		

Principal Dancers:

Frank Augustyn	Karen Kain	Sergiu Stefanschi
Vanessa Harwood	Charles Kirby	Hazaros Surmeyan
Mary Jago	Nadia Potts	Veronica Tennant
Stephen Jeffries	Tomas Schramek	

First Soloists:

Victoria Bertram	Rashna Homji	Wendy Reiser
Colleen Cool	James Kudelka	Clinton Rothwell
Joel Dabin	Gloria Luoma	David Roxander
Jacques Gorrissen	Linda Maybarduk	Mavis Staines

Second soloists:

Ann Ditchburn	Cynthia Lucas
Miguel Garcia	Constantin Patsalas

The Repertoire

Giselle (Coralli/Perrot/Petipa) 1952/3
Coppélia (Saint-Léon) 1952/3
Swan Lake (Petipa/Ivanov) 1954/5
The Nutcracker (Petipa/Franca) 1955/6
Giselle * (Coralli/Perrot/Petipa) 1956/7
Coppélia * (Saint-Léon) 1958/9
Romeo and Juliet (Cranko) 1963/4
The Nutcracker * (Petipa/Franca) 1964/5
La Sylphide (Bruhn) 1964/5
Swan Lake (Bruhn) 1966/7
Cinderella (Franca) 1967/8
Kraanerg (Petit) 1968/9
Giselle * (Coralli/Perrot/Petipa/Wright) 1969/70
The Sleeping Beauty (Nureyev) 1972/3
Coppélia * (Bruhn) 1974/5
Coppélia Act II (Saint-Léon) 1951/2
The Dance of Salome (Franca) 1951/2

Ballet Composite (Adams) 1951/2
Etude (Armstrong) 1951/2
Les Sept (Adams) 1951/2
Les Sylphides (Fokine) 1951/2
The Polovetsian Dances from Prince Igor (Fokine) 1951/2
The Nutcracker, Act II (Petipa/Franca) 1952/3
Ballet Behind Us (Adams) 1952/3
L'Après-Midi d'un Faune (Franca) 1952/3
Le Pommier (Franca) 1952/3
Swan Lake, Act II (Petipa/Ivanov) 1953/4
Jardin aux Lilas (Tudor) 1953/4
Gala Performance (Tudor) 1953/4
Dances from the Classics (Petipa/Ivanov) 1953/4
Barbara Allen (Dark of the Moon) (Harris) 1953/4
Offenbach in the Underworld (Tudor) 1954/5
Dark Elegies (Tudor) 1955/6

The Lady from the Sea (Leese) 1955/6
Les Rendezvous (Ashton) 1956/7
The Fisherman and his Soul (Strate) 1956/7
La Llamada (Moller) 1956/7
Post Script (Macdonald) 1956/7
Pas de Chance (Adams) 1956/7
Carnaval (Fokine) 1957/8
Winter Night (Gore) 1957/8
The Willow (Strate) 1957/8
Dances from the Sleeping Beauty
(Petipa/Franca) 1957/8
Ballad (Strate) 1958/9
Pineapple Poll (Cranko) 1959/60
The Mermaid (Howard) 1959/60
Death and the Maiden (Howard) 1959/60
Princess Aurora (Petipa/Franca) 1960/1
Barbara Allen * (Adams) 1960/1
Antic Spring (Strate) 1960/1
Pas de Six (Adams) 1960/1
The Remarkable Rocket (Gillies) 1960/1
Concerto Barocco (Balanchine) 1961/2
One in Five (Powell) 1961/2
Sequel (Strate) 1962/3
Time Cycle (Strate) 1962/3
Serenade (Balanchine) 1962/3
The Judgement of Paris (Tudor) 1962/3
Pas de Six from Laurencia (Chabukiane/Samsova)
1962/3
House of Atreus (Strate) 1963/4
Allegresse (Solov) 1963/4
Triptych (Strate) 1964/5
Pulcinella (Strate) 1965/6
The Rake's Progress (de Valois/Worth) 1965/6
Rivalité (Seillier) 1965/6
Solitaire (MacMillan) 1965/6
Adagio Cantabile (Poll) 1965/6
La Bayadère (Petipa, staged by Eugen Valukin)
1966/7
Eh! (Franca) 1966/7
Rondo Giocoso (Poll) 1966/7
Studies in White (Strate) 1967/8
La Prima Ballerina (Heiden) 1967/8
The Arena (Strate) 1968/9
Celebrations (Poll) 1968/9
Cyclus (Strate) 1968/9
Four Temperaments (Balanchine) 1968/9
Le Loup (Petit) 1969/70

The Lesson (Flindt after Ionesco) 1969/70
Brown Earth (Ditchburn) 1970/1
For Infernal Use as Well (Spain) 1970/1
Sagar (Spain) 1970/1
The Mirror Walkers (Wright) 1970/1
Fandango (Tudor) 1971/2
Evocation (Staged by Seillier) 1971/2
Intermezzo (Feld) 1971/2
Session (Iscove) 1971/2
The Moor's Pavane (Limon) 1972/3
Les Sylphides * (Fokine, produced by Celia
Franca and Erik Bruhn) 1973/4
Don Juan (Neumeier) 1973/4
Inventions (Patsalas)
Kettentanz (Arpino) 1974/5
Whispers of Darkness (Vesak) 1974/5
Offenbach in the Underworld (Tudor) 1975/6
Kisses (Ditchburn) 1975/6
Monument for a Dead Boy (van Dantzig) 1975/6
Le Coq d'Or (Beriozoff) 1975/6
La Fille Mal Gardée (Ashton) 1976/7
Afternoon of a Faun (Robbins) 1976/7
Shadows (Ditchburn) 1976/7
Monotones II (Ashton) 1976/7
Pas de Deux from The Nutcracker (Petipa) 1951/2
Pas de Deux from Don Quixote (Petipa) 1951/2
Pas de Deux from Giselle (Coralli/Perrot) 1951/2
Jeune Pas de Deux (Strate) 1956/7
Pas de Deux Romantique (Adams) 1960/1
Pas de Deux from Le Corsaire (Klavin, staged by
Galina Samsova) 1962/3
Pas de Deux from Don Quixote (Valukin) 1963/4
Pas de Deux from Don Quixote (Petipa, staged by
Svetlana Beriosova) 1963/4
Pas de Deux from Walpurgis Night (Lavrovsky,
staged by Galina Samsova) 1963/4
Pas de Deux (Cranko) 1964/5
Pas de Deux (Strate) 1964/5
Clair de Lune (Valukin) 1965/6
Mélodie (Valukin) 1966/7
Pas de Deux (Gordon) 1968/9
Phases (Strate) 1968/9
Pas de Deux from Flower Festival in Genzano
(Bournonville/Bruhn) 1973/4
Four Schumann Pieces (van Manen) 1976/7
* new production

Touring

Apart from a demanding touring programme throughout Canada, National the Ballet has visited Europe twice, and makes regular visits to the United States. Individual dancers of the company have been invited as guest artists to many parts of the world; Mary Jago (Royal Winnipeg Ballet); Karen Kain (London Festival Ballet); Sergiu Stefanschi (Columbus Ballet and Eliot Feld Ballet Company); Veronica Tennant (The New Orleans Ballet); Frank Augustyn (London Festival Ballet). In addition many members of the company have danced at international ballet festivals where they have won an impressive array of awards.

Les Grands Ballets Canadiens

The youngest of the professional Canadian ballet companies, Les Grands Ballets Canadiens, nevertheless, has a distinct national and personal style. It was founded in 1952, as a company to present performances for television from Montreal, but, since its inception, it has been renowned for the innovation and experiment of its choreography and is now a major performing company both at home and abroad.

Founder and Director, Ludmilla Chiriaeff still takes a lively interest and an active part in the running of both the company and its school. Born in Latvia, she studied dance with Alexandra Nicolaieva in Berlin, before joining Colonel de Basil's Ballet Russe and continuing her studies with such major figures as Michel Fokine and Leonide Massine. She later joined the Berlin Opera Ballet and, following World War II, she became première danseuse and choreographer with the Municipal Theatre of Lausanne in Switzerland. Shortly after, she founded her first dance company – Les Ballets des Arts de Genève. In 1952 she moved to Canada and, shortly afterwards, was invited to form Les Ballets Chiriaeff.

The company quickly gained a considerable reputation with its television appearances and, in 1954, it began to give a number of performances on the stage. Most of the repertoire consisted of works created by Ludmilla Chiriaeff herself, although, in 1953, Eric Hyrst joined the company as leading dancer, choreographer and artistic adviser. By 1958, the number of dancers had increased to 20 and this fact, combined with the increasing success enjoyed by the company, encouraged it to change its name to Les Grands Ballets Canadiens, an optimism which has since proved justified. At this time, it also began to receive financial support from federal, provincial and municipal authorities, giving it the status of Quebec's first professional company.

In 1959, the company gave its first performance abroad, at the Jacob's Pillow Dance Festival in the United States. It returned the following year and now performs regularly in the United States and tours frequently in other parts of the world.

The foundations of any major company lie eventually in the basis of a good school and this aspect has not been neglected by Les Grands Ballets Canadiens. The Ecole Superieure de Danse was founded by Ludmilla Chiriaeff and its work is continued through the Academy of Les Grands Ballets Canadiens. The training is concentrated at elementary level and, in 1975, with the co-operation of the Quebec Ministry of Education and the St Croix School Commission, it became possible to establish a system of full professional training within the normal education programme of the high school system. Further educational possibilities are extended by the company's choreographic workshop. This takes place annually and members of the company, as well as other young Canadian talent, are given the opportunity to present works they have created themselves with the full facilities of a professional performing group. Several of the resulting works have been incorporated into the regular repertoire.

It has been a constant aim of the company, since its inception, to foster and encourage Canadian talent. Moreover, it has always endeavoured to present an exciting and innovatory repertoire. These two aspects of Les Grands Ballets Canadiens have been perfectly conjoined in the appointment of Brian Macdonald as Artistic Director in 1974. A controversial figure in the world of dance, he was once described as 'possibly the world's worst choreographer'. Following his graduation from McGill University, he spent

Annette av Paul as Odette is partnered by Vincent Warren as Siegfried. Les Grands Ballets Canadiens is especially proud of its recent production of Swan Lake *with the original choreography of Marius Petipa and Lev Ivanov. Brian Macdonald believes that generations of dancers and audiences have grown up without ever seeing the original masterpiece, as it is such a popular work for choreographers to re-design. The company feels a special responsibility in the field of education and believes that by staging this work in its original form, it is providing a valuable opportunity for audiences and dancers.*

two years as music critic for the *Montreal Herald*. He joined the National Ballet of Canada in the year of its foundation, but a severe injury in the 1950s ended his career as dancer, but precipitated him into an early involvement with teaching and choreography. In 1956, he founded the Montreal Theatre Ballet. His insistence on the use of Canadian composers and designers anticipated the distinctive national character he later brought to Les Grands Ballets Canadiens. Renowned for his exceptional energy and the extraordinary demands he makes on himself, he was, during this period, also involved in teaching at the Banff School of Fine Arts and the National Theatre School, as well as creating a number of original works for CBS television. In 1958, he began an association with the Royal Winnipeg Ballet. During these years, he created a number of major works for this company and also directed Canadian productions of several musicals for the stage and television, including *Guys and Dolls*, *Carousel* and *Oklahoma*.

In 1962, he received a Canadian Council Award which enabled him to study abroad and this inaugurated a period of even more feverish activity and much travelling. For three years he was Artistic Director of the Royal Swedish Ballet and then of the, now defunct, Harkness Ballet in New York. Among the companies which include his works in their repertoires are the Royal Swedish Ballet, the Royal Danish Ballet, the Norwegian National Ballet, the Ballet of the German Berlin Opera, the London Festival Ballet, and the Ballet Théâtre Contemporain.

When he was appointed Artistic Director, he brought to Les Grands Ballets Canadiens his vast experience and an exciting and sophisticated choreographic style which had evolved over a period of years and within a broad geographical spectrum. Although he could never be called derivative, he draws freely on the styles and experiments of other choreographers, including Martha Graham, Jerome Robbins, Antony Tudor, George Balanchine and even Gene Kelly. His style is constantly changing and evolving and it is, therefore, difficult to define a characteristic Macdonald ballet. His works present a tremendous impression of energy and drive, typical of their creator and often demand a sparkling perfection of technique from the dancers. He is capable of delightful humour as in *Bawdy Variations*, but can also miscalculate badly and his tendency for excess can occasionally result in something bordering on vulgarity. His rich supply of new and imaginative ideas can also result in fragmentation, so that his works sometimes lack total artistic unity. However, his secure international reputation rests firmly on a constant stream of major works. His own individual approach has done much to ensure a distinctive identity for Les Grands Ballets Canadiens and this has been further consolidated by his encouragement of native talent.

Although contemporary developments in dance and the work of Brian Macdonald, in particular, form a major part of the company's repertoire, works by leading twentieth century choreographers, such as George Balanchine, William Dollar, John Butler and Anton Dolin, are also featured. Several of the world's great classics are also included and the company is particularly proud of its recent revival of *Swan Lake*, containing, as far as possible, the original Petipa and Ivanov choreography. This rather surprising project typifies the adventurous approach of the company and the varied repertoire generally demonstrates the qualities of vitality and fluidity for which it is renowned.

Right *Sonia Vartanian, Maniya Barredo, David La Hay and Marianne Rowe in a scene from* Lignes et Points, *which was created by Paige and Macdonald.*

Overleaf *Maniya Barredo and Alexandre Bélin in* Tam Ti Delam, *with choreography by Brian Macdonald to music by Gilles Vigneault.*

The Company

Founder and Director:	Ludmilla Chiriaeff
Artistic Director:	Brian Macdonald
Resident Choreographer:	Fernand Nault
Ballet Mistress:	Linda Stearns
Resident Teacher:	William Griffith

Principal Dancers:

Annette Av Paul	John Stanzel
Maniya Barredo	Sonia Vartanian
Alexandre Belin	Vincent Warren

The Repertoire

Allegro Brillante (Balanchine)
Artère (Chiriaeff)
Aurkhi (Nault)
A Yesterday's Day (Rabon)
Bagatelle (Chiriaeff)
Bawdy Variations (Macdonald)
Berubee (Paige)
Canadiana (Chiriaeff)
Cantate pour Une Joie (Macdonald)
Cantiques des Cantiques (Nault)
Carmina Burana (Nault)
Catulli Carmina (Butler)
Cérémonie (Nault)
Cinderella (Chiriaeff)
Combat (Dollar)
Concerto Barocco (Balanchine)
Coppélia (Hyrst/St Leon)
Cordes (Macdonald)
Danses Concertantes (Nault)
Divertissements Glazounov (Nault)
En Cage (Gradus)
Espagnola (Paige)
Etudes (Chiriaeff)
Exercises (Chiriaeff)
Farce (Chiriaeff)
Fête Hongroise (Chiriaeff)
Folies Françaises (Paige)
Four Temperaments (Balanchine)
Gehenne (Nault)
Giselle (Dolin)
Graduation Ball (Lichine)
Grand Pas de Deux Classiques (Caton)
Hip and Straight (Nault)
Hommages (Hyrst)
Icare (Hoving)
Initiation à la Danse (Chiriaeff/Gradus/
Belhumeur)
Introduction (Hyrst)
Jeu d'Arlequin (Chiriaeff)
Jeu de Cartes (Chiriaeff)
Jeu de Cartes (Macdonald)
La Belle Rose (Chiriaeff)
Labyrinthe (Chiriaeff)
La Corriveau (Paige)
La Couvée (Kuch)
La Fille Mal Gardée (Hyrst/Chiriaeff/Caton)
Pas de Quatre (Dolin)
Les Clowns (Chiriaeff)
Les Noces (Chiriaeff)
Le Spectre de la Rose (Fokine)

Les Sylphides (Fokine/Nault)
Liberté Temperée (Nault)
Lignes et Pointes (Macdonald/Paige)
L'Oiseau Phoenix (Chiriaeff)
Medée (Paige)
Memoirs de Camille (Caton/Chiriaeff)
Mobiles (Nault)
Nonagone (Chiriaeff)
On Est 00016 (Jackson)
Pantomime (Paige)
Pas De Deux (Balanchine)
Pas Rompu (Nault)
Payse (Chiriaeff)
Pierrot de la Lune (Chiriaeff)
Pile ou Face (Von Gencsy)
Pointes sur Glace (Conte)
Première Classique (Hyrst)
Prothalemium (Macdonald)
Quatrième Concert Royal (Chiriaeff)
Quintessence (Nault)
Rigodon (Paige)
Romeo and Juliet (Macdonald)
Sea Gallows (Hyrst)
Serenade (Balanchine)
Shining People of Leonard Cohen (Macdonald)
Sinfonietta (Salbaing)
Sombre Apparition (Paige)
Springwater (Messerer)
Suite Canadienne (Chiriaeff)
Swan Lake (Petipa/Ivanov)
Symphonie de Psaumes (Nault)
Tam Ti Delam (Macdonald)
The Firebird (Béjart)
Time Out of Mind (Macdonald)
Tommy (Nault)
Themes and Variations (Balanchine)
Tournament (Macdonald)
Trapeze (Sellier)
The Nutcracker (Nault)
The Swan of Tuenelo (Dolin)
Trianon (Hyrst)
Triomphe d'Aphrodite (Walker)
Trip (Butler)
Valses Nobles et Sentimentales (Hyrst)
Variations Diabelli (Macdonald)
Variations en Blanc (Chiriaeff)
Variations for a Dark Voice (Paige)
Variations for Four (Dolin)
Villon (Butler)

Touring

The company tours regularly in Canada and the
United States and has made several visits to other
parts of the world.

EUROPE

Lynn Seymour, one of the outstanding ballerinas of the twentieth century, is partnered by Rudolf Nureyev in Dances at a Gathering. *Created for Britain's Royal Ballet by Jerome Robbins, this delightful, abstract work is a favourite of both audiences and dancers. Rudolf Nureyev has a specially close association with the Royal Ballet and has danced frequently with it, besides staging a number of his own works.*

BELGIUM
The Royal Ballet
van Vlaanderen

An independent Flemish ballet company grew out of opera – an association common to many countries. The Flemish Opera was established in 1893 as a manifestation of a general cultural movement away from French political and artistic domination. By 1907, the company had its own building and a regular repertoire. It lacked, however, a ballet company and so only performed those operas without ballet intermezzi or simply omitted them.

To maintain its international status it was essential for the opera company to establish a ballet group. This feeling coincided with a period of new consciousness of ballet in Europe – the Ballets Russes of Diaghilev, Isadora Duncan's European tours and the developments in Central Europe led by Kurt Jooss. However, the future of ballet in Belgium looked bleak for there were no schools or teachers to supply dancers.

It was not until the 1923/4 season that a ballet company associated with the KVO (Flemish Royal Opera House) was begun under the leadership of Sonia Korty. In its first season an unbelievable 34 new works were created. Moreover, Sonia Korty experimented with new techniques and styles as well as the classical tradition.

The company continued to develop. The appointment of the Russian teacher Vladimir Karnetzky as ballet master in the 1930s directed the company towards classical ballet but new ballets continued to be created. Development was interrupted, but not halted, by World War II and soon after the war ended, ballet once again became popular. New works by various choreographers associated with the company were added to the repertoire.

In 1951 the Ballet School of the KVO was founded providing the company with a pool of professionally trained dancers. This was an important link in the establishment of a Flanders ballet company and incidentally made Antwerp the ballet centre of Flanders. The ballet school was progressively integrated into the municipal education system and in 1964 it became the Municipal Institute of Ballet.

The ballet company continued to evolve rapidly with a quick succession of choreographers and guest choreographers between 1958 and 1966 – Leonide Katchourowsky, Christian Foye, Heino Heiden, Bob Hamilton, Paolo Bortoluzzi, Frances Gionny, and Walter Gore. In 1966 André Leclair was appointed Director and together with Jeanne Brabants, head of the Municipal Institute of Ballet, he raised the level of the opera-ballet to international standards. New techniques and styles were again experimented with and introduced.

However, although the opera-ballet was flourishing, it was, nevertheless, only of secondary importance. In Brussels, Maurice Béjart's Ballet du XXième siècle, set up in 1960, was enjoying phenomenal success. In 1966, the Ballets de Wallonie had been founded as an independent company for the French speaking part of Belgium. The old question of Flemish cultural autonomy was once again raised in political circles. This, combined with the fact that the Municipal Institute of Ballet was producing highly-trained professional dancers for whom there was no future in Flanders, meant that it was imperative to establish an independent ballet company.

Discussions about establishing the ballet company, with a firm basis in the

school and built around the KVO dancers, began in 1966. Plans were drawn up and a work party investigated budgets, administration and, most important of all, the autonomy of the company.

Finally, on 2 December 1969, the company was created at a foundation ceremony in Brussels in the presence of Frans van Mechelen, Minister of Flemish Culture. Jeanne Brabants was appointed Director of the new company and André Leclair became the first choreographer.

The company consisted, at first, of the existing opera-ballet company supplemented by some former students of the Municipal Institute and some foreign dancers. The first performance, *Prometheus*, was given in Brussels on 10 September 1970 and was broadcast on television. After this excitement it was necessary to settle down to the hard work of establishing the company. Initially the repertoire consisted mainly of works from the opera-ballet but five new works were developed including Maurice Béjart's *Love Scene*, Jeanne Brabants' *Cantus firmus* and *La Ventana* by Hans Brenaa. The corps de ballet was gradually extended from 32 to 54 dancers. Help was sought from other countries and ballet-masters from the Royal Danish Ballet, the London Festival Ballet and the Nederlands Dans Theater offered assistance.

Besides performing works from the old repertoire and rehearsing the new ones, in the first year the company also danced 89 opera-intermezzi. The second year brought more rapid development. It began auspiciously with considerable success at the Summer Festival in Athens and this initiated a long series of foreign tours. The Ballet van Vlaanderen has since toured extensively in Europe and Latin America meeting with public and critical appreciation everywhere.

New ballets were constantly added to the repertoire – Jack Carter's *Cage of God*, Flemming Flindt's *The Lesson*, Charles Czarny's *Brandenburg 3*, Birgit Cullberg's *Miss Julie*, *Nepentha* by Alexander Roy as well as works by Balanchine, Witaly Osins, Kurt Jooss, Michael Howes, Moshe Efrati, Alain Davesne, Michel Fokine, David Lichine, Juan Corelli, Dame Ninette de Valois, John Butler and Sir Frederick Ashton.

The company continues to supply dancers for the KVO and in the 1976/77 season it took the major step of presenting its first full-length ballet, *Ulenspiegel, de Geus* with choreography by Jeanne Brabants and André Leclair to music specially commissioned from Willem Kersters.

The Ballet van Vlaanderen has established a pattern of producing works of all periods and countries – classical and contemporary, abstract and narrative ballets. It does, however, show a preference for modern works and plays a very important part in the encouragement of Flemish choreographers and composers. In fact, the company sees itself as an integral part of Flemish culture and is deeply involved in public dance education, drawing on its historical roots.

The Ballet van Vlaanderen is therefore a young company with a determinedly open mind about its future, yet with a strong sense of its cultural responsibilities and traditions. It is in the fortunate position of having a solid core of well-trained professional dancers and the fundamental support of a ballet school of more than 20 years standing. In 1977, in recognition of its services to Flemish culture, it was granted the title 'Royal'.

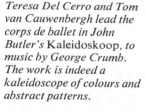

Teresa Del Cerro and Tom van Cauwenbergh lead the corps de ballet in John Butler's Kaleidoskoop, *to music by George Crumb. The work is indeed a kaleidoscope of colours and abstract patterns.*

The Company

Artistic Director:	Jeanne Brabants	
First Choreographer:	André Leclair	
Ballet Mistress:	Andrée Marlière	
Dance Teacher:	Marie-Louise Wilderijckx	

Principal Dancers:

Frieda Brijs	Aimé de Lignière
Patricia Carey	Christiane Meyten *
Roselinde De Craecker	Stefan Schuller
Josef Eyckmans *	Gilbert Serres
Winni Jacobs	Nanda Zervaes *
Christiane Latré	

Soloists:

Walter De Cock	Rudi Van den Berghe
Daniel Rosseel	Antoine Criscuolo *
Ben Van Cauwenbergh	* Opera group

The Repertoire

Acht (de Lignière) 1973
After Eden (Butler) 1977
Amelia (Brabants) 1973
Apollon Musagète (Balanchine) 1974
Arabesque (Brabants) 1970
Bach Brandenburg 3 (Czarny) 1971
Bartok 12 (Brabants) 1975
Cage of God (Carter) 1971
Cantus Firmus (Brabants) 1970
Concerto de Aranjuez (Leclair) 1970
Concerto for 8 (Czarny) 1974
Confrontatie (Leclair) 1972
Conservatoire (Bournonville) 1970
Daphnis and Chloë (Leclair) 1977
De Bijen (Osins) 1973
De Liefde van Don Juan (Leclair) 1974
Dialogue (Brabants) 1971
Divertimento (Leclair) 1971
Dream (Holmes) 1971
Een Dag aan het Hof van Bourgondië (Brabants) 1974
Ein-Dor (Efrati) 1973
Elegie (Brabants) 1975
Epitomé (Davesne) 1975
Façade (Ashton) 1976
Grand Hôtel (Brabants) 1977
Halewijn (Leclair) 1974
Images of Love (Glasstone) 1975
Kaleidoscoop (Butler) 1976
La Ventana (Bournonville) 1971

Leading Astray (Efrati) 1975
Liefdescène (Béjart) 1970
Miss Julie (Cullberg) 1972
Nachteiland (van Dantzig) 1971
Nepentha (Roy) 1973
Notturno (Leclair) 1973
Offenbach Folies (Leclair) 1974
Opus Vivaldi (de Lignière) 1977
Pas de Six (Brenaa) 1971
Petrouchka (Fokine) 1970
Pierlala (Brabants) 1974
Poëma (Brabants) 1975
Presto Vivo et Lento (Brabants) 1972
Prometheus (Leclair) 1970
Rencontre (Lichine) 1973
Rip van Winkle (Corelli) 1973
Ritus Paganus (Leclair) 1972
Salomé (Leclair) 1971
Salvé Anteverpia (Brabants) 1974
Satirische Suite (Leclair) 1973
The Green Table (Jooss) 1973
The Lesson (Flindt) 1971
The Rake's Progress (De Valois) 1972
Three Preludes (Stenvenson) 1977
Ulenspiegel, de Geus (Brabants/Leclair) 1977
Variomatic (Van Manen) 1971
Venusberg (Leclair) 1970
5 Evoluties (Leclair) 1972

Touring

Apart from touring throughout Belgium – appearing in nearly 90 towns – the Royal Ballet van Vlaaderen has visited England, Finland, France, Greece, East and West Germany, Holland, Italy, Poland, Portugal, Switzerland, Turkey, Yugoslavia, Costa Rica, Dominican Republic, Mexico, Nicaragua and Venezuela.

FRANCE
The Paris Opera

The Paris Opera was unquestionably the cradle of romantic ballet and perhaps it is not too far-fetched to claim that it was the cradle of ballet itself. Popular tradition usually credits the Sun King, Louis XIV, with founding ballet and undoubtedly the arts in general were much advanced during his reign. In 1661 he founded the Académie Royale de Danse and this led to the establishment of the Académie Royale de Musique ten years later. This, in turn, evolved into the Théâtre National de l'Opéra in 1871.

The first ballet, *Pomone*, was performed in 1671 and there has been an uninterrupted tradition of ballet ever since. The first director of the Academy, Jean Baptiste Lully, was appointed in 1672. Italian by birth, he was taken to the court of Louis XIV where he became a dancer and violinist. He appeared in a number of ballets with the king with whom he remained on friendly terms all his life. He was instrumental in setting up the Académie Royale de Musique, and composed the music for many ballets, including *Cadmus et Hermione* and *Proserpine*. Among the distinguished ballet masters of this time were Charles Louis Beauchamps, Louis Pécourt, Jean Lany, Gaetano and Auguste Vestris and Maximilien and Pierre Gardel.

France's most exciting contemporary dance company is the Ballet Théâtre Contemporain. Thérèse Thoreux and Itchko Lazarov are pictured in Felix Blaska's Danses Concertantes. *The costumes and decor were designed by Sonia Delaunay.*

All these were dancers, choreographers and teachers. Auguste Vestris, for example, was not only a virtuoso dancer, noted for his spectacular elevation and brilliant footwork, he also taught Fanny Elssler, Charles Didelot and Jules Perrot. The Parisian ballet has always been tremendously influential and the style of many major companies, from Denmark to St Petersburg, has been profoundly affected by the training of French teachers – a tradition clearly already established in the eighteenth century.

Maximilien Gardel is credited with being the first dancer to remove the cumbersome mask which was then a standard piece of stage equipment. It is said that he removed the mask during a performance in order to inform the audience that it was he, not Vestris, who had been scheduled to dance the role. He created a number of ballets for the Academy – *La Chercheuse d'Esprit*, *Le Déserteur*, *La Rosière*, *Le Coq du Village*.

Numbered amongst the dancers of this period were Marie Sallé, Madeleine Guimard, Louis Dupré and Marie Camargo who is famed for the shortening of her skirt, lowering the heels of her shoes and inventing the turnout. The choreographers were an equally distinguished group, including the revolutionary theorist and prolific choreographer Jean Georges Noverre and his pupil Jean Dauberval. Jean Dauberval created *La Fille Mal Gardée* in 1789, one of the oldest ballets still regularly performed, although the original choreography is no longer in existence.

With such a remarkable number of major figures, it is hardly surprising that the Paris Opera was the acknowledged leader of ballet in the eighteenth century. With the advent of romantic ballet in the nineteenth century the Paris Opera consolidated its leadership. The two major romantic ballets – *La Sylphide* and *Giselle* – were first performed at the Paris Opera in 1832 and 1841 respectively.

La Sylphide was created by Filippo Taglioni for his daughter Maria and she danced the title role at the première. Although there is evidence that other ballerinas had danced on full pointe before this occasion, Maria Tagalioni is often credited with being the first one to do so, and she certainly introduced a new style of delicate lightness and spirituality to ballet.

Giselle was based on a libretto by the romantic poet Theophile Gautier and the choreography was by Jean Coralli and Jules Perrot, perhaps the greatest choreographer of the period. Carlotta Grisi created the title role and Lucien Petipa, brother of the famous choreographer Marius, partnered her as Albrecht. *Giselle* was, and still is, an outstanding ballet because of its remarkable artistic unity – story, choreography and music blending harmoniously together, recurring themes and a systematic development throughout. The title role has been the aim of every aspiring dancer, since its première.

Besides Maria Taglioni and Carlotta Grisi, the other great ballerinas of the period also appeared at the Paris Opera. Fanny Elssler, Maria Taglioni's greatest rival, made her debut in Paris in September 1834 as Alcine in Jean Coralli's ballet *La Tempête* to a rapturous reception. Famed for her character dance, Fanny Elssler remained the sole star of the Paris Opera after Maria Taglioni accepted an invitation from the St Petersburg Imperial ballet in 1838. Fanny Cerrito also appeared with great success at the Paris Opera and Lucile Grahn quarrelled with August Bournonville partly as a result of her triumphant visits to Paris and Hamburg.

It was almost inevitable that the golden days of the Paris Opera, which had reached their apogee with romantic ballet, would come to an end. By the last quarter of the nineteenth century the Paris Opera Ballet had gone into a severe decline which continued until the early years of the twentieth century.

The revival of the Paris Opera Ballet dates from Jacques Rouche's appointment as director of the Paris Opera in 1914. As well as engaging guest stars such as Michel Fokine, Anna Pavlova, Olga Spessivtzeva and Bronislava Nijinska, he appointed Serge Lifar as director of the Paris Opera Ballet in 1929.

Serge Lifar was born in Kiev, and studied piano and violin at the Conservatory of Music as well as dance at the State School. In 1923 he joined Diaghilev's Ballets Russes and became premier danseur in 1925. While he was with the Ballets Russes he created the title roles in George Balanchine's *Prodigal Son* and *Apollon Musagète*. He joined the Paris Opera Ballet as Director and Ballet Master in the same year and remained there until 1944, receiving the title Professor in 1932. During this time he created a number of ballets including *Promethée* (1929), *Icare* (1935), *David Triomphant* (1936), *Le Roi Nu* (1936), *Alexandre Le Grand* (1937), *Oriane et le Prince d'Amour* (1938), *Le Cantique des Cantiques* (1938) and *Joan de Zarissa* (1942).

In 1944 he left the Paris Opera to become Artistic Director and choreographer of the Nouveau Ballet de Monte Carlo and remained there until 1947 including one season under the Marquis de Cuevas, when the company was renamed the Grand Ballet de Monte Carlo.

The following October he returned to the Paris Opera as Ballet Master, dancer and choreographer. Ballets he created during this second period in Paris include *Zadig, Escales, Lucifer, Endymion, La Naissance des Couleurs, Septuor, L'Inconnue, Le Chevalier Errant, Phèdre, Astrologue, Blanche-Neige, Les Fourberies, Cinéma, Variations, Grand Pas, Nauteos, Les Noces Fantastiques*, Prokofiev's *Romeo and Juliet, Le Chemin de Lumière, Le Bel Indifférent* and *Daphnis and Chloë*. Leading dancers during these years included Solange Schwarz, Yvette Chauviré, Nina Vyroubova, Marjorie Tallchief, George Skibine, Peter van Dijk, Alexandre Kalioujny, Michel Renault and Serge Lifar himself. Jean Babilée, Roland Petit and Renée Jeanmaire also began their careers with the Paris Opera Ballet. Serge Lifar gave his last performance as a dancer in 1956 and left the Paris Opera in 1958.

After Serge Lifar's departure, George Skibine became Director of the Paris Opera Ballet. During the four years he was Ballet Master he created *Concerto, Isoline, Atlantide*, his own interpretation of *Daphnis and Chloë, Facheuses Rencontres, Conte Cruel* and *Pastorale*, which was staged for the state visit

Cyril Atanassoff is one of the most elegant dancers of the Paris Opera. His fluid grace and lyrical poise can be clearly seen in this apparently effortless leap.

of the late President John F. Kennedy and his wife to Paris. Although he resigned as Ballet Master in 1962 he remained as guest artist and choreographer until 1964 when he joined the Harkness Ballet.

In 1963 Yvette Chauviré whose long association with the Paris Opera Ballet began with her studies at the school, was appointed Director. Michel Descombey succeeded George Skibine as Ballet Master in 1962.

Mainly due to the creative energy of Serge Lifar, the Paris Opera Ballet is now once again one of the world's major companies. The repertoire is a combination of traditional works and mainstream contemporary choreography. There are no resident choreographers – Serge Lifar, George Skibine, and Michel Descombey were all Ballet Masters as well as choreographers. The policy of the company is to present major works and it is felt that the stage of the Paris Opera is not the right place for young inexperienced choreo-

Below *The legendary Maria Taglioni was the most famous and best loved ballerina of the romantic period. She was especially renowned for her creation of the title role in her father's ballet* La Sylphide, *which was first performed at the Paris Opera on March 12, 1832 and later became an international triumph.*

graphers to try out new works. The company is proud of its great romantic heritage and regularly presents new versions and re-stagings.

The majority of company members graduated from the Ecole de Danse, where the child pupils are known as 'petits rats'. On leaving the school and entering the company the dancers, depending on their abilities, pass through five categories, stagiaires, quadrilles, choryphées, sujets and premiers danseurs. The company is run on very formal lines as befits an old-established national ballet. Nevertheless it remains a major force in the cultural life of France and a company of unvaryingly high standards and international importance. The stage of the Paris Opera has been a regular host to major companies from all parts of the world. As a result of this, many influences have combined to extend the dance vocabulary of the French dancers and broaden the repertoire. In 1976, Yuri Grigorovich was invited to stage his recently created and spectacular ballet, *Ivan the Terrible*.

In 1978 it will enter a new phase when Violette Verdy, for many years a star in the United States with the New York City Ballet, will return to the Paris Opera as Artistic Director.

The Company

Administrator:	Rolf Liebermann
Artistic Director:	Violette Verdy (from 1978)

Principal Dancers:

Cyril Atanassoff	Charles Jude
Patrice Bart	Dominique Khalfouni
Michaël Denard	Noëlla Pontois
Jean Guizerix	Ghislaine Thesmar

Soloists:

Florence Clerc	Marie-Christine Mouis
Elisabeth de Mikhnevitch	Jacques Namont
Claude de Vulpian	Olivier Patey
Katia Grey	Georges Piletta
Françoise Legré	Francine Richard
France Merovak	Christiane Vlassi
Claire Motte	Francesca Zumbo

The Repertoire

Agon (Balanchine)
Capriccio (Balanchine)
Circus Polka (Robbins)
Conservatoire (Bournonville, staged by Hans Brenaa)
Coppélia (Saint-Léon/Lacotte)
Défilé du Corps de Ballet (Aveline)
Four Temperaments (Balanchine)
Giselle (Perrot/Alonso)
Hommages à Varese (Charrat/Butler/Kenten/Blaska)
Ivan the Terrible (Grigorovich)
Il y à juste un instant (Carlson)
Jeux (Flindt)
La Vivandière (Lacotte)
La Sylphide (Taglioni/Lacotte)
Le Sacre du Printemps (Béjart)
Night Shadow (Balanchine)
Notre Dame de Paris (Petit)

Orphée (Balanchine)
Orphée et Eurydice (Balanchine)
Pas de Quatre (Alonso)
Pas de Quatre (Dolin)
Scherzo Fantastique (Robbins)
Shéhérazade (Petit)
Soir de Fête (Staats)
Spectacle de Ballets (Béjart)
Suite de Danses (Clustine)
Swan Lake (Bourmeister)
Symphonie Concertante (Descombey)
Symphony in C (Balanchine)
The Firebird (Béjart)
The Prodigal Son (Balanchine)
The Sorcerer's Apprentice (Schmucki)
Un jour ou deux (Cunningham)
Variations on a simple theme (Macdonald)
Webern Opus V (Béjart)

Ballet Théâtre Contemporain

It is very appropriate that this company is called the 'Contemporary Ballet Theatre'. The word 'contemporary' is not just descriptive but is used very specifically and precisely. From its inception, the company has had a clear idea of its role, not only as part of French cultural life, but as a mirror reflecting the constant change and re-adjustment of modern man. It has always aimed at portraying the present through the medium of dance.

The Ballet Théâtre Contemporain was founded in 1968 as a national centre for choreography by the Ministry for Cultural Affairs. France was, at that time, at the height of a decentralization programme so the company was established at Amiens rather than Paris. This location proved fortuitous for the company's development and later educational projects.

Es, le huitième jour, *with choreography by Michel Descombey and music by Karlheinz Stockhausen, is perfectly suited to the Ballet Théâtre Contemporain. Neither a narrative nor an abstract ballet, it is a philosophical reflection on contemporary life.*

Un poco piu ma non troppo, by Claudine Allegra, is a delightful blend of caricature and fantasy. It is a short ballet to music by Walter Carlos after Rossini, Purcell, Bach and Beethoven.

The founders of the Ballet Théâtre Contemporain like to think of themselves as being, in one way at least, like Diaghilev, described as a man who perceived 'l'odeur d'époque'. Like Diaghilev, they are constantly aware of the present – shifts in mood, the drama of ordinary social life, the confusion which surrounds us all. If this makes the Ballet Théâtre Contemporain sound serious and pessimistic, it must also be added that, with the enthusiasm and energy of youth, they see an essential counterbalance of hope and optimism expressed through both the dancer and the dance.

Another fundamental aspect of the company is its total view of the creative process. It aims to act as a meeting place for the plastic arts – the music, choreography and design are seen as an integrated part of the process of creating a ballet. The composer, choreographer and designer collaborate to produce a communal creation. However, the company prides itself that the quality of musical composition is such that it can also exist as a valuable independent art form. Similarly, the ballets are designed by painters and sculptors. A fine example is the spectacular setting and costumes designed for *Danses Concertantes* by Sonia Delaunay.

These are splendidly ambitious aims and, when it is realized that they necessarily involve the constant creation of new works, seem to court diaster and chaos. However, the dancers are expected to satisfy the most exacting standards and combine the energy of youth with strict, almost military discipline and resolute attack with subtle interpretation. The dancers themselves are, after all, the central core of this overall artistic view.

The repertoire is very varied ranging through all kinds of moods and emotions – the despair of *Nuits*, the lyrical purity of *Aquathème*, the vivacity of *Hopop* and the caricature of *Un Poco Piu ma non Troppo*.

The Ballet Théâtre Contemporain believes that dance is a popular art form

112

not just the prerogative of an informed few. Consequently, the company organizes debates, lectures, meetings, demonstrations and films with a view to reaching the largest possible audience.

The Ballet Théâtre Contemporain has achieved enormous popularity not only in France but among the varied cultural and artistic backgrounds of the many countries it has visited in North and South America, Europe, North Africa and the Far East.

The Company

Director:		Jean-Albert Cartier
Director of Choreography:		Françoise Adret
Ballet Master:		Raoul Celada

Principal Dancers:

Muriel Belmondo — Itchko Lazarov
Jean-Claude Giorgini — Martine Parmain
Noriko Kubota — James Urbain

Soloists:

Odile Carrard — Régina Rylls
Jean Marion

Dancers:

Ritva Ahlfors	Gilles Estran	Edith Muller
Ariane Asscherick	Phillipe Giraudeau	Véronique Murillo
Yannick Blanchard	Emilio Gritti	Bernard Olivier
Dominique Boivin	Itoshi Ito	Joëlle Pederencino
Charline Bourbon	Monique Marion	Edouard Saint-Denis
Catherine Brunet	Françoise Michaux	Véronique Simottel
Alain Courtaux	Philippe Muhl	
Régine Coste	Ariel Mulard	

The Repertoire

Agitor (Araiz) 1975
Amériques (Schmucki) 1971
Aquathème (Adret) 1968
Astral (Guiliano) 1970
Bakyla (Blaska) 1969
Cantate Profane (Sparemblek) 1969
Cycle (Adret) 1973
Dangerous Games (Macdonald) 1969
Danses Concertantes (Blaska) 1968
Déserts (Descombey) 1968
Eonta (Adret) 1969
Es, le Huitième Jour (Descombey) 1973
Hai Kai (Babilée) 1968
Hi-Kyo (Butler) 1971
Hopop (Sanders) 1969
Hymnen (Descombey, Deshayes, Garnier, Roux, Schmucki) 1970
Intersection II (Saint-Denis) 1975
Itinéraires (Butler) 1970
Kill What I Love (Butler) 1973

La Légende des Cerfs (Skibine) 1970
Le Rossignol (Adret) 1972
Le Soleil des Eaux (Skibine)
Mobilissimo (Goliard)
Nuits (Efrati) 1972
Pasdanses (Sanders and Goliard) 1972
Pas de Trois (Fielden) 1973
Rags (Macdonald) 1975
Renard (Lecocq) 1972
Requiem (Adret) 1971
Saints and Lovers (Sanasardo) 1975
Salomé (Lazzini) 1968
Sans Titre (Lubovitch) 1972
Trauma (Neumeier) 1973
Un Poco Piu ma non Troppo (Allegra) 1795
Violostries (Descombey) 1969
Whisky-Coca (Sanders) 1973
7 Pour 5 (Adret) 1972
For children: *Le Grenier Enchanté* (Ponelle) 1971

Touring

Canada, United States, Mexico, Venezuela, Colombia, Ecuador, Peru, Brazil, Uruguay, Argentina, Chile, Great Britain, Germany, Belgium, Poland, Luxemburg, Switzerland, Spain, Portugal, Italy, Greece, Tunisia, Morocco, Canary Islands, Cyprus, Iran, India, Thailand, Singapore, Indonesia, Philippines, Korea and Japan.

GREAT BRITAIN & IRELAND
The Ballet Rambert

A company totalling 33 people which included 15 soloists and no corps de ballet, the Ballet Rambert celebrated its fiftieth birthday in June 1976. This celebration represented fifty years of profound influence on the development of ballet, not only in its native Britain, but directly and indirectly in many other parts of the world. The Ballet Rambert is rightly ranked among the 'greats', not least because of its tenacity, its reputation for enthusiastic experiment, its constant development, change and adaptability and the unique opportunities it has generously offered to young, unknown artists – dancers, choreographers, musicians and designers – many of whom, in the course of those 50 years, have become international celebrities.

Glen Tetley created his powerful work, Ziggurat, especially for the Ballet Rambert, who gave the first performance in November 1967. It is a ballet of emotional density and is rich in imagery, so it is especially well suited to the company. The striking designs were by Nadine Baylis.

The Ballet Rambert's first performance, although it was not known by that name then, was *A Tragedy of Fashion* included as a part of Nigel Playfair's revue, *Riverside Nights* at the Lyric Theatre, Hammersmith in West London, in June 1926. It was a new ballet designed by Sophie Fedorovitch, to music by Eugene Goòssens and with choreography by Frederick Ashton who was, at that time, a pupil at the Rambert Ballet School and who was one of the many names associated with this remarkable company destined for a long and distinguished career. This performance in 1926 was important, not just because it was the first given by the Rambert company, nor even because it was the first of Sir Frederick Ashton's many works, but because it marked the birth of British ballet.

The history of the Ballet Rambert is linked inextricably with the forceful personality of Dame Marie Rambert. She was born in Warsaw, Poland in 1888, and showed remarkable talent as a dancer from an early age. By the time she was 16 she had begun to consider the possibility of becoming a professional dancer. Her decision was influenced by her admiration and respect for the work of Isadora Duncan and it does not seem far fetched to suggest that her refreshing attitude to experiment dated from this time. However, in 1905 she was sent by her parents to Paris to study medicine. It is fortunate for the world of dance that she was too young and, instead, she continued with her dancing, earning herself something of a reputation in fashionable Parisian salons. She attended a summer course at Jacques Dalcroze's School of Eurhythmics in Geneva and, in fact, remained there for a further three years.

In 1912 she joined Diaghilev's Ballets Russes to assist Nijinsky in teaching the complex rhythms of Stravinsky's *Le Sacre du Printemps*. She continued to teach eurhythmics and to dance with the company until 1914, when she left Paris and went to live in London.

For the next six years she continued her own studies, taught in schools and private houses and continued to establish her considerable reputation with a new recital programme. She married the English playwright, Ashley Dukes, in 1918. Two years later she opened her own school of dancing. In 1926, she and her students appeared in *A Tragedy of Fashion* and the Marie Rambert Dancers, as the company was then called, began its famous career. A year later, Ashley Dukes bought a disused church hall in Notting Hill Gate in West London and converted it to a small theatre and a studio for the school. By 1930, the Ballet Club at the Mercury Theatre was established and this remained the company's headquarters for some 30 years. It was moreover

the first permanent company and school in Britain.

The repertoire at first consisted of excerpts from famous ballets and new works by young choreographers, including Frederick Ashton. The company and all aspects of its repertoire continued to expand and change. Nijinsky's ballet *L'Après-Midi d'un Faune* was presented in its original version. The Rambert's production of *Giselle* became deservedly famous as well as much later an electrifying version of *Don Quixote*, a ballet which suffered a long and undeserved obscurity in Europe, until relatively recently.

Marie Rambert was always quick to recognize and foster new talent and it was she who discovered and encouraged Antony Tudor, later associated with so many other major companies, including the Royal Ballet London, the

116

American Ballet Theatre, the National Ballet of Canada and the Royal Swedish Ballet. His remarkable ballet *Dark Elegies*, created to Mahler's *Kindertotenlieder* song cycle, in 1937, is still included in the current repertoire. Another now famous name associated with the Ballet Rambert is Ronald Hynd. He was trained at the Rambert School and was a soloist in the company. He later became a principal dancer with Britain's Royal Ballet, and

eventually a distinguished choreographer creating such works as *The Fairy's Kiss* for the Dutch National Ballet, *Dvořák Variations* and *The Nutcracker* for the London Festival Ballet, and *The Merry Widow* for the Australian Ballet. Others include Andrée Howard, Harold Turner, John Gilpin, Celia Franca, Lucette Aldous and of course Sir Frederick Ashton, and many more too numerous to mention.

The Ballet Rambert's economic troubles began during World War II. In spite of help from the Arts Council of Great Britain and the inclusion of new productions, by 1966, the costs of a large touring company had become prohibitive. It seemed as if financial problems would force the company to disband. Happily, a grant from the Arts Council and the indomitable will and courage of Dame Marie Rambert averted this catastrophe. She set about a complete and ruthless revision of the company with the assistance of Norman Morrice, her principal choreographer. The 'New Ballet Rambert', consisting of just 17 soloists and no corps de ballet, was designed to concentrate on contemporary works. Ballets from the old repertoire suited to the new style of the company were also included, among them Tudor's *Dark Elegies*. Marie Rambert remained Artistic Director, Norman Morrice became Associate Director, John Chesworth became Assistant to the Directors and Leonard Salzedo became Musical Director.

The new company gave its first performance on November 28, 1966 at the Jeanetta Cochrane Theatre, amidst great public and critical speculation and excitement. That season included four works new to the company – Pierre Lacotte's *Numeros* and *Intermède*, John Chesworth's *Time Base*, and *Night Island* with choreography by Rudi van Dantzig. Also included were Kenneth MacMillan's *Laiderette* as well as *Dark Elegies* and two other Antony Tudor ballets, *Jardin aux Lilas* and *Judgement of Paris*. The 'New Ballet Rambert' had certainly made an unequivocal statement about its intentions. Yet, in essence, it was not unlike the early experimental days of the Ballet Club at the Mercury Theatre in the 1930s.

Public and critical response to the new company was mixed and it took some time for audiences to 'catch up' with the developments. Indeed, some of the regular following of the old company were completely lost to the revised 'Ballet Rambert' but at the same time, a vast new audience was accumulating. The company appealed enormously to young people, many of whom had never previously shown any interest in ballet. This aspect of the company developed further in 1967 and 1968 when Collaboration One was founded. This was a workshop for new choreographers giving them the opportunity to work with professional dancers. An important part of this workshop was co-

Leigh Warren makes a dramatic leap in Christopher Bruce's Black Angels, *a gripping work based on the myth of the fallen angels and the archetypal war between good and evil. This was his second work to music by George Crumb — he created* Ancient Voices of Children *for the Ballet Rambert in 1975.*

operation between the Ballet Rambert and the Theatre Design Department of the Central School of Art and Design, giving novice designers a unique opportunity to work in real theatre conditions.

During this time there was a stream of new productions. Among them were Glen Tetley's *Pierrot Lunaire* in January 1967 and *Ricercare* in February 1967, Norman Morrice's *Hazard* in June 1967 and Anna Sokolow's *Deserts* in July 1967. 1968 brought 'legitimate' and quite phenomenal success in London's West End. Another crop of new works was added to the repertoire. These included John Chesworth's *Tic-Tack* and *Pawn to King 5;* Norman Morrice's *1–2–3* and *Embrace Tiger and Return to Mountain*, specially created for the company by Glen Tetley, whose early development as a choreographer was considerably enriched by his association with the Ballet Rambert. In 1969, the company was invited to Dortmund, Vienna, Berlin and Verona and rose splendidly to the challenge of a European tour.

The phenomenal flow of new material continued and the five new works presented by the Ballet Rambert in November 1970 and May 1971 were all from choreographers within the company, refuting totally, earlier charges that the company was excessively influenced by developments in American ballet. These were Norman Morrice's *The Empty Suit* and *That is the Show*, Joseph Scoglio's *Metaflow*, Jonathon Taylor's *'Tis Goodly Sport* and Christopher Bruce's *Wings*. Moreover, in the autumn the Ballet Rambert gave two world premières, *Rag Dances* by Glen Tetley and Norman Morrice's *Solo*.

1972 marked yet another step forward in the world of dance by this pioneer company. Previously, most ballets, even the newly created works, had been designed for the proscenium stage. *Dance for New Dimensions*, performed in March 1972, was specially created for the open stage. This was such a successful production, a second version was performed as part of the Fanfare for Europe festivities in 1973, to celebrate Britain's entry into the European Economic Community. Later other ballets were created to explore the challenge of the open stage, including Christopher Bruce's *Weekend* and Norman Morrice's *Spindrift*, both in 1974. The company, of course, continued to perform works for the proscenium stage. The American choreographer, Louis Falco was invited to create *tutti-frutti* for the Ballet Rambert.

In 1974, Norman Morrice ended his twenty-one years of association with the company. John Chesworth became Artistic Director and, in 1975, Christopher Bruce was appointed Associate Director .The change in leadership did not bring about a change of pace. 1974 saw the London première of *Escaras* by Manuel Alum and Jonathon Taylor's *Almost an Echo* and the new ballets of 1975 included Joseph Scoglio's *Night Dances*, Lindsay Kemp's *The Parades Gone By;* Cliff Keuter's *Table* and *Musete di Taverni* and Christopher Bruce's highly successful *Ancient Voices of Children*. In 1976, Christopher Bruce's eleventh creation for the company was presented – *Promenade* to two sonatas for flute and harpsichord by Bach. The same year saw the addition of another new work, by the young American choreographer Sara Sugihara, herself new to the Ballet Rambert.

By now the Ballet Rambert has established its new identity as an exciting, controversial and experimental contemporary company. Yet as it pioneers new ways of presenting ballets, as well as creating seven or eight new works each year, it retains a sense of continuity, not least through the personality of Dame Marie Rambert, with the beginnings of 'the old company', so auspiciously marked by the première of the unknown Frederick Ashton's first ballet.

The Company

Founder Director:		Marie Rambert DBE
Director:		John Chesworth
Associate Director:		Christopher Bruce

Rehearsal Director and Classical Ballet Teacher:	Gary Sherwood	Choreologist:	Dora Frankel

Dancers:	Catherine Becque	Zoltan Imre	Robert Smith
	Blake Brown	Gerard Jouanneau	Sara Sugihara
	Christopher Bruce	Judith Marcuse	Lenny Westerdijk
	Lucy Burge	Sarah Newton	Sylvia Yamada
	Nelson Fernandez	Sally Owen	

The Repertoire

Ancient Voices of Children (Bruce)
Black Angels (Bruce)
Blind-Sight (Morrice)
Collaboration Three (Brown/Blaikie/Caroll/Imre/ Marcuse/Owen/Scoglio/Smith/Warren/ Westerdijk)
Dance for New Dimensions (Avrahami/Bruce/ Chesworth/Curtis Jones/ Law/Morrice/Scoglio/ Taylor)
Dark Elegies (Tudor)
Deserts (Sokolow)
Duets (Bruce)
Embrace Tiger and Return to Mountain (Tetley)
Four According (Chesworth)
Freefall (Tetley)
George Frideric (Bruce)
Girl with Straw Hat
H (Chesworth)
Hazard (Morrice)
Judgment of Paris (Tudor)
Les Saltimbanques (Scoglio)
Listen to the Music (Taylor)
Living Space (Bruce)
Metaflow (Scoglio)
Moveable Garden (Tetley)
Musical Offering (Imre)
Opus 65 (Sokolow)
Pawn to King 5 (Chesworth)

Pierrot Lunaire (Tetley)
Promenade (Bruce)
Rag-Dances (Tetley)
Reflections
Ricercare (Tetley)
Running Figures (North)
Solo (Morrice)
Table (Keuter)
Take a Running Jump
That is the Show (Morrice)
The Act (Hodes)
The Empty Suit (Morrice)
The Parades Gone By (Kemp)
Sea Whisper'd Me (Morrice)
There was a Time (Bruce)
Tick-Tack (Chesworth)
'Tis Goodly Sport (Taylor)
tutti-frutti (Falco)
Weekend (Bruce)
Window (Sugihara)
Wings (Bruce)
Ziggurat (Tetley)
1-2-3 (Morrice)
Bertram Batell's Sideshow
(A programme of dance and music for the entertainment of children of all ages).

Touring

Since their first venture outside Great Britain in 1969, the Ballet Rambert has established quite a gruelling yearly schedule – two London seasons, regional tours, foreign tours and the creation of at least six new ballets.

1969	Dortmund, Vienna, Berlin and Verona
1970	Premio Roma Festival and the Israel Festival
1971	Bergen Festival and the Kupio Dance Festival in Finland
1972	Poland
1973	Helsinki, Copenhagen, Northern France and Dusseldorf
1974	Austria, Yugoslavia and Germany
1975	Germany, (May) including performances at the Wiesbaden Festival, *Danza* 75 in Venice, Romania, Hungary, Germany, Luxembourg and France
1976	Lausanne Festival, Holland Festival and Paris, Flanders Festival

The Royal Ballet

The Royal Ballet is probably Britain's best known and best loved company. Unquestionably, it has earned a high position in the world of ballet, ranking in importance with such long-established companies as the Bolshoi Ballet and the Royal Danish Ballet. Among the five or six companies generally accepted as the best in the world, only the American ones are younger than the British company.

The story began with Dame Ninette de Valois, a woman of intense tenacity, vision and energy who, even today, although she is retired, maintains an active and lively interest in the company she founded. She studied with several leading teachers, including Edouard Espinosa and Enrico Cechetti. After several years in revues and as première danseuse of the Royal Opera, Covent Garden, she joined Diaghilev's Ballets Russes where she quickly became a soloist. She left the company in 1925 but she still danced occasionally with it for a further year. In 1926, she founded her own school in London, the Academy of Choreographic Art, with a view to the eventual establishment of a company. The students gave occasional performances and, in 1928, Ninette de Valois persuaded Lilian Baylis, the remarkable director of London's world-famous Old Vic Theatre, to allow occasional short ballets to precede the evenings' plays.

Lilian Baylis was an extraordinary woman with a rare ability to encourage new talent and draw out performances of the highest quality. In fact, many of Britain's greatest actors and actresses owe an immense debt of gratitude to her. Apart from running the Old Vic in conditions of extreme financial insecurity, she organized the reconstruction of the Sadler's Wells Theatre, inviting Ninette de Valois to form a permanent ballet company to perform at the two theatres on alternating weeks. Thus the Vic-Wells Ballet was established in January 1931, as part of Lilian Baylis' extensive organization, which also presented Shakespearean plays and opera sung in English as alternative entertainment to the rather seedy options open to ordinary people. All these activities functioned well away from the West End of London where the major theatres were situated. Finances were extremely precarious and Lilian Baylis is reputed to have made curtain speeches chastising the audiences for not attending Monday performances in adequate numbers.

The first full-length ballet performance of the new company was given on 5 May, 1931. The programme consisted of *Les Petits Riens, Danse Sacré et Danse Profane, Hommages aux Belles Viennoises, The Jackdaw and the Pigeons, Faust Scène de Ballet, Bach Suite, The Faun* and a Spanish solo. The small company included Ursula Moreton, Freda Bamford, Ninette de Valois herself and Anton Dolin as a guest artist. At the same time, Ninette de Valois closed down her Academy of Choreographic Art and opened a new school at the Sadler's Wells Theatre.

The music for the first performance was conducted by Constant Lambert, who shortly afterwards, became the company's Musical Director and conductor. He remained with the company until three years before his death and excercised enormous influence upon its development. His devotion to the company was phenomenal and his perspicacious and expert criticism was greatly valued.

Much of the early repertoire consisted of ballets created by Ninette de Valois. Some of these works were unremarkable, but among them were two particularly impressive creations, *Job* and *The Rake's Progress*. The former, presented at the Old Vic on September 22, 1931, was based on William Blake's illustrations from the *Book of Job*. The quality of the choreography was variable but the ballet contained some quite masterly episodes, including a

Margot Fonteyn's and Rudolf Nureyev's partnership is one of the best known and best loved in the world. Margot Fonteyn's extraordinary grace and lyrical fluency have delighted supporters of the Royal Ballet since she began her career in the Vic-Wells Company in the 1930s. Her dancing achieved new dimensions in the 1960s, when she formed her celebrated association with ex-Kirov dancer, Rudolf Nureyev. His powerful and dramatic technique have made him a truly international star, although he remains most closely associated with the Royal Ballet.

The Rake's Progress *is
generally accepted as Dame
Ninette de Valois' finest
work. The title role became
uniquely that of Robert
Helpmann, premier danseur
with the Sadler's Wells
Ballet, now the Royal Ballet,
from 1934 to 1950. He is
now Director of the
Australian Ballet.*

spectacular scene where Satan, danced by Anton Dolin, flung himself over a flight of steps. *The Rake's Progress*, first performed at the Sadler's Wells Theatre on 20 May, 1935, is generally considered to be Ninette de Valois' finest work. It is based on a series of paintings and engravings by the English artist, William Hogarth, published in the early eighteenth century. It presents a moral tale of the Rake who, on inheriting a fortune, leaves the countryside for London, where he is rapidly tricked out of his money. Ruined by gambling, he ends up in Bedlam, a notorious London lunatic asylum, where he dies in the arms of a girl he has betrayed but who is still capable of pity for him. The 'living reproductions' of the original prints were immensely impressive and the final scene is one of the most dramatic and exciting in British ballet. The role of the Rake was created by Walter Gore and that of the betrayed girl by Alicia Markova.

In addition to presenting her own works, Ninette de Valois also commissioned ballets from Frederick Ashton who was closely associated with the early days of the Ballet Rambert. His neo-classical style provided an excellent contrast to her own approach. In 1933, he created *Les Rendezvous* and, not long afterwards, he became attached to the Vic-Wells Ballet. In addition, several of the great classics were commissioned from Nicholas Sergeyev. Former regisseur and Ballet Master at the Maryinsky Theatre, he left Russia in 1918, rifling the theatre files before he left. Although he was unpopular in St Petersburg, and Soviet authorities have found little to say in his favour subsequently, he played a very important part in the preservation and dissemination of many of the great Russian classics. Among the ballets staged by the Vic-Wells company from Sergeyev's notes between 1933 and 1939, were *Coppélia, Giselle, The Nutcracker, Swan Lake* and *The Sleeping Beauty*. This provided a solid foundation to the repertoire and also did much to preserve choreography which might otherwise have been lost forever. Furthermore, Ninette de Valois also added several works by Michel Fokine, including *Carnaval, Le Spectre de la Rose* and *Les Sylphides*. Other ballets with which the Vic-Wells Company was particularly successful during these years were *The Haunted Ballroom* and *Checkmate* by de Valois and *Apparitions, Nocturne, Les Patineurs* and *Horoscope* by Ashton.

The company has been fortunate in its dancers. In 1932, Alicia Markova appeared with the Vic-Wells Ballet beginning an important association. She had joined the Ballets Russes, when only 14 years old and remained with the company until Diaghilev's death in 1929. Her delicacy and lightness won her the admiration of audiences throughout the world during her long dancing career and her association with several major companies in Europe and the United States was a major influence on the development of Western ballet.

She made her debut with the Vic-Wells company in *Swan Lake* Act II, partnered by Anton Dolin. She created a number of leading roles in the new works presented during the early 1930s and was the first English dancer to undertake the title role in *Giselle* and Odette–Odile in *Swan Lake*. In the same year, 1934, she also danced in a revival of *The Nutcracker*. Anton Dolin partnered her in her first interpretation of Giselle and it was partly the success of this association which encouraged the two dancers to found the Markova-Dolin Ballet in 1935, which eventually developed into the London Festival Ballet in 1950. Between 1931 and 1935, he was the Vic-Wells Ballet's principal dancer.

By the time these two major figures left the company, it had acquired several promising young dancers and also experienced performers from other companies, including Pamela May, June Brae, Mary Honer, William Chappell, Harold Turner and Michael Somes. In addition, the Australian dancer, Robert Helpmann had joined the school in 1933 and appeared in the corps de ballet in *Coppélia* while still a student. Within nine months he proved capable of taking over the role of Satan in *Job*, from Anton Dolin. In 1934, he created the role of the Master of Treginnis in *The Haunted Ballroom*. By this time it was apparent that he was the natural successor to Anton Dolin and future premier danseur of the company. He occupied this position until 1950 when he resigned from the company.

A successor to Alicia Markova was equally apparent. In 1934, Margot Fonteyn took over the mime role of Young Treginnis in *The Haunted Ballrooms* from Freda Bamford, and the following year, she danced the part of the Creole Girl in a revival of *Rio Grande* at the Vic-Wells. She made a great impression in both these roles and after Alicia Markova's departure, she was trained to take over the ballerina roles. On January 19, 1937 she danced her first Giselle, at the age of 17. She was still immature and had not yet achieved the superb technical proficiency for which was later so famed. However, her simplicity and charm at the beginning of Act I, and the agonizing dramatic intensity of her mad scene convinced audiences that she was going to become one of the world's greatest ballerinas. At the age of 17 she was too lively and her dancing too full of youthful exuberance for her interpretation in Act II to be wholly convincing, but it was not long before she achieved the quality of supernatural mystery required.

It has often been remarked that the arts in Britain flourished during World War II. Perhaps this paradoxical situation was brought about by a need for something beautiful, stable and entertaining to counterbalance the horror and austerity of everyday life. Whatever the cause, the Sadler's Wells ballet certainly gave performances of a higher standard than ever before. The company had changed its name when it had confined its activities to the Sadler's Wells Theatre, leaving the Old Vic completely free to present plays. The company toured extensively during the war years. The Sadler's Wells Theatre was requisitioned but two other theatres in London, the New and the Princes, provided temporary accommodation. The size of audiences increased but the company suffered acutely from a shortage of male dancers.

It is fortunate that a firm and varied repertoire had been established during the 1930s because few new works could be staged in war-time. In 1943 Frederick Ashton was granted special leave from the Royal Air Force to create *The Quest*, which was staged at the New Theatre on April 6. The part of Pride was the first major role of the young Scottish dancer, Moira Shearer who became an international film star two years later in *The Red Shoes*. Other works added to the repertoire at this time included Frederick Ashton's *Dante Sonata* and *The Wanderer*, Ninette de Valois' *The Prospect Before Us*, and *Orpheus and Eurydice* and the first three ballets created by Robert Helpmann, *Comus*, *Hamlet* and *Miracle in the Gorbals*. At one time the company was giving nine performances each week, which included three on Saturdays. However, this period of intense activity was not without problems. A visit to Holland, sponsored by the British Council, coincided with the German invasion. The company escaped unharmed but it lost the scenery, costumes and scores for several major items of the repertoire. Among these were the scenery and costumes for *Façade*, a one-act ballet created Frederick Ashton to the music originally composed by William Walton as an accompaniment to poems by Edith Sitwell. It was first produced by the Camargo Society in 1931 and almost immediately taken into the repertoire of the Ballet Rambert, and this version remained with it for many years. Frederick Ashton first staged *Façade*, with the addition of the Country Dance, for the Vic-Wells company in 1935. After the loss in Holland, new costumes and scenery were designed by John Armstrong for a performance in July 1940, but these were greatly inferior to his originals. Two more dances were added to the choreography, although one was later dropped. *Façade* is sometimes thought of as marking the beginning of British ballet because it was the first major creation

Cinderella *was the first of Sir Frederick Ashton's full-length ballets. Here, he and Robert Helpmann portray the Ugly Sisters. This charming and lovely ballet has remained a tremendous favourite and is particularly popular with younger audiences for whom it often serves as their introduction to ballet.*

Above *La Fille Mal Gardée,*
created by Sir Frederick
Ashton, features in the
repertoires of both the
Royal Ballet and the
Sadler's Wells Royal
Ballet. The choreography
incorporates traditional
British folk dance elements
besides passages for
virtuoso classical dancers.

Above right *Lynn Seymour*
and Anthony Dowell dance
the roles of Natalia
Petrovna and Beliaev in Sir
Frederick Ashton's ballet
A Month in the Country.
Their subtle interpretation
and the superb choreography
of their duets as Beliaev's
repulsion changes to
passionate ardour, have
made the roles uniquely
their own. Lynn Seymour is
a dancer of rare emotional
force and remarkable
dramatic ability and these
talents have been fully
exploited in this work.

of Frederick Ashton, who was responsible, in many ways, for the development of a national identity for British ballet. When World War II ended, the Sadler's Wells Ballet found itself in a stronger position than seemed possible. All the leading male dancers who had been engaged on active service, returned to London, unscathed and eager to continue their careers. The Arts Council of Great Britain, which had grown out of the Council for the Encouragement of Music and the Arts, founded in 1939 to assist the arts during war-time, was organizing the establishment of permanent, subsidized opera and ballet companies at London's prestigious Royal Opera House at Covent Garden. The Sadler's Wells Ballet was invited to become the permanent dance company and, in 1946, it moved to Covent Garden, re-opening the opera house with a performance of *The Sleeping Beauty* starring Margot Fonteyn and Robert Helpmann. No suitable opera company was in existence at that time, so that the Sadler's Wells Ballet increased the number of dancers and gave performances every evening. When an opera company was formed, only half the number of performances could be given and the need for a second auditorium at Covent Garden quickly became apparent.

After the transfer to the Royal Opera House, Ninette de Valois did not create any more original works. She commissioned a number of new works from several British choreographers and, during the 1950s, she revived two works from the Ballets Russes' repertoire, *Petrouchka* and *The Firebird.* These were staged with great care by Serge Grigoriev, former regisseur with Diaghilev, and by his wife Lubov Tchernicheva, a leading dancer with the company. Careful attention to details of choreography, costumes, scenery and lighting reproduced the original productions as far as possible and, as was the case with the great classics of Imperial Russia, the Sadler's Wells Ballet was responsible for the preservation of these great works.

When Frederick Ashton returned from the Royal Air Force, he became the company's chief choreographer. He formed a close association with Margot Fonteyn which, over many years, developed a characteristic style. He created many works for her particular talents and style and she responded naturally to his neo-classicism. In 1946, he created *Symphonic Variations*, considered one of the great masterpieces of British ballet. The decor was designed by Sophia Fedorovitch, whose association with British Ballet and Frederick Ashton began with *A Tradegy of Fashion* in 1926. A superb theatrical designer, she created an abstract, mathematical decor and simple costumes eminently suited to the lyrical, plotless choreography.

In 1948, he created the first of his own versions of several major classics, *Cinderella*. This was followed by *Daphnis and Chloë* in 1951, a one-act ballet originally created by Michel Fokine. The role of Chloë was superbly created by Margot Fonteyn, Michael Somes danced Daphnis and the part of the Pirate Chief was undertaken by Alexander Grant, who later became internationally renowned as a character dancer. This was followed by *Sylvia* in 1952 and *Ondine* in 1958, the title role becoming uniquely Margot Fonteyn's. Frederick Ashton commissioned a new score from the composer Hans Werner Henze and simplified the original complicated plot by Jules Perrot and Fanny Cerrito. The ballet had some remarkable romantic effects and the scene where Ondine, a water sprite, dances with her shadow, when she sees it for the first time, was the most striking of all.

In 1960, he created a new version of *La Fille Mal Gardée*, possibly the oldest surviving ballet in the world, although it had undergone many changes in both Europe and Imperial Russia. The subject was excellently suited to Frederick Ashton's particular style. Apart from one mime scene he requested Tamara Karsavina to reproduce, he did not use any of the extant choreography. He followed the original story exactly and created a charming and humorous ballet. In Mother Simone's delightful clog dance he incorporated steps from traditional folk dance. The simple-minded Alain was triumphantly created by Alexander Grant. Although many leading dancers have since taken the roles of Lise and Colas, they remain closely identified with their creators, Nadia Nerina and David Blair. Frederick Ashton's version of *La Fille Mal Gardée* remains one of the most popular works in the repertoire and has been successfully presented by other companies, including the National Ballet of Canada as part of its twenty-fifth anniversary celebrations in 1976.

For many years, Margot Fonteyn was the unsurpassed prima ballerina of the company. Since 1959 she has been a guest artist but continued to appear very frequently with it. Her dancing gained a new vitality in the 1960s when she formed a world-famous partnership with the former Kirov dancer, Rudolf Nureyev. This association began at a gala performance organized in London and, in 1963, he partnered Margot Fonteyn, 19 years his senior, in *Giselle*, *Le Corsaire Pas de Deux*, *Les Sylphides*, *Swan Lake* and *Marguerite and Armand*, in which he created his first leading role outside the USSR. In spite of his immaturity in both technique and artistry, it was clear that a special rapport existed between the two dancers and he benefited enormously, in the following years, from the greater experience of his partner. Together with Margot Fonteyn he was given the status of a more or less permanent guest artist from 1963 and, in spite of his many activities with several companies throughout the world, he has a specially close relationship with the Royal Ballet.

When the Sadler's Wells Ballet moved to The Royal Opera House in 1946, Ninette de Valois, with characteristic foresight and energy, set up a second company in the old theatre, called the Sadler's Wells Opera Ballet. This was intended to provide a professional performing background for the developments of young dancers and choreographers who would later be promoted

The Vic-Wells Ballet's first ballerina was the incomparable Alicia Markova. Here she is partnered in The Nutcracker *by premier danseur Anton Dolin. Their successful partnership led them to establish their own company, the Markova-Dolin Ballet, in 1935.*

to the main company. Among those who graduated from the Sadler's Wells Opera, later Theatre, Ballet to the senior company were Svetlana Beriosova, David Blair, Stanley Holden, Maryon Lane, Donald MacLeary, Nadia Nerina and Annette Page. The second company was also responsible for providing dancers for opera performances. Under the direction of Peggy van Praagh, the Sadler's Wells Theatre Ballet began to extend beyond its original purpose and started to gain a regular audience of its own. Two choreographers closely associated with this stage of its development were the late John Cranko and Kenneth MacMillan, now Director of The Royal Ballet. Among their early works specially created for it were *Pineapple Poll* and *The Lady and the Fool* (Cranko) and *Danses Concertantes* and *House of Birds* (MacMillan).

When John Field was appointed Director in 1955, the company underwent a major change. Touring became its chief activity and full-length ballets, such as *Swan Lake* and *The Sleeping Beauty*, were added to the repertoire. Most of the year was spent in the provinces presenting these ballets and also works by the senior company's choreographers, including *The Two Pigeons* and *La Fille Mal Gardée*. The London seasons were very much reduced in length. In spite of the undoubted value of this enterprise, by the end of the 1960s, it became apparent that major re-organization was necessary for both companies, involving a drastic reduction in the number of dancers. The touring company ceased to exist and was replaced instead by the Royal Ballet New Group. This consisted of 25 soloists from the main company and no corps de ballet. The soloists varied and the idea was that dancers would be interchangeable between the Covent Garden company and the New Group, although this caused vast administrative problems. The repertoire obviously could no longer include the major classics which had featured so sucessfully in the old Sadler's Wells Theatre Company's programmes. Instead, a number of smaller-scale works by contemporary choreographers were presented. Besides ballets by Kenneth MacMillan, the repertoire included Joe Layton's *The Grand Tour*, Hans van Manen's *Grosse Fuge* and Glen Tetley's *Field Figures*. Audiences do not adapt rapidly or readily to change and the New Group failed to maintain the loyalty and affection of the old following. Moreover, although it was an exciting venture and, in many ways, an artistic success, a new following was slow to establish itself and was much smaller.

Consequently, it was decided in 1974, to re-establish a touring company on more conventional lines. The number of dancers was increased and the repertoire was extended accordingly, to include those classics suited to the smaller provincial theatres. The company's London base is still the Sadler's Wells Theatre and it recently changed its name to the Sadler's Wells Royal Ballet. This name both distinguishes it from the Royal Ballet and identifies its roots.

Under the direction of Peter Wright, who was a member of the Sadler's Wells Theatre Ballet from 1949 to 1954, a balanced repertoire has been built up. This ranges from *The Sleeping Beauty* Act III to Lynn Seymour's *Rashomon* and includes works by George Balanchine, Kenneth MacMillan, Glen Tetley, Rudolf Nureyev and Frederick Ashton. This variety is challenging for the dancers and has proved extremely popular throughout Britain. The appearances of guest artists, such as Galina Samsova, Maina Gielgud, Robert North and Egon Madsen, testify to the major status of the company.

Besides its function of ensuring that London does not monopolize dance activity in England, the Sadler's Wells Royal Ballet also feels a special responsibility for younger audiences. Recently, Peter Wright organized a project entitled *Journey Through Ballet*, which, when it was tried out in Bristol, proved both popular and valuable. It aims to introduce children to ballet and give them some idea of the preparations which take place before a performance can be given. The success of the first presentation of *Journey Through Ballet* has encouraged the company to continue the project in other parts of the country.

While these adventurous activities were taking place with the Sadler's Wells companies, the main company was changing too. Ninette de Valois was awarded the DBE in 1951 and the same honour was accorded to Margot Fonteyn eight years later. Frederick Ashton was awarded a knighthood in 1962 and, most important of all, in 1956, the company was granted a Royal Charter. It's name was changed to the Royal Ballet and the Sadler's Wells School became the Royal Ballet School.

Dame Ninette de Valois retired from the directorship of the Royal Ballet in 1963 and was succeeded by Frederick Ashton. He continued as Artistic Director for seven years, although he would have preferred to concentrate on the creative rather than administrative aspects of the company. His responsibilities prevented him from creating as many new works as he would have liked. However, a total of over 70 works is no small achievement. At his instigation several major ballets were added to the Royal Ballet's repertoire. Shortly before her death, Bronislava Nijinska revived her two great masterpieces *Les Biches* and *Les Noces*, in December 1964 and March 1966, respectively. Three George Balanchine ballets were also staged during these years – *Ballet Imperial*, *Serenade* and *Apollon Musagète*.

The present Director of the Royal Ballet is Kenneth MacMillan, whose association with the company began at the Sadler's Wells School. He entered the Sadler's Wells Theatre Ballet in 1946 and joined the Covent Garden company two years later. In 1952, he returned to the smaller company and made his choreographic debut with *Somnabulism*, the following year. Other works followed and, in 1956, he staged his first ballet at Covent Garden, *Noctambules*. In 1961, he created *The Invitation* for the touring company and this has recently been revived very successfully in the Royal Ballet's repertoire. It was created specially for the talents of the young dancer Lynn Seymour and provided her with tremendous scope for her fine dramatic abilities. Four years later he responded to the challenge of creating

Two exceptionally attractive dancers, Antoinette Sibley and Anthony Dowell, formed a most successful partnership at the Royal Ballet. They are pictured here in Sir Frederick Ashton's Thais.

a full-length version of *Romeo and Juliet*. Originally created by the Soviet choreographer, Leonid Lavrovsky, the ballet was greatly admired and many versions have been staged by Western choreographers, including Kenneth MacMillan's former colleague, John Cranko. *Romeo and Juliet* was one of Kenneth MacMillan's finest creations and his sensitive handling of the duets between the lovers was exceptionally exquisite. The role of Juliet was particularly suited to Lynn Seymour and was also performed by Antoinette Sibley and Merle Park. The special talents of Margot Fonteyn did not accord well with MacMillan's passionate and dramatic Juliet and she was not at ease in the role. Consequently, he created a version specifically for her, which remains one of her finest roles.

From 1966 to 1969, Kenneth MacMillan was Director of the Ballet of the German Berlin Opera. During these years he staged *The Sleeping Beauty* and *Swan Lake* and created a number of new works. Among these was a one-act version of *Anastasia*, which he later used as Act III for the longer version he created for the Royal Ballet in 1971. In 1970, he was appointed Artistic Director of the Royal Ballet. He continues his creative work, including new ballets for other companies, such as the Stuttgart Ballet, whilst maintaining and extending the Royal Ballet's classical foundations. He has also invited major contemporary choreographers to stage their works at Covent Garden and create new ones for the company. These have recently included Hans van Manen's *Adagio Hammerklavier*, John Neumeier's *Humoresque* and Glen Tetley's *Voluntaries*.

Since the triumphant success of the company's visit to the United States in 1949, the Royal Ballet has toured extensively. It has danced all over the world and its many stars have been invited to appear as guest artists with other major companies, including the Bolshoi Ballet. Many of the world's leading dancers have, in return, been invited to appear at Covent Garden and recently, these have included Mikhail Baryshnikov, Richard Cragun, Marcia Haydée, Natalia Makarova, Julia Farron, Pamela May and Margot Fonteyn. In addition, Rudolf Nureyev has danced many leading roles as well as staging his own versions of several Kirov classics, such as *The Nutcracker* and *Raymonda* Act III.

Audiences throughout the world have a special affection for the Royal Ballet, and its wide and varied repertoire and gifted principals ensure that this will continue.

The Company
The Royal Ballet

Director:	Kenneth MacMillan	**Principal Regisseur:**	Michael Somes
Ballet Master:	Donald MacLeary	**Senior Teacher:**	Gerd Larsen
Ballet Mistress:	Jill Gregory	**Principal Choreologist:**	Christopher Newton

Principal Dancers:			
	Michael Coleman	Ronald Emblen	Ria Peri
	Lesley Collier	Ann Jenner	Derek Rencher
	Laura Connor	Desmond Kelly	TV Lynn Seymour
TV	Vergie Derman	Gerd Larsen	Brian Shaw
TV	Anthony Dowell	Monica Mason	Antoinette Sibley – Retired 1979 age 40
	David Drew	TV Merle Park	Wayne Sleep
	Wayne Eagling	Georgina Parkinson	Alfreda Thorogood
	Leslie Edwards	Jenifer Penney	David Wall

Soloists:			
	David Adams	Rosalind Eyre	Rosemary Taylor
	Christopher Carr	Graham Fletcher	Anita Young
	Sandra Conley	TV Garry Grant	
	Wendy Ellis	Marguerite Porter	

Coryphées:	Sally Ashby	Julie Lincoln	Jacqueline Tallis
	Paul Benson	Susan Lockwood	Hilary Tickner
	Belinda Corken	Barbara Lower	Julie Wood
	Judith Howe	Anthony Molyneux	Christine Woodward
	Sally Inkin	Suzanna Raymond	
	Jennifer Jackson	Mark Silver	

The Repertoire

Adagio Hammerklavier (van Manen)
Afternoon of a Faun (Robbins)
X *A Month in the Country* (Ashton)
Anastasia (MacMillan)
Concerto (MacMillan)
Dances at a Gathering (Robbins)
Elite Syncopations (MacMillan)
Enigma Variations (Ashton)
Humoresque (Neumeier)
La Bayadère (Petipa, staged by Rudolf Nureyev)
La Fille Mal Gardée (Ashton)
Monotones (Ashton)
Manon (MacMillan)

Rituals (MacMillan)
Romeo and Juliet (MacMillan)
Song of the Earth (MacMillan)
Swan Lake (Petipa/Ivanov/Ashton)
Symphonic Variations (Ashton)
The Concert (Robbins)
The Dream (Ashton) *TV 1979 (Dowell & Park)*
The Four Seasons (MacMillan)
The Invitation (MacMillan)
The Nutcracker (Nureyev)
The Taming of The Shrew (Cranko)
Triad (MacMillan)
Voluntaries (Tetley)

Touring Major tours throughout the world.

The Company
Sadler's Wells
Royal Ballet

Director:	Peter Wright	**Principal Repetiteur:**	Brenda Last
Assistant to the Director:	John Auld	**Company Teacher:**	Hilary Cartwright
Ballet Master:	Ronald Plaisted	**Choreologist:**	Elizabeth Cunliffe

Principal Dancers:	David Ashmole	Vyvyan Lorrayne	Lois Strike
	Margaret Barbieri	Carl Myers	Marion Tait
	Brenda Last	Peter O'Brien	

Soloists:	Christine Aitken	June Highwood	Jeanetta Laurence
	Bernd Berg	Murray Kilgour	David Morse
	Brian Bertscher	Ashley Killar	Peter Millar

Coryphées:	Ian Owen		
	Kim Reeder		
	Paul Waller		

The Repertoire

Birdscape (Morse)
Checkmate (de Valois)
Concerto (MacMillan)
Coppélia (Petipa/Cecchetti, staged by Peter Wright)
Four Temperaments (Balanchine)
Gemini (Tetley)
Grosse Fuge (van Manen)
La Fille Mal Gardée (Ashton)
Las Hermanas (MacMillan)
Les Patineurs (Ashton)
Les Rendezvous (Ashton)

Lulu (Carter)
Prodigal Son (Balanchine)
Rashomon (Seymour)
Raymonda Act III (Nureyev after Petipa)
Solitaire (MacMillan)
Summertide (Wright)
The Lady and The Fool (Cranko)
The Sleeping Beauty Act III (Petipa, staged by Peter Wright)
The Two Pigeons (Ashton)
Tilt (van Manen)

The London Festival Ballet

The story of the London Festival Ballet begins with Alicia Markova. She had often danced with the Ballet Rambert in its early days during its short London theatre seasons. Later she added to her considerable reputation as the first prima ballerina of what was then called the Sadler's Wells Ballet, starring in major classics such as *Les Sylphides, Coppélia, The Nutcracker* and *Swan Lake*, partnered, very often, by Stanislas Idzikovsky. In the early 1930s, Sadler's Wells staged a revival of *Giselle* specially for her. She was partnered by Anton Dolin and this marked the beginning of an association that was to be of great importance to British ballet.

In 1935, they left the Sadler's Wells Ballet to form their own company, the Markova-Dolin Ballet, which disbanded in 1938 and reformed in 1945. In 1949 under the management of Julian Braunsweg, Alicia Markova, Anton Dolin and a corps de ballet toured the British Isles. The tour was so successful and so popular, they decided to establish a more permanent and organized arrangement. The new company was called the Festival Ballet, a name suggested to Alicia Markova by the Festival of Britain due to take place in 1951.

The company was inaugurated by a provincial tour in the summer of 1950 and a London season at the Stoll Theatre the following October. The repertoire consisted mainly of the standard major classics of the nineteenth century and also featured the ballets of Fokine and Massine – a logical choice, considering the training and traditions of the founders.

Great artists, then as now, featured frequently. Famous names of the past included Alexandra Danilova, Yvette Chauviré, Tatiana Riabouchinska, Nathalie Krassovska, Mia Slavenska, Beryl Grey, Tamara Toumanova and Leonide Massine. Nor did the company fail to encourage its own stars, among them the well-known dancers Belinda Wright, John Gilpin, Toni Lander, Flemming Flindt and Oleg Briansky.

Another early policy decision was to tour abroad, starting with a visit to Monte Carlo. Since then, the Festival Ballet has toured extensively throughout Europe, North and South America, the Middle East, the Far East and Australia. No other British company can claim such an impressive record and the Festival Ballet has acted as a sort of unofficial British ballet ambassador in many parts of the world.

From its inception in 1950 to 1960, the Festival Ballet consolidated its position as a leading British company. Its loyal and sizeable following expected sparkling performances of mainstream, traditional ballet, and it was not disappointed. Unlike the Ballet Rambert, the Festival Ballet was not famed for innovatory choreography and experiment in dance. Some new ballets were presented, but generally they were not particularly successful.

In 1960, Anton Dolin resigned. (Alicia Markova left the company in 1952, although she returned as guest ballerina on a number of occasions.) This, combined with growing financial anxiety, brought some changes in the company. Greater emphasis was placed on the company's own stars – Lucette Aldous and Galina Samsova, John Gilpin and André Prokovsky. The company also acquired a new full-length ballet, *The Snow Maiden*. The choreography was by Vladimir Bourmeister and it was designed by two other Soviet artists, Gennady Epishin and Yury Pimenov. The Festival Ballet also presented Bourmeister's version of Act II of *Swan Lake* at the same time.

In 1965 Julian Braunsweg invited Vladimir Bourmeister to present a new version of *Swan Lake* in its entirety. Unfortunately, Bourmeister was not

Manola Asensio and the late Paul Clarke dance in Ronald Hynd's The Sanguine Fan. *The title refers to a red fan which becomes confused with two similar ones in the course of a love story concerning twin brothers and the lady with whom they are both in love.*

permitted to come to London. The new version of *Swan Lake* was concocted in a rather haphazard fashion by several different people. When it was finally presented at London's New Victoria Cinema it met with little success and much criticism.

In spite of the two successful seasons at the Festival Hall in the summer and winter of each year and Julian Braunsweg's constant care and attention, the failure of *Swan Lake* was a crushing blow to the company's critical financial situation. As in so many other cases in British dance and opera, the Arts Council of Great Britain provided a grant to rescue the Festival Ballet from collapse. The theatrical impresario Donald Albery became administrator and the company was reorganized and rearranged, although still under the leadership of Lucette Aldous, Galina Samsova, John Gilpin and André Prokovsky. Among the developments which followed was a new version of *The Sleeping Beauty*, and the whole repertoire in general was revised and expanded.

In 1968 Donald Albery retired, leaving the Festival Ballet much more secure financially. Beryl Grey, who had been an adviser on the 1967 production of *The Sleeping Beauty*, was invited to become the Artistic Director. A further change in the fortunes of the company permitted the repertoire to be extended and strengthened even more. The company acquired the London Coliseum for its Spring season and quickly began to make full use of its much greater size and excellent facilities. *Swan Lake* was again revised, by Beryl Grey herself – this time with much greater success. She also invited other choreographers to produce new versions of traditional works and she acquired Borkowsky's *Don Quixote*. Among these productions were Mary Skeaping's *Giselle*, Jack Carter's *Coppélia* and Rudolf Nureyev's *Sleeping Beauty*.

Wisely, Beryl Grey decided to build on the company's established and popular classical repertoire, extending the range and providing works to demonstrate the brilliance and technique of the principal dancers. Massine's ballets continued to figure in the repertoire – *Le Beau Danube*, *The Three Cornered Hat*, *Gaîté Parisienne* and *Parade*. Similarly, the major works of Fokine remained prominent – *Les Sylphides*, *Petrouchka*, *The Polovetsian Dances from Prince Igor*, *Scheherazade*, *Le Coq d'Or* and *Le Spectre de la Rose*. The company continued to perform many of the works which had helped to build its reputation – Balanchine's *Night Shadow* and *Bourée Fantasque*, Lifar's *Noir et Blanc*, *Cinderella*, *Graduation Ball* and a variety of divertissements as well as the full-length and one-act ballets. Other ballets suited to the character of the company were also presented and assimilated into the repertoire; Harald Lander's *Etudes*, and Antony Tudor's *Echoing of Trumpets*, for example.

But it must not be assumed that the Festival Ballet relies only on tried and true favourites, however charming and successful these may be. New

Left *Manola Asensio leaps across the stage in the London Festival Ballet's much discussed revival of Fokine's* Le Coq d'Or. *The ballet has remained unperformed for a number of years and Beriozoff's 1976 version caused much comment because of alterations in the middle scene. Most of the original choreography has been carefully preserved.*

Inset *Dame Alicia Markova, shown here in* The Dying Swan, *was one of the founders of the London Festival Ballet and made frequent guest appearances until she retired from the stage.*

Harald Lander's themeless ballet Etudes *is a demonstration of the classical technique — from the basic plié to the full range of allegro. The precision and polish of the company is excellently suited to this sparkling display.*

choreography has not been ignored. A particularly fruitful association for the company has been with Barry Moreland whom Beryl Grey invited to create works for it. One exceptionally successful new addition to the repertoire was his two-act ballet, *Prodigal Son* (*In Ragtime*), to an arrangement of music by the popular American composer Scott Joplin. The leading role was created for Paul Clarke, one of the Festival Ballet's most versatile principals, who died tragically at the age of 29 in 1976.

Other one-act ballets of Barry Moreland include *Dancing Space*, *In Nomine* and *Summer Solstice*. Also included in the repertoire are several ballets and divertissements by the choreographer Ronald Hynd – *Dvořák Variations*, *The Fairy's Kiss*, *Mozart pas de deux*, *The Sanguine Fan* and a new version of *The Nutcracker*, and a new production of *Les Sylphides* by Alicia Markova and in 1977 Rudolf Nureyev's *Romeo and Juliet* was included.

The Festival Ballet celebrated its twenty-fifth birthday in 1975 with Rudolf Nureyev's new production of *The Sleeping Beauty*, and enjoyed further celebrations in 1976 to mark the acquisition of a permanent home. For a quarter of a century the company endured considerable difficulties because it was so itinerant. Now that the rehearsal rooms, the wardrobe and offices are all at one location they look forward with confidence and optimism to a more stable but still exciting future.

The Company **Artistic Director:** Beryl Grey, CBE
Administratioe Director: Paul Findlay

134

Beryl Grey resigned 1979
New Director – John Field

Ballet Mistress:	Joan Potter	**Choreologist:**	Bronwen Curry
Principal Dancers:	Manola Asensio	Gaye Fulton	Patricia Ruanne
	Liliana Belfiore	Carole Hill	Juan Sanchez
	Peter Breuer	Nicholas Johnson	Noelle Taddei
	Kerrison Cooke	Peter Mallek	Dudley von
	Alain Dubreuil	Margot Miklosy	Loggenburg
	Eva Evdokimova	Noleen Nicol	
Character Principals:	Terry Hayworth	Ken Wells	
	David Long		
Senior Artists:	Linda di Bona	Vivien Loeber	
	Robert Brassel	Judith Rowann	
Soloists:	Valerie Aitken	Raya Lee	Karen Smith
	Nigel Burgoine	Kenneth McCombie	Nini Stucky
	Freya Dominic	David Picken	John Travis
	Diane Hunwin	Loma Rogers	Frederick Warner

The Repertoire

Cinderella (Stevenson)
Coppélia (Saint-Léon/Petipa/Carter)
Don Quixote (Cervantes/Petipa/Gorsky/ Borkowski)
Giselle (Skeaping after Perrot/Coralli/Petipa)
The Nutcracker (Ivanov/Hynd)
The Sleeping Beauty (Petipa/Nureyev)
Romeo and Juliet (Nureyev)
Swan Lake (Grey after Petipa/Ivanov)
Prodigal Son (*In Ragtime*) (Moreland)
Bourée Fantasque (Balanchine)
Conservatoire (Bournonville/Vangsaa)
Dances from Napoli (Bournonville/Vangsaa)
Dancing Space (Moreland)
Designs for Strings (Taras)
Dvořák Variations (Hynd)
Echoing of Trumpets (Tudor)
Etudes (Lander)
Gaîté Parisienne (Massine)
Graduation Ball (Lichine)
In Nomine (Moreland)
La Peri (Darrell)
Le Beau Danube (Massine)
Le Coq d'Or (Fokine/Beriozoff)
Le Spectre de la Rose (Fokine/Beriozoff)
Les Sylphides (Fokine/Markova)
Mendelssohn Symphony (Nahat)

Night Shadow (Balanchine)
Noir et Blanc (Lifar)
Parade (Massine/Cocteau)
Pas de Quatre (Dolin)
Paquita (Mazilier/Casenave)
Petrouchka (Fokine/Beriozoff)
Piège de Lumière (Taras/Heriat)
Polovetsian Dances from Prince Igor (Fokine/ Trunoff)
Scheherazade (Fokine/Trunoff)
Summer Solstice (Moreland)
The Fairy's Kiss (Hynd)
The Sanguine Fan (Hynd)
The Three Cornered Hat (Massine)
The Witch Boy (Carter)
Variations for Four (Dolin)
Black Swan (after Petipa)
Grand Pas Classique (Gsovsky)
La Esmeralda (Beriozoff)
Le Corsair (after Saint-Léon)
Mozart pas de deux (Hynd)
Pas de Trois (Balanchine)
Romeo and Juliet pas de deux (Ashton)
Soirée Musicale (Taras)
Spring Waters (Messerer)
Tchaikovsky pas de deux (Balanchine)
Three Preludes (Stevenson)

Touring

The Festival Ballet has toured extensively and made many repeat visits. It has danced in festivals and theatres in Cyprus, Czechoslovakia, Denmark, France, Germany, Greece, Hungary, Italy, Norway, Poland, Portugal, Romania, Spain, Sweden and Yugoslavia. It has visited the Middle East and the Far East, including Japan, Malaysia, Singapore and South Korea. It has travelled throughout North and South America four times, and in 1975 it made an extremely successful, extended tour of Australia.

The Scottish Ballet

Nigel Spencer and Judith Mohekey appear in a scene from Peter Darrell's recent creation, Othello. *Shakespeare's plays have been a constant source of inspiration to choreographers all over the world.*

The origins of the Scottish Ballet – a company which has now established a clear national identity – had nothing to do with Scotland at all. It began life in quite a different guise as an English company called the Western Theatre Ballet, giving its first performance at the Theatre Royal, Bristol, on June 18, 1956. It was founded by Elizabeth West and Peter Darrell, who were also the company's first Artistic Directors, as a reaction to London's dominance in the arts. Elizabeth West had a broad theatrical background as well as training and experience in dancing and choreography and Peter Darrell was

136

one of the original members of the Sadler's Wells Theatre Ballet and later joined the London Festival Ballet, where he created *Harlequinade*.

This small, enterprising company was able to undertake a tour of the West of England a year later. The repertoire consisted of five ballets – *The Prisoners*, *Celeste and Celestina*, *Tableaux Vivants*, *Pulcinella* and *Peter and the Wolf*. The last two were created for the company by Elizabeth West who afterwards concentrated on the administrative side of the company. Peter Darrell ceased to be co-director in 1959 in order to concentrate on choreography, although he continued to lead the company with Suzanne Musitz, Brenda Last, Anna Paskevskaya and Jean Cebron.

The company quickly established a reputation for lively and interesting performances and it was not long before it was invited to Europe where it visited Belgium, Holland, Italy and Spain as well as touring Britain, appearing for short seasons in London.

In 1962 Elizabeth West was killed in an Alpine accident near the Matterhorn, and Peter Darrell once again took on the responsibilities of directing the company. He remained the principal choreographer, becoming famous as a pioneer of dramatic ballets. He was the first British choreographer to ask playwrights to write scenarios for his ballets.

Other choreographers whose works were included in the repertoire at the time were Meriel Evans, Walter Gore, Gillian Lynne, who created *The Owl and The Pussycat* for the company, Laverne Meyer, Ray Powell and Clover Roope, who created *Orfeo and Euridice* and Bach's *Partita Rencontre Imprevu* for the company. Also, Tamara Karsavina staged a revival of Fokine's *Carnaval* for the company. In 1963, the company made its American debut at the Jacob's Pillow Dance Festival.

In the late 1960s the Scottish Arts Council invited the Western Theatre Ballet to move to Scotland. In 1969 the Scottish Ballet came into existence under the continuing artistic direction of Peter Darrell. Since then the company has moved deliberately in the direction of establishing itself as a national ballet on the international scene. However, no-one can accuse it of being parochial – of the 38 dancers, six are native Scots and the others come from New Zealand, England, Nigeria, Singapore, Australia, South Africa, China, Japan, Wales and Greece. The Scottish Ballet is a fine example of the cross-pollinations of training, traditions and influences which are so valuable, particularly to young developing companies.

The move to Scotland involved more changes than simply a new location. Peter Darrell revised the company's repertoire, planning to include some of the famous classics which he believes to be an essential part of the repertoire of any major ballet company.

The first and, in some ways, the most ambitious of these important additions to the repertoire was *Giselle*. This production retained the traditional choreography whilst presenting the themes of the ballet in a new and refreshing way. Thus the production of *Giselle* represented the quintessence of the Scottish Ballet and its intention to present modern themes and concerns by means of classical dance.

In 1971 the company staged *Tales of Hoffman* with choreography by Peter Darrell. This lavish spectacle was so successful that the American Ballet Theatre invited Peter Darrell to produce it in the United States in 1972.

The Scottish Ballet could hardly neglect *La Sylphide* and this was the next major production, followed shortly afterwards by *The Nutcracker* which like the productions of so many companies, has been a feature of the Christmas seasons and introduced many younger audiences to classical ballet. 1977 continued this process with Peter Darrell's production of *Swan Lake* based on the traditional Petipa/Ivanov choreography.

Peter Darrell, however has not lost the pioneering spirit of his earlier

Above and above right *Two sculptural poses from* Belong *demonstrate the contemporary aspect of the Scottish Ballet's work. The dancers are Andrea Durant and Nigel Spencer.*

innovatory days with the Western Ballet Theatre. Dramatic contemporary works still form a very important part of the company's repertoire and include *Three Dances to Japanese Music* by Jack Carter, *Ways of Saying Bye Bye* by Toer van Schayk, *Intimate Pages* by Harold King, all premièred by the Scottish Ballet, as well as André Howard's *La Fête Etrange* and Flemming Flindt's *The Lesson.* Peter Darrell himself has continued to create for the company and the current repertoire includes *O Caritas, Jeux* and *The Scarlet Pastorale* which he created especially for Dame Margot Fonteyn when she appeared with the Scottish Ballet as guest artist during a tour of Great Britain in 1975.

It can, perhaps, be said that Dame Margot Fonteyn's appearances as guest artist in 1974 and 1975 marked recognition of the Scottish Ballet as a company of international standing. In fact, the list of guest artists in the 1975/6 season is impressive – Anthony Dowell, Margot Fonteyn, Maina Gielgud, Anna Marie Holmes, Neïls Kehlet, Peter Mallek, Ivan Nagy, Rudolf Nureyev, Chinko Rafique, Jorge Salavisa and Augustus van Heerden.

The 1975/6 seasons also involved a busy programme of activities throughout Great Britain – a long season at Glasgow's Theatre Royal, a London Season at the Sadler's Wells Theatre, opened with a Royal Gala Performance before Princess Margaret, a second London season at the Coliseum and a summer season in Edinburgh where, for the first time, a joint repertoire of opera and ballet was presented by the Scottish Opera and the Scottish Ballet.

The Scottish Ballet has always been eager to encourage young dancers and aims, eventually, to set up a ballet school in association with the company. However, the formidable cost of such a project has precluded this, although a series of scholarship classes is taught by the company's Ballet Mistress, Cecilia Barrett. Each year private ballet schools submit leading pupils for auditions and those selected attend two weekend classes throughout the year, on condition they attend two classes per week with their own teachers as well. These classes have proved a successful compromise and three of the company's own dancers – Eleanor Moore, Kenneth Burke and Elizabeth Peden graduated from them.

In line with its aim of becoming an integral part of the arts in Scotland, the Scottish Ballet has also developed the Movable Workshop. A group of dancers provides workshop sessions in dance, improvisation and movement techniques at a non-vocational level in Schools and Colleges of Education and Physical Training throughout Scotland.

The Scottish Ballet has a fine record of achievement in the field of ballet education in its short history, but it is conscious that the foundations of any major company are in its school and the establishment of a ballet school is therefore a priority.

A young company with an impressive list of successes, the Scottish Ballet likes to compare itself with the Stuttgart Ballet. John Cranko and Peter Darrell, old friends from Sadler's Wells, had much in common and it is hoped that Peter Darrell will follow John Cranko's spectacular achievement in Stuttgart, by transforming his own company also into one of world acclaim and leadership.

The Company

Artistic Director:	Peter Darrell	**Choreologist:**	Julie Haydn
Ballet Mistress:	Celilia Barrett	**Opera Ballet Master:**	Jim Hastie
Ballet Master and Principal Teacher:	Gordon Aitken		

Dancers:

Anne Allan	Robin Haig	Noriko Ohara
Linda Anning	Vincent Hantam	Elizabeth Peden
Graham Bart	Richard Holland	Kim Petts
Sarah Beck	Simon Laing	Ruth Prior
Kenneth Burke	Kit Lethby	Patricia Rianne
Brian Burn	Elaine McDonald	Yuji Sato
Veronica Butcher	Nicola Maclaurin	Kenneth Saunders
Roy Campbell-Moore	Henny Man	Nigel Spencer
Gillian Chatt	Christopher Mercer	Dianne Storer
Chua Kah Joo	Patricia Merrin	Mary Storey
James Cowie	Judith Mohekey	Paul Tyers
Gavin Dorrian	Eleanor Moore	Anastasio Vitoros
Andrea Durant	Jeanette Newell	

The Repertoire

Beauty and the Beast (Cranko) 1966
Beauty and the Beast (Darrell) 1969
Cage of God (Carter) 1967
Carnaval (Fokine) 1958
Dancing Floor (Carter) 1974
Flower Festival at Genzano Pas de Deux (Bournonville) 1973
Giselle (Coralli/Perrot) 1971
Grand Pas Gitane (Darrell) 1974
Harlequinade Pas de Deux (Petipa, staged by John Gilpin) 1975
Intimate Pages (King) 1974
Jeux (Darrell) 1963
Le Fête Etrange (Howard) 1971
La Sylphide (Bournonville, staged by Hans Brenaa) 1973
Las Hermanas (MacMillan) 1966
La Ventana (Bournonville, staged by Hans Brenaa) 1968

Mary Queen of Scots (Darrell) 1976
O Caritas (Darrell) 1975
Othello (Darrell) 1976
Paquita (Mazilier/Petipa, staged by Roland Casenave) 1975
Pas de Quatre (Dolin) 1975
Peepshow (Gore) 1971
Soirée Musicale (Tudor) 1973
Sonate à Trois (Béjart) 1959
Street Games (Gore) 1961
Sun into Darkness (Darrell) 1966
Tales of Hoffman (Darrell) 1972
The Lesson (Flindt) 1967
The Nutcracker (Ivanov/Darrell) 1973
The Scarlet Pastorale (Darrell) 1975
Three Dances to Japanese Music (Carter) 1973
Valse Excentrique (MacMillan) 1957
Variations for Four (Dolin) 1975
Ways of Saying Bye Bye (van Schayk) 1973

Touring

Apart from successful seasons in various parts of Great Britain, the Scottish Ballet toured Australia and New Zealand in 1974 (guest artist Dame Margot Fonteyn) and opened the Madrid Festival Season in 1975 (guest artist Rudolf Nureyev).

The Irish Ballet

The Irish Ballet is one of the youngest national ballet companies in the world but its history might have been very different. In the early 1930s an Irish-woman, Edris Stannus, who had been a soloist with Diaghilev's Ballets Russes, and had later opened a ballet school in London, attempted to establish an Irish ballet company at Dublin's Abbey Theatre. She met with no success and, discouraged, she returned to London. Edris Stannus adopted the name Ninette de Valois and was the founder and Artistic Director, until 1964, of London's Royal Ballet.

This incident seems to have initiated an unfortunate pattern of setbacks for the establishment of an Irish ballet company. A few years after Dame Ninette de Valois' lack of success, a group of Irish dancers made another attempt to set up a company at the Gaiety Theatre. They gave performances on occasional Sunday evenings but, in spite of their imagination and determination, World War II ended their activities.

When the war was over, a company, called the Cork Ballet Group, was started. Later called the Cork Ballet Company, this group of dancers struggled on with inadequate facilities and almost no money. In 1959, some of the dancers, all of them amateurs, formed the Irish Theatre Ballet. Still facing daunting obstacles, this company managed to survive for five years and to travel to many parts of Ireland.

Kathleen Smith and Richard Collins as Yerma and Juan in Domy Reiter-Soffer's dramatic creation, based on the tragedy by Federico Garcia Lorca. With this ballet, the company has achieved critical recognition and established a new direction for future developments.

Finally, nine years later, the Arts Council in Dublin made a small subsidy available to form Ireland's first national ballet. The company's first performance was given at the Cork Opera House in 1974. By the following year the company had added 10 new productions to its repertoire. Under the artistic direction of Jean Denise Moriarty, the company decided on an ambitious policy of artistic integration – extending choreography and music to extra depths and dimensions. A wide range of styles was explored; performances of pas de deux from *Giselle* and *The Sleeping Beauty;* works by established contemporary choreographers – *Asparas* and *Biedermeier Dances* by Peter Darrell of the Scottish Ballet and Anton Dolin's *Pas de Quatre*; and works created by Joan Denise Moriarty herself and by the company's Artistic Advisor, Domy Reiter-Soffer.

Such a policy for a fledgeling company was perhaps too ambitious and there were, inevitably, failures, In spite of the vitality of the dancers, *They Come They Come*, created by Joan Denise Moriarty, was a laboured production and inexperience was probably the fault in *Le Corsair Pas De Deux*. However, it is not reasonable to expect a company to have explored its resources fully and recognized its limitations in such a short period and without making any mistakes.

1976 marked the beginning of a new maturity for the Irish Ballet Company, with the première in June of Domy Reiter-Soffer's *Yerma* at the Abbey Theatre, Dublin. The ballet was based on the tragedy by Federico Garcia Lorca and the music was George Crumb's *Ancient Voices of Children*, already used for other works, notably Christopher Bruce's intensely moving creation for the Ballet Rambert. With *Yerma*, the Irish Ballet has achieved its aim of total theatrical experience – George Crumb's magnificent score, Reiter-Soffer's evocative, subtle and shocking choreography, and Patrick Murray's designs.

The première of *Yerma* was received with both public and critical acclaim and such a major advance in the company's reputation promises an interesting future.

The Company

Artistic Director:	Joan Denise Moriarty
Artistic Advisor:	Domy Reiter-Soffer
Ballet Master:	David Gordon

Dancers:

Joanna Banks	Kathleen McInerney	Dennis Spaight
Richard Collins	Melanie Morgan	Rosemary Stacey
Anna Donovan	Sally Morris	Oliver Tessier
Babil Gandara	Kathleen Smith	Michael Woolsey

The Repertoire

Asparas (Darrell)
Biedermeier Dances (Darrell)
Billy the Music (Moriarty)
Bluebirds Pas De Deux (Petipa, reproduced by David Gordon
Caprice for 12 (Neubauer)
Contrast in Time (Beck)
Devil to Pay (Moriarty)
Don Quixote Pas De Deux (Petipa, reproduced by Richard Collins)
First Impressions (Gordon)
Flights of Fancy (Hurde)
Grand Pas Gitane (Darrell)

Images (Beck)
Jingle-Rag Jingle-Tag (Reiter-Soffer)
La Esmeralda Pas De Deux (Gilpin)
Loveraker (Reiter-Soffer)
Other Days (Reiter-Soffer)
Overture (Moriarty)
Pas de Quatre (Dolin)
The Prisoners (Darrell)
They Come, They Come (Moriarty)
Timeless Echoes (Reiter-Soffer)
West Cork Ballad (Moriarty)
Women (Reiter-Soffer)
Yerma (Reiter-Soffer)

ITALY
La Scala

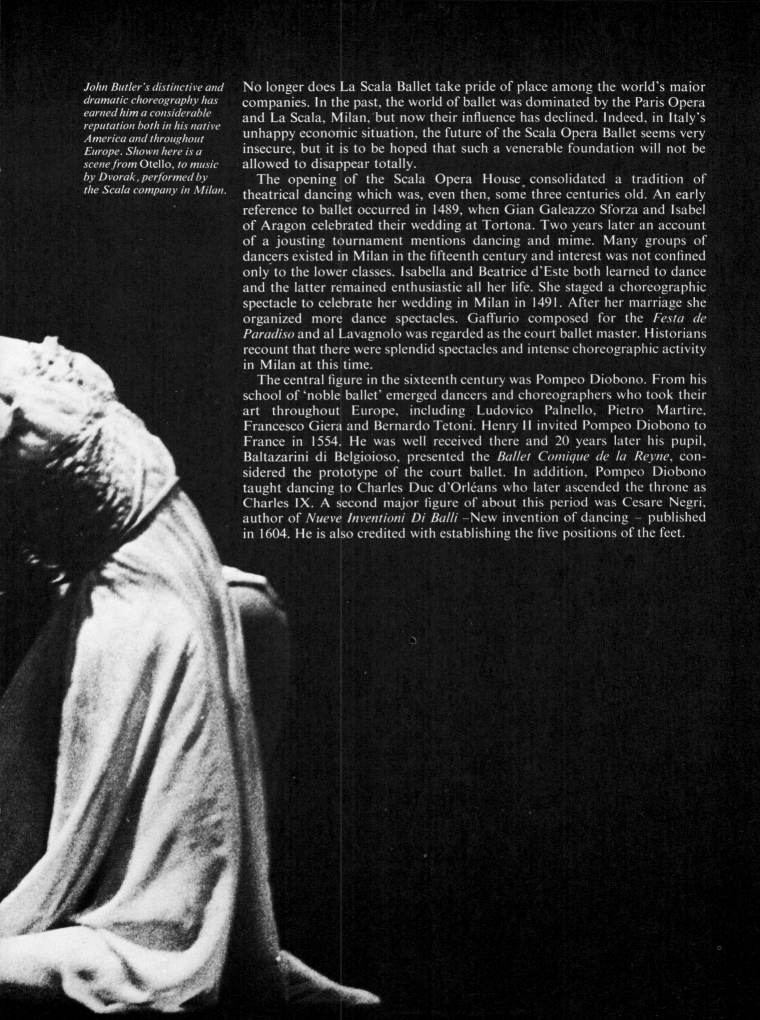

John Butler's distinctive and dramatic choreography has earned him a considerable reputation both in his native America and throughout Europe. Shown here is a scene from Otello, *to music by Dvorak, performed by the Scala company in Milan.*

No longer does La Scala Ballet take pride of place among the world's major companies. In the past, the world of ballet was dominated by the Paris Opera and La Scala, Milan, but now their influence has declined. Indeed, in Italy's unhappy economic situation, the future of the Scala Opera Ballet seems very insecure, but it is to be hoped that such a venerable foundation will not be allowed to disappear totally.

The opening of the Scala Opera House consolidated a tradition of theatrical dancing which was, even then, some three centuries old. An early reference to ballet occurred in 1489, when Gian Galeazzo Sforza and Isabel of Aragon celebrated their wedding at Tortona. Two years later an account of a jousting tournament mentions dancing and mime. Many groups of dancers existed in Milan in the fifteenth century and interest was not confined only to the lower classes. Isabella and Beatrice d'Este both learned to dance and the latter remained enthusiastic all her life. She staged a choreographic spectacle to celebrate her wedding in Milan in 1491. After her marriage she organized more dance spectacles. Gaffurio composed for the *Festa de Paradiso* and al Lavagnolo was regarded as the court ballet master. Historians recount that there were splendid spectacles and intense choreographic activity in Milan at this time.

The central figure in the sixteenth century was Pompeo Diobono. From his school of 'noble ballet' emerged dancers and choreographers who took their art throughout Europe, including Ludovico Palnello, Pietro Martire, Francesco Giera and Bernardo Tetoni. Henry II invited Pompeo Diobono to France in 1554. He was well received there and 20 years later his pupil, Baltazarini di Belgioioso, presented the *Ballet Comique de la Reyne*, considered the prototype of the court ballet. In addition, Pompeo Diobono taught dancing to Charles Duc d'Orléans who later ascended the throne as Charles IX. A second major figure of about this period was Cesare Negri, author of *Nueve Inventioni Di Balli* –New invention of dancing – published in 1604. He is also credited with establishing the five positions of the feet.

At this time, Milan had two theatres – the Salon Margharita and the Comedy. The first was opened by Margaret of Austria in 1598, with a huge dance spectacle staged by Cesare Negri. All dance activity continued to take place at the Salon Margharita for, throughout the seventeenth century, afficionados of comedy disdained ballet.

In France, ballet thrived at the court but in Italy, dance was a complementary part of theatrical performances. It also became a private diversion in gentlemen's homes and clubs. In 1748, Casanova went to the opera at the Ducal Theatre to contact Marina, a 'comic dancer' and an old flame. Little more is known of this encounter but it is probable that she was one of many young women who travelled around Europe under the specious name of 'ballerina'. However, many authentic dancers and grand ballerinas performed at il Ducal during the half century of its life. Jean Georges Noverre produced many ballets, five created specially. Incidentally, the Ducal Theatre can boast of presenting the first operatic attempts of the young Mozart.

However, the first most important name associated with dance at the Ducal Theatre was Gasparo Angiolini. He was both a musician and a choreographer and created one of the world's major dance works – *Don Giovanni* to the music of Gluck. At this time the cultural horizons of Milan were enlarging. Much of this was due to Giuseppe Parini whose interests inclined towards the theatre. He was also the librettist at the Ducal and supplied Mozart with the text for the serenata *Ascanio in Alba*. His interests, however, were not confined to music and opera and he also collaborated with Gasparo Angiolini. The ubiquitous Casanova re-appeared at this time, falling in love with Angiolini's wife, the beautiful actress and dancer Teresa Fogliazzi.

Gasparo Angiolini succeeded Hilverding as Ballet Master to the Imperial Theatre in St Petersburg in 1765. It was during his first visit to Russia that the famous quarrel between Angiolini and Jean Georges Noverre erupted. The argument arose from a preface in Noverre's programme for three of his ballets in which he proclaimed himself the father of ballet d'action. Angiolini pointed out the chronological priority of his *Don Giovanni* but, in fact, attributed the title to Hilverding who was the first to crystallize the concept some 10 years previously. The quarrel continued with an open letter from Noverre and the controversy raged for years.

The confrontation of the two adversaries could not continue. Although he staged *Sacrificio Di Dircea e Arianna nell'isola di Nasso*, very successfully at the Ducal Theatre in 1772 and 1774, Angiolini went to Vienna to two important musical theatres placed at his disposal by the Emperor of Austria. Noverre remained at the Ducal Theatre from 1774 until 1776, when it burned down. It has never been decided whether the 'Duel of the Ducal' was resolved in favour of the French or Italian master, but it is significant that Angiolini returned to Milan in 1780 and remained at La Scala until the last year of the century, staging many triumphant successes.

La Scala's inaugural evening on August 3, 1778, presented a mixed programme including two ballets. Reports of the time said that the spectacles of the opening night would make it the most celebrated musical theatre in the world. The Archduke Ferdinand and his consort were present to see more than 50 dancers led by the choreographer Claude Le Grand and Caterina Curtz. Claude Le Grand, principal dancer and Ballet Master, possessed a reputation far in excess of his merits. Far more important was the influence of Guiseppe Canziani who was not given an important position in the hierarchy of the new theatre. He had gained most of his experience in Venice and later staged some of his works at La Scala.

On December 26, 1778, another dancer and choreographer, Sebastien Gallet, made his Milan debut at La Scala in *La Festa Campestre* by Canziani. He commenced his career at the Paris Opera and remained there for seven years but was forced to leave by the jealousy and intrigue which characterized it for so long. He travelled around the capitals of Europe and returned to La Scala in 1785 when he danced in *The Rape of the Sabines* and *Ludovico il Moro*. The return of Gasparo Angiolini was very important for the theatre. Between *La Scoprimento di Achille*, in 1779 and *Amore e Psiche*, 10 years later, he staged about 30 ballets. He also wrote nearly all the music. These were all new works and he never re-staged his main works from his Viennese period. Gluck's *Don Giovanni*, with choreography by Massine, was not performed at La Scala until 1959.

Gaspara Angiolini was succeeded by his son Pietro who had joined the Scala company as a dancer in 1782. He was not as talented a composer or choreographer as his father but he was industrious and presented a number of new works until 1826.

The last years of the eighteenth and the first years of the nineteenth centuries brought rapid changes. Huge spectacles involving vast mechanical contrivances were staged. In one evening, up to four ballets might be performed and some of these had between five and seven acts each. The subjects of the ballets and the dancing became more ambitious, although the realization did not always match the ideal and records show that audiences at a number of performances made their displeasure evident, by hissing and shouting. Dancers were organized into ranks and some were given the status of soloists. Generally, works were presented for one season only, with little chance of a revival. A few people resisted this trend towards lengthy stagings. Paolo Franchi produced a number of shorter works between 1786 and 1808, but these were soon forgotten. Several others, such as Giovanni Monticini, Antonio Muzzarelli and Luigi Dupen, suffered the same fate.

The dispute between classicists and romantics was acutely felt in Milan. The two choreographers, Gaetano Gioja and Salvatore Vigano, oscillated from one style to the other as the public demanded. Their period of leadership at La Scala was very successful, Gioja remaining until 1824. Master of heroic ballets, he staged his own work *Caesar in Egypt* and the première was attended by Napoleon. The French neo-classicist, Clerico, presented a number of well-received ballets during this highly successful period, including *Hamlet*, *Cleopatra* and *Macbeth*.

Salvatore Vigano was undoubtedly one of the most important figures associated with La Scala during the early part of the nineteenth century. He went to Milan at the height of his artistic strength after a brilliant career as a dancer, in conjunction with his wife the Spanish ballerina, Maria Medina. He began his period at La Scala somewhat modestly and timidly. The first work he presented, in December 1811, was a revival of the ballet *Gli Strelizzi*, which he had created in Venice in 1809. This was followed by a succession of very successful works including *Riccardo Cuor di Leone*, *Noce di Benevento*, which was the first of his ballets which really captured the public's interest, *Dedalo*, *Otello*, *La Vestale* and *Titani*.

Salvatore Vigano came from a family of dancers with a musical background. He was the nephew of Luigi Boccherini. It is hardly surprising, therefore, that he was a very musical choreographer and was especially clever at blending the works of several different composers for one of his ballets. Sometimes he composed the music himself and one of his best known ballets, *Prometheus*, was composed especially for him by Ludwig van Beethoven in 1801. His early interest in literature enabled him to create very dramatic ballets and many of them used colossal technical effects which were very popular. *Titani* was the last and most remarkable of these spectacular presentations and marked the end of his creative life in 1819. He died on August 10, two years later.

Overleaf Romeo and Juliet has proved to be one of the most popular ballets of the twentieth century among audiences and companies alike. Unquestionably, one of the best loved versions is John Cranko's, which was originally created for the Scala company in 1959. It achieved major success when it was staged for the choreographer's own company, the Stuttgart Ballet, in 1962.

In 1817 and 1820, two French choreographers, Jean-Pierre Aumer and Louis Henry joined the Scala company, marking the end of the classical period. Louis Henry, in particular, created many works for the company, especially *Elery and Zulmida* in 1826 and *Silfide* in 1828. He had also created *La Fée et le Chevalier* for the dancer Armand Vestris in Vienna in 1823. The ballerina on that occasion was La Brugnoli, an Italian trained dancer. It is claimed that she danced en pointe in that work and was the first to do so, preceding Maria Taglioni by nine years. There is certainly evidence that La Brugnoli rose on full pointe in a production of *Dircea* at La Scala in 1826, but there are many claimants to the title of originator of this style and it is unlikely that the controversy will ever be resolved satisfactorily. La Brugnoli appeared regularly at La Scala, dancing with her husband in ballets by Henry and others, until 1830.

Other popular ballerinas of the time were Elisa Vaque-Moulin and Teresa Héberlé who excelled in *Silfide*, an Italian ballet with music by Luigi Carlini. Sadly, she died while still quite young in 1840. *Silfide*, surpassed the dance dramas of Vigano and it is claimed that it profoundly influenced the history of ballet throughout the world. It certainly pre-dated Filippo Taglioni's more famous *La Sylphide*, premièred at the Paris Opera on March 12, 1832. This version reached La Scala in March 1841 when Maria Taglioni was invited to visit Milan.

Thirty years of constant new choreography persuaded the management of La Scala to establish a permanent ballet company rather than seasonal, made-up companies as had been the custom. As a result, the Imperial Regia Academia di Ballo alla Scala was established in 1813 and was one of the first professional schools associated with a musical theatre. From its inception the school set about building a reputation that would make it a foremost force in European ballet.

The impresario, Benedetto Ricci, organized the school and invited the assistance of some foreign ballet masters, particularly Louis La Chapelle and Charles Villeneuve, followers of Noverre, and who had both been principal dancers at La Scala. The first class took place in 1813 with eight female and four male pupils. Among these were Margherita Bianchi and Francesco Saverio Marente whose careers at La Scala continued until 1856.

Shortly after the founding of the school Carlo Blasis joined the Scala company. This first appearance was in Vigano's *Dedalo*, in 1818. He made his debut as a choreographer the following year with *il Finto Fendatario*, which was hissed by the audience throughout the performance. However, he was an elegant danseur noble and became a principal dancer with La Scala until 1823. During this time he wrote two textbooks – *An Elementary Treatise upon the Theory and Practice of the Art of Dancing*, in 1820, and *The Code of Terpsichore*, in 1828. In these he codified the techniques of both dancing and teaching dancing and his theories remain the foundation of classical ballet today. In 1837 he was appointed Director of the Academy where he had taught for some very valuable years. His influence cannot be overestimated and many famous dancers owe an immense debt of gratitude directly or indirectly to his teaching. He died in 1878, leaving the world of ballet and the Scala company in particular, very much stronger than he had found them.

His value was not, however, fully appreciated during his lifetime. Owing to jealousy and intrigue he was replaced by Augusto Huss in 1851 who was replaced in turn by Giovanni Casati in 1868, who remained Ballet Master until 1883. Casati's thematic range was extensive. He created romantic ballets, such as *Il Diavolo a Quattro*, reproduced historical ballets, such as *Sardanapolo* and less easily categorized works, such as Shakespeare's *Midsummer Night's Dream*.

However, it was the ballerinas of the nineteenth century who most com-

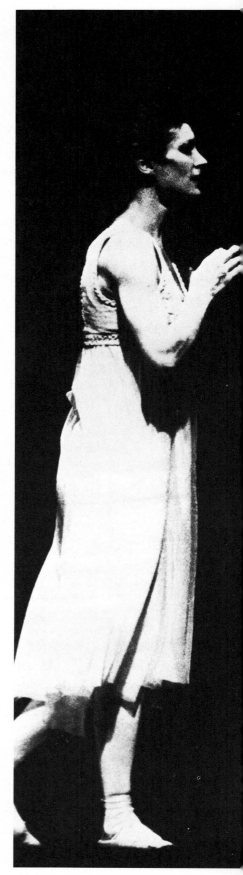

pletely embodied the spirit of romanticism. Most of the great ballerinas of the period appeared at La Scala. Maria Taglioni danced her triumphant interpretation of *La Sylphide* in 1841, rivalling in popularity Italy's own great ballerina, Fanny Cerrito. The latter's contemporary, the Austrian dancer, Fanny Elssler was also immensely popular at La Scala. After her triumphant tour of America she returned to La Scala in December 1843 and danced there during the next two years. However, during the production of *Faust*, she broke her contract and returned to Vienna. Her role was taken over by Augusta Maywood, the first American dancer to gain an international reputation. She became ballerina at La Scala in 1848 and retired from the stage in 1863. The 'Danish Sylphide' Lucile Grahn appeared at La Scala in December 1843 and about two years earlier, August Bournonville had danced in *Kenilworth Castle* on a much acclaimed Italian tour. The Russian dancer, Elena Andreyanova, visited La Scala in 1846, where she danced in Casati's revival of *Il Diavolo a Quattro*. The list of guest stars is completed by the visit of Arthur Saint-Léon and Lucien Petipa, brother of the more famous Marius. The only famous figure of the period who did not appear at La Scala seems to have been Carlotta Grisi.

Of all the foreign guests, the 'Divine Maria' – Taglioni – was the most popular and received with the greatest enthusiasm. She was at the peak of her career and appeared in all her major roles. Italy was not dependent on guest artists, however. At the end of the century a newspaper reported that 'There are 150 active Italian ballerinas of whom half have come from the Milan School'. Carolina Rosati was one of these and was especially noted for her interpretations of the leading roles in *Giselle* and *Esmeralda*. Like many Italian ballerinas of the time, she was a guest artist at St Petersburg where she created the title role in Petipa's *Pharoah's Daughter*. She also visited London where she replaced Lucile Grahn in Jules Perrot's *Pas de Quatre*. Her greatest rival was Amalia Ferraris who, at the age of 13, was acclaimed 'the new Taglioni'. Sofia Fuoco was also a very popular Italian dancer, famous for her success in a revival of *Catarina* at La Scala, originally created in London for Lucile Grahn. Perhaps the most loved dancer however, was Carolina Pochini, a true Blasis dancer, who became La Scala's prima ballerina before she was 18 years old.

A few years later, another star, Caterina Beretta, appeared. She made her debut in Milan in 1855 and later made a sensational impression in Paris and St Petersburg. She returned to La Scala for the 1859 to 1861 seasons, alternating in the leading roles with Carolina Pochini and another leading ballerina, Olimpia Priora, daughter of the choreographer Egidio. After this, she returned to Russia until 1902, when she was appointed Director of the Milan ballet school. She continued in this position until 1908, three years before her death. Her demanding, and inflexible teaching helped form many leading dancers of the twentieth century, including Anna Pavlova, Tamara Karsavina and Olga Preobrajenska in Russia and Pierina Legnani and Cia Fornaroli in Italy. It is not possible to enumerate all the ballerinas of this period but they included Claudine Cucchi, Amina Boschetti, Virginia Zucchi and La Brianza, famous for her performance in *The Sleeping Beauty* in St Petersburg in 1890.

The great choreographer of the last decade of the nineteenth century was Manzotti. He created *Pietro Micca* and *Excelsior* and adapted Vigano's works. *Excelsior* was an international success in Paris, London and the United States. He became ambitious and wanted to make the *Divine Comedy* into a ballet. He created a 'choreographic poem', *Amor*, which required a cast of 614 people, 12 horses, two oxen and an elephant. It ran for 44 performances. *Sport*, the third ballet of the trilogy also ran for 44 nights in 1897.

After the grandiose works of Manzotti the company began to decline. There were imitators but they tended less towards dancing and more towards mechanical spectacle and sheer numbers. Some of Manzotti's works were revived but, generally, it was an extremely arid time for creation.

In January 1911 a small Russian company, under the leadership of Ida Rubinstein, visited La Scala. A member of Diaghilev's Ballets Russes, she was a powerful force in the changing world of dance in the early twentieth century, providing financial support for choreographers, composers and painters. The company presented two ballets, *Cléopâtre* and *Scheherazade*, both by Fokine. However the audiences of Milan, accustomed to flamboyant spectacles, disliked them and considered *Cléopâtre* indecent. When the company returned to Milan in 1929, the audience's response was even more negative.

The reception which greeted the even more illustrious company, Diaghilev's Ballets Russes, was no better. Diaghilev, always an ambitious man, had determined to conquer La Scala. A visit to the Lirico in 1920 had left the Milan audiences uncomprehending and uninterested. When the company visited La Scala in 1927, the intelligentsia recognized the importance of the event but the ordinary public remained unmoved. Among the programmes prepared for the visit were Massine's *Cimarosiana*, criticized as pedestrian, *The Firebird*, *Swan Lake* and part of *The Sleeping Beauty*. Diaghilev presented some of the major works of the repertoire with original choreography by Massine and Fokine and all his stars, Olga Spessivtzeva, Alexandra Danilova, Lubov Cerniceva, George Balanchine, Leonide Massine and Serge Lifar. The scenery was designed by Léon Bakst, Natalia Goncharova and Constantine Korovine. Nevertheless, the public remained obdurate. For years it had been used to dictate what it wanted and reckoned that the dancing and scenery of Blasis, Vigano and Taglioni remained unsurpassed.

Meanwhile, the last ballet of any note presented by the Scala company was *The Golden Willow* in 1914. For two seasons, 1916 to 1918, the war prevented any ballet performances and in 1917, the school closed. In 1918, *Old Milan* was presented but it was a poor effort to return to the former days of grand ballet. Otherwise, La Scala remained more or less closed until 1921 when it was re-opened mainly due to the efforts of Arturo Toscanini. Olga Preobrajenska took over the leadership of the ballet but she left in 1924 and was replaced by Nicola Guerra, but he quarrelled with the dancers who formed a small company under the leadership of the principal dancer, Ettore Caorsi.

On September 15, 1925, Enrico Cecchetti returned to La Scala and began its revival. He returned to Milan after many years abroad during which time his brilliant teaching had enriched the Imperial Ballet in Russia, the Ballets Russes and ballet in Britain and Poland. He chose Cia Fornaroli as prima ballerina. She had been a favourite pupil and was a highly experienced dancer, having danced with the Metropolitan Opera Ballet New York and the Teatro Colón in Buenos Aires. She appeared in many ballets including Pick Mangiagalli's *Mahit* in 1923 and *Petrouchka*, *Le Rossignol* and *Hansel and Gretel* in the 1926/7 season. Her greatest success was in *Il Convento Veneziano* by Pratesi-Casella. In 1928 she was appointed Director of the school but continued to dance until the early 1930s, when she left Italy because of political persecution of her husband. In 1936, Fokine returned to La Scala and a flood of new works and revivals followed. Among these were Margherita Wallman's revival of *Coppélia* in 1937 and a shortened version of *The Nutcracker* in 1938, staged by the former Bolshoi and Ballets Russes dancer Margherita Froman. *Mahit* was revived and the Hungarian choreographer, Gyula Hàrangozó's *Mirage* was presented in 1939.

The 1940s added further to the repertoire. *The Sleeping Beauty* was presented in 1940 and that season also included *La Boutique Fantasque* and *The Firebird*. Contemporary works were also being performed and in 1942 Aurelio Milloss staged *The Miraculous Mandarin* and Erika Hanka created ballets to music by Honegger and Carl Orff's *Carmina Burana*. The expressionism of Aurelio Milloss was an important step in the development of ballet at La Scala.

In 1943, the company toured provincial theatres for the first time in its history. Several difficult years followed as the Scala Theatre was being rebuilt. The ballet company was re-organized by Aurelio Milloss in conjunction with Ugo Dell'Ara. He was appointed Ballet Master in 1947 and remained at La Scala until 1956, creating many works, including *The Winter's Tale* based on a story by Dostoyevsky.

The re-opening of La Scala coincided with an upsurge of artistic activity throughout the world. In addition, the public took a renewed interest in ballet, providing much needed support. The idea of an autonomous ballet company independent of the opera took root in 1948 and was consolidated in 1953. A succession of foreign ballet companies visited La Scala bringing fresh ideas and innovations. In 1953 George Balanchine's New York City Ballet presented works like *Four Temperaments*, *The Cage* and *Afternoon of a Faun* with stars like Tanaquil Le Clerq, Maria Tallchief, Nora Kaye, Patricia Wilde, Nicholas Magallanes, Andre Eglevsky and Francisco Moncion. The New York City Ballet returned in 1965 with Suzanne Farrell, Allegra Kent, Melissa Hayden and Jacques d'Amboise in more recent Balanchine works such as *Bugaku*.

In 1954, the Sadler's Wells Ballet presented a classical programme including *The Sleeping Beauty*, *Swan Lake* and *Les Patineurs*. Margot Fonteyn, partnered by Michael Somes, interpreted the roles of Aurora and Odette-Odile. Other well-known dancers from Britain included Nadia Nerina, Svetlana Beriosova and Violette Elvin. In 1965, the Royal Ballet returned with Kenneth MacMillan's *Romeo and Juliet* and Margot Fonteyn and Rudolf Nureyev in *La Bayadère*. The company also danced *The Dream* by Frederick Ashton and Kenneth Macmillan's *The Invitation*. In addition to the two great stars, the company included Nadia Nerina, Merle Park, Annette Page, Lynn Seymour, Antoinette Sibley, Christopher Gable, Anthony Dowell and David Blair.

The Paris Opera company also visited La Scala in 1948. The programme included Fokine's *Daphnis and Chloë* and several ballets by Serge Lifar. The visits of these companies inspired the Milan dancers, who began life in the New Scala Theatre with new versions of Ravel's *Bolero* and *Petrouchka* by Milloss. In 1948 Massine staged *Le Sacre du Printemps* and this was restaged several times during the 1950s and 1960s.

In 1950 the Russian teacher, Vera Volkova became Director of the school but in 1951 she left to join the Royal Danish Ballet in Copenhagen. She was replaced by the British teacher Esmée Bulnes who remained Director until 1969. During this time some of pupils were invited to the Bolshoi School in Moscow.

Ballets such as *Love the Magician* and *Peter and the Wolf* were added to the repertoire and guest artists such as Margot Fonteyn and Yvette Chauviré were regularly invited to appear at La Scala. Tamara Toumanova, Galina Ulanova and Alicia Markova also appeared there.

Milloss returned to the company after a short interval and continued his policy of introducing more unusual ballets, such as *The Wooden Prince*. The new theatre was ideally suited to the works of George Balanchine and, beginning with *Concerto* in 1952, many of his ballets have been presented, including *Serenade*, *Allegro Brillante* and *Four Temperaments*. Other contemporary choreographers also staged their works at La Scala. Roland Petit mounted *Le Jeune Homme et La Mort* in 1965 and Jean Babilée presented *Till Eulenspiegel*, *Balance à Trois* and *Auditorium*. Roland Petit first went to La Scala in 1963 for an evening dedicated to him. *The Four Seasons*, *Le Loup*,

La Chambre and *Spanish Rhapsody* were performed. He returned in December of the same year to present *Les Desmoiselles de la Nuit*. In 1967 he staged *L'Eloge de la Folie* and in the autumn of the following year, *L'Extase*.

More recently, several ballets with choreography by Rudolf Nureyev have been performed and he has danced in several of them. They include *La Bayadère*, *The Sleeping Beauty* and *The Nutcracker*, which starred Italian dancers. The visit of the Bolshoi Ballet in 1970, confirmed the importance of La Scala. The company presented three full-length works, *Swan Lake*, *The Nutcracker* and *Spartacus*. The dancers included Maya Plisetskaya, Nicolai Fadeyecev, Natalia Bessmertnova, Nina Timofeyeva and Yekaterina Maximova.

The company at La Scala has proved itself to be a sensitive mirror of the evolution of ballet. It is to be hoped that the unsatisfactory economic situation will not prevent it from continuing to demonstrate its adaptability and development and that the stage of La Scala will remain open to the other great companies of the world.

The Ballet of La Scala was particularly pleased to include several of Rudolf Nureyev's works in its repertoire. Among these were The Sleeping Beauty *and* The Nutcracker, *shown here, in which he made guest appearances.*

NETHERLANDS
Nederlands Dans Theater

The Nederlands Dans Theater began in 1959 as a movement against the apparent direction of European ballet. In particular, the American teacher and choreographer Benjamin Harkavy, grew dissatisfied with the traditional opera-ballet and the lack of opportunities for ambitious, young choreographers. At that time he was Ballet Master with the Nederlands Ballet, which later became the National Ballet. Some of the dancers felt equally dicontented and in 1959 the Nederlands Dans Theater was founded by Benjamin Harkavy to channel these feelings of frustration in a positive and creative direction.

The new company not only had a clear artistic policy of presenting contemporary works and progressive choreography, but it also expressed the intention of bringing about irreversible changes in the world of ballet generally. The two choreographers of the opening programme were Rudi van

The music and designs for the Nederlands Dans Theater's An American Beauty are by Burt Alcantara and William Katz, respectively, who have both been closely associated with the Louis Falco Dance Company in the United States. The choreography is by Jennifer Muller. At one time it seemed as if the influence of American artists was causing a lack of balance in the Dutch company's repertoire, but this is now no longer a problem.

Dantzig and Hans van Manen but when Benjamin Harkavy returned to the United States, they returned to the National Ballet.

The most influential figures in the development of the young company were the American choreographers, Glen Tetley, John Butler and Anna Sokolow. Glen Tetley, in particular, benefited considerably from his experiences in Europe, developing an assurance of approach during his time in Holland, with the Ballet Rambert in London and with the Stuttgart Ballet in West Germany. He was invited to the Hague as guest artist in 1962 and this began a close association with the company, both as a dancer and as a choreographer. He staged a number of earlier works, including the successful *Pierrot Lunaire* and has since created works especially for the Dans Theater as well as mounting ballets originally created for other companies, including *The Anatomy Lesson, Mythical Hunters, Mutations* with Hans van Manen and *Game of Noah*.

A further result of the collaboration between the contemporary American choreographers and the company was that Rudi van Dantzig and Hans van Manen felt challenged and so began serious experiments with choreography themselves. The particular qualities of the company are due, to a considerable extent, to its association with Hans van Manen and Glen Tetley. They, in fact, have collaborated on *Mutations*, premièred during the 1969/70 season.

All the ballets in the repertoire are by contemporary choreographers and between 10 and 12 new works are presented each season. The company regards the choreographer as central to the dance activity and the planning and organization of the ensemble. Everything is arranged to provide the choreographer with the right artistic climate, creative dancers and the necessary co-operation. Such emphasis on the rich diversity of choreography makes exceptional demands on the dancers. For this reason, they are trained to high standards in both classical and modern dance techniques. The Nederlands Dans Theater is particularly renowned for the vitality and precision of its dancers.

This close relationship focused on the creative process of the choreographer, has resulted in the crystallization of a very specific aesthetic concept. The modernity of the Dans Theater does not, therefore, result from the support of underlying literary themes, nor is it dependent upon the compulsory use of avant-garde music, but rather it springs directly from the choreography. Furthermore, this has created, not only a wide range of dance vocabulary, but a new artistic awareness of dance images independent of tradition and of plot.

The influence of American choreographers on the Dans Theater has always been profound and, in the early days, was most successful and productive. However, at the beginning of the 1970s this influence was starting to threaten

the balance of the repertoire which tended to be dominated by the works of American choreographers, particularly those of Jennifer Muller and Louis Falco. His colleague, the composer and musician, Burt Alcantara, was also closely associated with the company.

The balance was restored when Jiri Kylian joined the company. As co-director with Hans Knill he has been partly responsible for extending the range of works presented and as resident choreographer he has provided a new creative force. The first ballet he created for the Nederlands Dans Theater, *Verklärte Nacht*, has done much to return the company to the direction of experiment and innovation. Schönberg's music was inspired by a poem about a woman's confession of her infidelity and the comforting reassurance of the man she loves which transfigures her emotional and spiritual darkness – hence the title of the music. Jiri Kylian's ballet is a kind of abstraction of both the music and the poem which inspired it. There are three characters, called simply He, She and The Other, but each is danced by two people. Thus, with poetic conciseness, two separate aspects of each character are revealed simultaneously to the audience. Sometimes the two dancers seem to present the same qualities, as in the parallel opening duets, but subtle differences of interpretation are noticeable. At other times the two dancers seem quite different, even opposite and a particularly revealing trio involves both manifestations of The Other with only one aspect of She. *Verklärte Nacht* is undoubtedly one of the most poetic and striking explorations of self-awareness and self-recognition in any art form. Jiri Kylian makes very particular use of his dancers. Each character-couple in this work is perfectly matched technically but the notable differences in actual appearance are exploited to develop the theme.

Members of the company have also recently begun creating works – a situation which is always indicative of healthy development. In particular, Nils Christe shows a talent for charming, light-hearted, inventive and humorous works and Eric Hampton displays a smoothness and control in *Overcast*, which promises an interesting future.

Further balance in the repertoire has been achieved by the presence of guest choreographers. Informed opinion seems to be divided on the question of resident and guest choreographers. Perhaps the ideal situation is a solid core of 'company' works with the addition of some new creations by other choreographers to prevent stagnation and to take advantage of developments and experiments happening elsewhere. This certainly seems to be the present position of the Nederlands Dans Theater. For the Holland Festival in 1976, the company invited Gerhard Nohner and Jonathon Taylor to create works for it and these have now been taken in to the regular repertoire.

The company once again seems to be adhering more closely to its performing policy. New works are regularly presented, usually at the Royal Theatre in The Hague or the Circus Theatre in Scheveningen, and are only taken into the permanent repertoire when they can be considered artistic successes.

Apart from regular performances in The Hague and at Scheveningen, the company frequently tours abroad and is particularly popular in Britain and the United States. Since its foreign debut at the Théâtre des Nations in 1963 and its visit to the Festival of Two Worlds in Spoleto in 1966, the company has visited three continents and many European cities.

It seems almost inevitable that any new and adventurous company which achieves acclaim and success in its early years, has to face a period of readjustment and consolidation afterwards. The Nederlands Dans Theater has moved on to the next phase of development which promises a new maturity and self-assurance without losing its pioneering spirit and imaginative creativity.

The Company

Artistic Director:	Hans Knill	**Ballet Masters:**	Hanny Bouman
Co-Director:	Jiri Kylian		Simon Mottram

Dancers:	Roslyn Anderson	Bonnie Mathis	Eric Hampton
	Moira Bosman	Susan McKee	Gérard Lemaitre
	Arlette van Boven	Jeanne Solan	Ric McCullough
	Shane Carroll	Karen Tims	Johann Meijer
	Kathleen Fitzgerald	Eve Walstrum	Joost Pelt
	Sheri Gaia	Jon Benoit	Paul Porter
	Marly Knoben	Hugo Bregman	Michael Sanders
	Sabine Kupferberg	Nils Christe	Gerald Tibbs

The Repertoire

An American Beauty Rose (Muller)
Arena (Tetley)
Carmino Burana (Butler)
Concertina (van Manen)
Concerto Grosso (Czarny)
De Maan in de Trapeze (van Manen)
Deranged Songs (Taylor)
Elegia (Kylian)
Grosse Fuge (van Manen)
Journal (Falco)
Juice (Sappington)
Light Part XI (Takei)
Metaforen (van Manen)
Moves (Robbins)
Mutations (Tetley/van Manen)

Mythical Hunters (Tetley)
Nouvelles Aventures (Flier)
Recital for Cello and 8 Dancers (Harkavy)
Septet Extra (van Manen)
Stoolgame (Kylian)
Strangers (Muller)
Symfonie in D (Kylian)
The Anatomy Lesson (Tetley)
Three Pieces (van Manen)
Tofuba in Scherzogrofi (Christe)
Torso (Kylian)
Unterwegs (Bohner)
Valkuil (Sanders)
Verklärte Nacht (Kylian)
Visage (Harkavy)

Touring

Italy, Britain, United States, Mexico, Australia, France, Denmark, Switzerland, West Germany.

Scapino Ballet

The name of the company is taken from a character in the Commedia dell'Arte, an Italian precursor of pantomime, popular in Europe from the sixteenth to the eighteenth centuries. Actors improvised within a given framework, presenting familiar stock characters such as Harlequin, Columbine and Pantalon. Scapino was the connecting link between the different parts of the play, explaining the action to the audience or commenting light-heartedly on the development of the plot. Scapino Ballet has the same kind of purpose – to inform young people about ballet during or before performances and to draw them into the theatrical event.

Since Hans Snoek, who was actually a woman named Johanna, founded the Scapino Ballet in 1945, thousands of Dutch children have been introduced to the principles of dance. It is actually one of the oldest theatre companies in the Netherlands.

The company has evolved a number of activities since its foundation. Its Italian namesake disappeared from the Commedia dell'Arte because his brief appearances could not encompass all that was necessary. Similarly, the ballet company recognized further needs in its education programme and set about teaching and explaining more thoroughly about such fundamentals as the choreography and music.

At present the company has six areas of activity. The first of these is a creative hour which takes place in schools. A professional dance teacher talks to small groups of pupils with the aid of photographs, records and other aids. Various forms of dancing – ballet, jazz, folk dance – are presented to the children. The teacher also tells them about choreography and explains in particular about the specific performance which the children will later visit.

The second activity is a demonstration given by a team of two female dancers, one male dancer and a sound technician. The company has three such teams who each give two demonstrations daily. The dancers demonstrate various forms of dancing using costumes and music to give vitality to the information.

From left to right, *Lieven Verkruisen, Anne van Tol and Robin Woolmer of Scapino Ballet's larger performing company, dancing a scene from* Concerto Grosso. *The choreography by Charles Czarny was inspired by sports and acrobatics.*

Anne van Tol and Robert Craset pictured in Hans van Manen's Variomatic, *created to music by Lennox Berkeley. The repertoire presents a mixture of family entertainment and more serious dance pieces.*

The company also provides a scheme which it calls a 'do-dance'. This is a combination of demonstration and class activity. The children are given 45 minutes after the professional demonstration to sample dance for themselves and attempt to create their own movement and forms stimulated by what they have just seen.

The company also runs a longer day-project. The aim of this is to familiarize children with the workings of the theatre. The children's own teacher, dance teachers and one demonstration group co-operate and the project is centred around a particular theme. The children are divided into four groups – scenery, costumes, dancers and orchestra – and assigned tasks. At the end of the day the four groups re-assemble and give an impromptu performance. The demonstration group also shows how professional dancers work.

A larger project is known as Scapino 10. Ten dancers form the company and it performs regularly in small theatres, local halls and other places which have insufficient accommodation for larger companies. A special repertoire has been organized which needs only a small stage and a minimum of scenery and lighting.

The larger company, known as the Scapino Ballet, performs in all the major theatres in the Netherlands. As well as school performances, intended for children aged between nine and sixteen, the company also presents adult programmes and family performances. The repertoire includes both classical and contemporary works and full-length ballets like *Coppélia* are regularly presented. Ballets have been created for the company by such well-known choreographers as Maurice Béjart, Charles Czarny, Hans van Manen, Roberto Trinchero and Armando Navarro.

Government, provincial and municipal authorities provide grants to assist the Scapino Ballet's education programme, and the Amsterdam city council provides financial aid to support the studios.

The company has travelled abroad giving both adult and youth performances with great success.

The Company
Scapino Ballet

Artistic Director:	Armando Navarro	**Ballet Mistress:**	Marian Sarstädt
Ballet Master:	Fernand Daudeij	**Repetiteur:**	Anne van Tol

Dancers:	Laura Atwood	Marja Ruurs	Henk Knaap
	Lisa Bendelac	Marijke Schulte	Stephane Laurent
	Martha Denton	Mary Siegel	Peter Sawtell
	Molly Gorden	Anne van Tol	Carlos Serrano
	Mary Hammel	Carla Wouters	Adrian Sichel
	Margreet Hoogendijk	Cor Adelphos	Lieven Verkruisen
	Deborah Lynn	Franklin Bobadilla	Alan Watson
	Grada Peskens	Henk van Boven	Robin Woolmer
	Patricia Renzetti	Robert Craset	

The Company
Scapino 10

Leader:	José Gutierrez		

Dancers:	Karin Chen	Marcelle Kramer	Cees Brandt
	Ruth Eman	Karin Maessen	Tony Cathlin
	Annelies Hermans	Saskia van der Kruck	Johan Smid
	Angèle Keizer	Maurice Berger	

The Repertoire
Scapino Ballet

Ah, Vous Dirais-je, Maman! (Béjart) 1976
Ajakaboembie (van Manen) 1971
Assortimento (van Manen) 1973
Bach-Brandenburg-Three (Czarny) 1973
Concerto Grosso (Czarny) 1974
Coppélia (Navarro) 1971
Divertimento (Trinchero)
Halve Symphonie (Navarro) 1974
Hatweeoh (Sanders) 1976

Interviews (Gosschalk) 1975
Out of the Blue (Hampton)
PG Suite (Hampton) 1975
Soft Floor Show (Hampton) 1973
Sunny Day (Czarny) 1973
The Nutcracker (Navarro) 1975
Twenty-four Bare Feet (Czarny) 1976
Variomatic (van Manen)

The Repertoire
Scapino 10

Aerobatics (Gutierrez) 1976/7
Birds of Shining Plumage (Gosschalk) 1976
Carambole (Gutierrez) 1976
Coffee for Five (Tuerlings) 1976
Impressions (Sanders) 1976

Push (Hampton) 1974
Santa Claus Ballet (Gutierrez) 1976
Screenplay (Sanders) 1975
Sunny Day (Czarny) 1975

Touring	Austria, Belgium, Italy, France, Norway, U.S.A. Finland, Germany.

PORTUGAL
The Ballet Gulbenkian

In 1961 the Calouste Gulbenkian Foundation which had, for some time, expressed a desire to support ballet in Portugal, stated 'after studying a variety of projects to subsidise a new organization to promote ballet, it was desirable to develop ballet, not dependant on a single individual or the caprices of a few people. Teachers, dancers, critics, choreographers and musicians should devote some of their energy to this'. Since its beginning this has been the aim of the Ballet Gulbenkian.

The Portuguese Dance Centre, founded in 1960, requested the Foundation to subsidise its general running and maintenance until 1965, which it duly did. The centre began by setting up a special course for dancers, directed by the British teacher and choreographer Norman Dixon, a former principal of the Ballet Rambert. This course became the core of the Experimental Ballet Group, founded by the Portuguese Dance Centre in February 1961. Norman Dixon was the first Artistic Director and was replaced by John Auld in 1964. In the five seasons under John Auld's direction, this group staged many performances both in Lisbon and in other parts of the country.

In 1965 the Centre decided to make quite profound alterations to the Experimental Group. Financial and administrative difficulties meant that the group was not fulfilling the expectations of the Foundation. It was decided that the Experimental Group and the Portuguese Dance Centre should be inte-

grated and transformed into the Gulbenkian Ballet Group from October 1965. In order to provide a permanent home for the company, a theatre with a modern auditorium was planned to be built next to the Head Office and Museum of the Foundation.

Maria Madalena de Azeredo Perdigao was appointed Musical Director. Walter Gore, former Ballet Master with the Frankfurt Opera, Artistic Director of the London Ballet and of the Australian Theatre Ballet and choreographer for the Ballet Rambert and the Sadler's Wells Ballet, was appointed Artistic Director. John Auld, who had been assistant to the Artistic Director of the London Festival Ballet, where he was also a principal dancer, as well as director of the Experimental Group, became Ballet Master. On December 23, 1965, the new company gave its inaugural performance at the Vasco Santana Theatre in Lisbon. The performance, John Auld's version of *Coppélia*, also celebrated the anniversary of the Gulbenkian Foundation and was dedicated to its personnel.

About a month later, on January 25, 1966, the company gave its first official performance. The programme consisted of Fokine's classic, *Carnaval*, and two works by Walter Gore, *Eaters of Darkness* and *Mosaic*. In the programme notes for the inaugural performance, Walter Gore explained at length the aims of the new Gulbenkian Ballet Group. Whilst recognizing the time and work involved he expressed the desire of the company to become one of Europe's leading dance groups. He also stated that the company would combine classical and modern repertoire in order to present an extensive programme with a firm basis in disciplined technique. While recognizing the need to establish internal cohesion in the company, he also hoped that Portugal would eventually produce choreographers of international standard, who would create works of universal appeal. He also remarked on the importance of opening a school to train professional dancers. The Ballet Gulbenkian today is, in many ways, still concerned with these ambitious aims.

Walter Gore remained Artistic Director until December 1969. During these four years, the company presented 52 works. Ten of these were from the traditional repertoire – *Coppélia*, *Carnaval*, *La Fille Mal Gardée*, *Les Sylphides*,

The Gulbenkian Ballet pictured in Symphony of Psalms. *The choreography is by Milko Sparemblek and the music by Igor Stravinsky.*

Giselle, Swan Lake Act II, Polovetsian Dances from Prince Igor, Aurora's Wedding, The Firebird *and* Le Beau Danube. Gore presented 25 of his own works, seven by Portuguese choreographers – Agueda Sena, Francis Graça and Carlos Trincheiras – and 10 from other choreographers – Norman Dixon, John Auld, Nini Theilade, Michel de Lutry and Milko Sparemblek. A number of Portuguese artists collaborated with the company during this time. In 1968, John Auld ceased to be Ballet Master and this post was temporarily filled by Roland Casenave.

After its first season the company began to give performances outside Lisbon, thereby following the policy of cultural decentralization initiated at the time of the Experimental Group. In 1969, it made an extended tour of Angola and Mozambique and danced in opera performances in Paris and Rome. Walter Gore left the Gulbenkian Ballet Group in 1969. Under his direction, the company had achieved unity and acquired and consolidated professional authenticity. This new-found professionalism permitted the company to work with guest choreographers, including such major figures as Serge Lifar and Leonide Massine.

The season following Walter Gore's departure was very reduced, particularly the traditional repertoire which only included *Petrouchka* and *Raymonda Divertissement* and rehearsals of *Les Sylphides* and *Giselle*, under the direction of Anton Dolin, who was working with the company for the first time. At this time, the two Portuguese dancers, Carlos Trincheiras and Agueda Sena,

became members of the company and three foreign choreographers were invited to Lisbon – Michel Descombey, Juan Corelli and Milko Sparemblek. Geoffrey Davidson was appointed Ballet Master and continued in this capacity until 1972. In this year too, the company was invited to Japan to dance at Expo 70 in Osaka. Milko Sparemblek had staged three of his works for the Gulbenkain Ballet Group – *The Miraculous Mandarin* and *Sinfonia da Reqùiem* in 1967 and *Gravitation* in 1970. The collaboration between him and the company was so successful that he was invited to become Artistic Director in October 1970. Yugoslavian by birth and Parisian by adoption, Milko Sparemblek had a wide experience as dancer, choreographer and ballet master with various well-known companies – Janine Charrat, Ludmilla Tcherina, Ballet du XXème Siècle, Ballet Théâtre Contemporain, Harkness Ballet and opera-ballets in Paris, Amsterdam, Marseilles and the New York Metropolitan Opera House.

Under the direction of Milko Sparemblek, the Gulbenkian Ballet Group turned towards contemporary dance without abandoning the discipline of classical ballet. He maintained a deliberately open mind towards classical technique and other kinds of dance, including ethnic and folk dance, in an endeavour to bring together all these varieties in the synthesis of a new repertoire. He believed that European ballet was undergoing a re-awakening and that this was most successfully brought about by choreographers who did not reject tradition but, at the same time, remained open to influences from America and from the Orient.

In the four and a half years the company was under his direction, Milko Sparemblek staged 44 works anew. Only one of these – *The Nutcracker* – was from the traditional repertoire. He presented 12 of his own works and 11 by Portuguese choreographers – Carlos Trincheiras, Agueda Sena, Armando Jorge, Fernando Lima and António Rodrigues. The remaining works were by 20 other choreographers including Lar Lubovitch, John Butler, Paul Sanasardo, John Chesworth, Michel Descombey and Jorge Garcia.

Walter Gore's original policy for the company had by this time become somewhat modified and augmented by the developments and changes that had taken place. The number of traditional works in the repertoire was considerably reduced. More emphasis was placed on collaboration with choreographers from abroad, particularly the major figures of contemporary dance in the United States. Milko Sparemblek also felt that the influence on the company of the Artistic Director was inevitably so strong, that the number of his works presented should be reduced by half.

In 1972 the Cuban teacher and choreographer, Jorge Garcia, became Ballet Master. It was at this time too, that the company began to expand internationally. It returned to Southern Africa and later visited South America and made European tours. It also continued its policy of cultural decentralization within Portugal.

With the departure of Milko Sparemblek in April 1975, the second chapter in the history of the Gulbenkian Ballet Group closed. The company took quite a revolutionary step in its administration then. The responsibility for artistic direction was entrusted to a committee elected by the dancers and which, at present, consists of the Ballet Master, Jorge Garcia, choreographer and teacher, Carlos Trincheiras, dancer and choreographer, Armando Jorge and two dancers, Isabel Santa Rosa and Ger Thomas. At the beginning of the 1975/76 season, the company decided to call itself the Ballet Gulbenkian which it felt corresponded better to its character and which was already in use in its performances abroad.

This new phase in the company's history has again brought about some modifications to its policies. More attention is again being given to the traditional repertoire, without prejudicing contemporary works. Portuguese choreographers are specially encouraged in line with Walter Gore's original aims. Also efforts are being made to attract new sectors of the public to ballet in Portugal. This educational aspect has taken several practical forms. The number of performances each season is increasing. Performances, discussions and lectures are given in factories, schools and colleges throughout Portugal. Children and young poeple are particularly encouraged by arrangements for special price tickets and free entry to observe lessons. The Ballet Gulbenkian has not yet been able to open a school. As is so often the case, financial considerations have prevented this. The company has assisted the work of public schools and studios, however, by setting up two training schemes. The first of these, begun in 1969, is an introductory course for children and the second, established in 1974, is an intensive course for young dancers over the age of 18, to assist with professional training. A choreographic studio, founded in 1972, also exists to encourage members of the company to create their own works. The resources of the company are available to the young choreographers who enjoy complete liberty to create new works. Eighteen small ballets have been presented by the studio and four of them are now included in the company's repertoire.

The company has yet to resolve the problem of balancing the classical and contemporary aspects of the repertoire. The size of the company and the nature of the principals has always made this a difficult matter. However, this is something that time will settle.

The Ballet Gulbenkian has encouraged Portuguese choreographers whilst, at the same time, insisting on an international standard. Twenty-four works by eight Portuguese choreographers have been developed and integrated totally with the 95 contemporary works by 29 international choreographers in the repertoire. The company succeeds in being a delightful blend of both Portuguese and cosmopolitan. In his programme notes in 1966 Walter Gore said: *Among other things, the choreographer must take into account the [fact that the] language of ballet is universal. He cannot confine himself to the idiom and music of each country.*

Over 10 years later, this is still the policy of the Ballet Gulbenkian.

The Company

Committee for Artistic Direction:	Jorge Garcia Carlos Trincheiras Armando Jorge Isabel Santa Rosa Ger Thomas	Ballet Master:	Jorge Garcia
Dancers:	Marta Atayde Graça Barroso Maria José Branco Ulrike Caldas Palmira Camargo Luisa Duarte Helena Lozano Lúcia Lozano	Colleen O'Sullivan Isabel Queiroz Isabel Santa Rosa Penelope Wright Soren Backlund Carlos Caldas Sean Cunningham David Hygh	Armando Jorge Fernando Leonardo Miguel Lyzarro Jair Morais Erich Payer Expedito Saraiva Ger Thomas Vasco Wellenkamp

The Repertoire

Adsum (Sena) 1975
Algumas Reacções de Algumas Pessoas Algures No Tempo ao Ouvirem a Notíca da Vinda do Messias (Lubovitch) 1970/1
Amargo (Sena) 1972/3
Amor de Perdição (Trincheiras) 1967/8
Ancient Voices of Children (Sparemblek) 1971/2

A Ressaca (Gore) 1967/8
Arquipélago III (Trincheiras) 1971/2
Aurora's Wedding (Petipa) 1968/9
Beauty and the Beast (Auld) 1967/8
Caminhos do Tempo (Carey) 1970/1
Canto da Solidão (Jorge) 1973/4
Carnaval (Fokine) 1965/6

Catulli Carmina (Butler) 1972/3
Concerto (Sena) 1970
Concerto in G Major (Wellenkamp) 1975
Configuration (Gore) 1967
Continuum Sobre Um Tema de Akutagawa
(Sparemblek) 1971/2
Contrastes (Banovitch) 1971/2
Coppélia (Auld) 1965/6
Desportistas (Gore) 1968/9
Dulcineia (Trincheiras) 1970/1
Duo (Fernandes) 1975
Duo (Garcia) 1973/4
Eaters of Darkness (Gore) 1965/6
Encruzilhada (Graça) 1967/8
Ensaio de Dança e Movimento (Gore) 1968/9
Epitafio para Gesualdo (Sparemblek) 1970/1
Euridice (Cullberg) 1975
Evocacões (Hurde) 1972/3
Feira (Gore) 1967
Ginevra (Gore) 1965/6
Giselle (Coralli/Perrot) 1967 (Dolin) 1970 (Garcia)
1973
Grand Pas de Quatre (Garcia after Perrot) 1975
Gravitacão (Sparemblek) 1970
Happening (Rodrigues) 1972/3
História de Amor (Gore) 1968/9
Homage to Florbela (Dixon) 1965/6
Hoops (Gore) 1965/6
Hossana Para Um Tempo Novo (Jorge) 1975
Il Ballo delle Ingrate (Gore) 1965/6
Il Combattimento di Tancredo e Clorinda (Gore)
1965/6 (Sparemblek) 1973/4
Instantãneo (Sena) 1968/9
Inter-Rupto (Trincheiras) 1972/3
Judas (Sena) 1967/8
Kinesis (Taylor) 1972/3
La Fille Mal Gardée (Auld) 1965/6
Lamentos (Trincheiras) 1975
Le Beau Danube (Massine) 1968/9
Les Sylphides (Fokine) 1965/6
Limbo (Gore) 1965/6
Majísimo (Garcia) 1973/4
Mascaras de Ostende (Corelli) 1970
Metamorphoses (Lima) 1971/2
Missa em Jazz (Descombey) 1972/3
Mosaic (Gore) 1965/6
Movimentos Sinfónicos (Jorge) 1970/1
Night Sound (Butler) 1972/3
O Baile dos Mendigos (Sanasardo) 1973/4
O Bando 1965/6 (O Encrontro 1967)
O Campo da Morte (Gore) 1967/8

O Crime de Aldeia Velha (Sena) 1967
Odisseia do Ser (Kuch) 1971/2
O Lodo (Trincheiras) 1968/9
Opus 43 (Sparemblek) 1972/3
O Ser Magico (Gore) 1965/6
Os Ultimos Segundos Do Ultimo Sonho De . . .
(Trincheiras) 1975
O Triunfo de Afrodite (Sparemblek) 1975
O Trono (Trincheiras) 1970
Parade (Gore) 1967/8
Pas de Six Classique (Auld) 1965/6
Passacaglia (Sparemblek) 1970/1
Pawn to King 5 (Chesworth) 1970/1
Peepshow (Gore) 1965/6
Petrouchka (Fokine) 1970 (Lazowsky) 1974
Psyche (Theilade) 1967
Quadros Soltos (Gore) 1967
Raymonda (Divertissement) (Petipa, re-created by
Armando Jorge)1970
Ritual de Sombras (Butler) 1970/1
Ritual One (Hughes) 1972/3
Salade (Lifar) 1967/8
Sassenach Suite (Gore) 1965/6
Satélites (Trincheiras) 1973/4
Simple Symphony (Gore) 1967
Sinfonia da Requiem (Sparemblek) 1967
Sky Well (Nather) 1971/2
Street Games (Gore) 1967/8
Suite de Bach (Descombey) 1970
Swan Lake Act II (Petipa directed by John Auld)
1967 (Directed by Roland Casenave) 1971
Symphonic Variations (Garcia) 1975
Symphony of Psalms (Sparemblek) 1971/2
Tekt (Sparemblek) 1973/4
Tempos Modemos (Sena) 1968/9
The Dances of Boyce (Gore) 1967
The Firebird (Lifar) 1968/9
The Miraculous Mandarin (Sparemblek) 1967, 1971
The Nutcracker (Dolin) 1970/1
The Polovetsian Dances from Prince Igor (Fokine,
re-created by Nicolas Beriozoff) 1968/9
The Siegfried Idyll (Sparemblek) 1973/4
The Wedding (Gore) 1965/6
Tres Movimentos (Garcia) 1972/3
Tres Poemas e Poslúdio (Sparemblek) 1970/1
Variações Sem Sentido (Theilade) 1967/8
Verdi Suite (Gore) 1967
Visões Fugitivas (Gore) 1967/8
Whirligogs (Lubovitch) 1973/4
Wop-Bop-A-Loobop (Hurde) 1973/4

Touring

1969	Angola, Mozambique, Paris, Rome
1971	Angola, Mozambique, Rhodesia, Malawi, Spain
1972	Brazil
1973	Spain, Britain, France, Italy, Yugoslavia

DENMARK
The Royal Danish Ballet

The Royal Danish Ballet, along with such companies as the Bolshoi and the Kirov, the British Royal Ballet, American Ballet Theatre and the New York City Ballet, is unquestionably one of the most important of the major companies of the world. It also has the distinction of being the oldest of these.

As in so many countries, the origins of the Royal Danish Ballet lie in the court ballets of the sixteenth and seventeenth centuries. When the first truly Danish Theatre, the Lille Grönegade Theatre was opened in 1722, ballet made the transition from the court to the stage. Foreign teachers, dancers and choreographers were invited by successive managements to build up a popular repertoire. For a long time the ballet scene in Denmark was dominated by the Italians and later by the French. Although this was still true when the Royal Theatre, still the home of the Royal Danish Ballet today, was opened in 1748, a number of Danish dancers were being trained and attracting notice.

A few years later, a more or less regular training programme was established at the Royal Theatre. The official school was founded in 1771 by Laurent who came from the Paris Opera and was one of the most important figures in the early days of Danish Ballet. He remained in Denmark for the rest of his life, training many of the Danish dancers, who, in their turn, influenced the development of the Royal Theatre's ballet company.

In 1775, the Italian, Vincenzo Galeotti, became Ballet Master at the Royal Theatre and continued to dance there, appearing in his own production of *Romeo and Juliet* at the age of 78. He became a naturalized Danish citizen in 1781 and years later became the first Danish dancer to receive the Knight's Cross of Dannebrog. During his long association with Danish ballet, Vincenzo Galeotti established a large international repertoire. He presented a wide range of works including dramatic ballets derived from literary sources and from Norse folklore as well as comic divertissements. *Les Caprices du Cupidon et le*

Maître de Ballet, first produced in 1786, was hardly ever out of the company's repertoire and can still be performed with the original choreography. It was still regularly danced in Denmark in the version staged by Harald Lander with music by Jens Lolle, during the 1960s.

In 1792, the French dancer Antoine Bournonville came to Copenhagen from the Gustav III Theatre in Stockholm, as guest artist. He remained in Denmark as a permanent member of the company and he became the leader of the Royal Danish Ballet in 1816. In the seven years of his leadership the Copenhagen ballet declined into a very poor condition because he was a weak administrator and an unimaginative choreographer.

In 1829 he was replaced by his son, August Bournonville, who was responsible for establishing the distinctive national character the company has today, as well as the renaissance the company enjoyed in the nineteenth century. He was born in Copenhagen in 1805 and was trained by his father, appearing at the Royal Theatre in 1843. He went to Paris and studied there for eight years, appearing at the Paris Opera from 1824 to 1828. He established a quite considerable reputation and seemed destined for international fame when he decided to return to Denmark and raise the status of Danish ballet. Naturally hard working, a gifted choreographer, and an internationally trained dancer, he was exactly what was needed by the Royal Danish Ballet.

August Bournonville was very much part of Danish cultural life in the nineteenth century and a close friend of other figures in the arts, such as the author Hans Christian Andersen and the sculptor Bertel Thorvaldsen. His work reflects the flourishing of romanticism taking place in literature and painting as well as in the performing arts.

He established a company of his own pupils and a repertoire of his own ballets. His works ranged from the lively *Napoli*, based on a folk tale, to the romantic *La Sylphide* and the classic French purity of *Conservatoire* (*Konservatoriet*). He also drew on Danish folk tradition with ballets like *Et Folkesagn*, set in sixteenth century Jutland and recounting the triumph of the beautiful Hilda over the trolls. The music for this romantic tale was composed by Niels William Gade and Johan Peter Emilius Hartman, and the wedding dance, from Act III, is often played at Danish weddings today. August

The Bournonville repertoire is a carefully preserved and highly valued heritage for The Royal Danish Ballet. Here, the company performs Conservatoire (Konservatoriet), *created in 1849. The action takes place at the Paris dance school of the Conservatory and mixes personal reminiscence with humorous intrigue.*

Bournonville worked with some of the finest Danish composers, including Hans Christian Lumbye.

He was a brilliant dancer and created many parts for himself in his early ballets. These parts are typified by their elevation, precision, lightness and fast, invigorating pace and these have remained characteristics of the Royal Danish Ballet, famous particularly for its male dancers. Female dancers have always been weaker, especially in the major classical roles, although Bournonville created a tradition of lively national dance requiring rapid neat footwork. Of the ballerinas he trained, Lucile Grahn is probably the most famous. She danced her first role, Sabi in *Jocko the Brazilian Ape*, before her tenth birthday and Bournonville created his version of *La Sylphide* for her, known as *Sylfiden* in Denmark. After successful guest appearances in Paris and Hamburg, she quarelled with Bournonville and left Denmark. She became an internationally renowned guest artist with the Paris Opera and appeared in Jules Perrot's famous *Pas de Quatre* with Fanny Cerrito, Carlotta Grisi and Maria Taglioni. Betty Schnell was also trained by Bournonville but found fame when she left ballet to become an actress, creating the roles of Nora and Hedvig in Ibsen's plays *The Doll's House* and *The Wild Duck*.

August Bournonville retired in 1877. For 40 years he had struggled to achieve recognition for the dignity and validity of his art. A despotic and fiercely energetic man, he left Denmark a ballet company of which it was rightly very proud. His spirit continued to dominate Danish ballet for nearly half a century after his death in 1879. Some of his works still feature in the repertoires of numerous international companies, either in their entirety or as excerpts – *La Sylphide*, *Napoli*, *Conservatoire*, *Flower Festival at Genzano* and *La Ventana*.

Almost immediately after Bournonville had left, the Royal Danish Ballet began to go into a decline. Hans Beck and Valborg Borchsenius kept quite a lot of Bournonville's repertoire alive but the company suffered from the absence of an original choreographer and later from its isolation from the exciting activities happening in the rest of Europe, particularly Diaghilev's Ballets Russes. Although Michel Fokine lived in Copenhagen for a while and worked with the Royal Swedish Ballet during this period, he was only asked to re-create three of his ballets in Denmark – *Les Sylphides* (known as *Chopiniana* in Denmark), *Petrouchka* and *The Polovetsian Dances from Prince Igor*.

The second renaissance in Danish ballet took place in the 1930s under the leadership of Harald Lander. A pupil of Hans Beck and trained in the Danish-French Bournonville tradition, he studied in the United States with Michel Fokine, in Mexico and in Russia. From 1932 to 1951 he was Ballet Master at the Royal Theatre during which time he revived the repertoire, including the works of Bournonville, and kept a firmer control on the administration of the company. He also produced a number of adaptations of ballets from international repertoire, notably *Coppélia* (a specifically 'Danish' version) and *Swan Lake*. As a choreographer, he was neither as prolific nor as original as Bournonville, but he created more than 25 ballets for the company. His most famous work, *Etudes*, created in 1948, has featured successfully in the repertoires of many other companies.

Harald Lander's fame was rather eclipsed by that of his two wives. He married Margot Gerhardt who, as Margot Lander, was one of the Royal Danish Ballet's greatest female dancers. The nomenclature of dancers in the Royal Danish Ballet is unusual. For the first year after graduating from the school, a dancer is called an aspirant. If he or she is then accepted into the company as a permanent member, he or she becomes a ballet dancer. There is only one rank above this – soloist. There have only been two exceptions to this – Margot Lander and her partner Børge Ralov, who were named prima ballerina and premier danseur. Although Margot Lander enjoyed a con-

siderable reputation in Denmark, she was not well known abroad. Harald Lander's second wife, Toni, gained a considerable international reputation after she left Denmark, with both the London Festival Ballet and American Ballet Theatre.

Two of the most famous dancers trained by Harald Lander are Erik Bruhn who, after a brilliant career as a premier danseur is now Resident Producer with the National Ballet of Canada, and Flemming Flindt who was an outstanding dancer with the London Festival Ballet and the Paris Opera before he returned

Anna Laerkesen and Henning Kronstam dance La Sylphide. *Known as* Sylfiden *in Denmark, it is the most famous of August Bournonville's works. He originally took the role of James and Lucile Grahn danced the sylph.*

169

Above *Mette Hønnigen and Peter Martins appear in a scene from Flemming Flindt's* Den Unge Mand Skal Giftes. *He has based several of his works on plays by Ionesco. The first and, perhaps the most famous, of these was* The Lesson.

Opposite *Lucile Grahn, known as the Danish sylphide, was one of the four or five internationally famed ballerinas of the nineteenth century. She was trained by August Bournonville and danced in St Petersburg and most of the capitals of Europe. In London, she appeared in Jules Perrot's* Pas de Quatre *with Maria Taglioni, Carlotta Grisi and Fanny Cerrito.*

to Denmark as Ballet Master, while still in his twenties, and after became Artistic Director of the Royal Danish Ballet.

In 1951 Harald Lander invited Vera Volkova to Copenhagen and she became the principal teacher of the 'Russian Style' to the Royal Danish Ballet. Shortly afterwards Harald Lander left Copenhagen and became Ballet Master at the Paris Opera and later an international choreographer. He returned to Denmark in 1962 and re-staged *Etudes*, which had not been performed there since he left, and also presented a new ballet, *The Triumph of Love*.

The departure of Harald Lander left the Royal Danish Ballet much weaker choreographically for some time. Happily, the company has a history of successful association with some of the world's leading contemporary choreographers. Beginning with Fokine's presentation of three of his works in 1925, the company has benefited from a succession of international choreographers – the ubiquitous George Balanchine who staged *Serenade* and *Apollon Musagete*. Vida Brown presented *Symphony in C*, and John Taras staged *Designs for Strings*. Frederich Ashton created his *Romeo and Juliet* for the Royal Danish Ballet and staged *La Fille Mal Gardée*. Anton Dolin, David Lichine and Jerome Robbins presented *Pas de Quatre*, *Graduation Ball* and *Fanfare*, respectively, for the company. Birgit Cullberg created *Moon Reindeer* for it as well as staging *Miss Julie* and *Medea*. Other choreographers who created or re-staged works for the Royal Danish Ballet include Roland Petit, Kenneth MacMillan and Elsa Marianne von Rosen. Of course, during this time, choreographers from within the Royal Danish Ballet were creating new works, notably Niels Bjørn Larsen (appointed Director in 1961), Erik Bruhn, Kirsten Ralov and Flemming Flindt.

August Bournonville's true heir did not emerge until 1965, when Flemming Flindt was appointed Artistic Director, He began his training at the Ballet School and continued from the age of 16 until he was 18 at the Paris Opera's school, under the direction of Harald Lander. At the age of 19 he joined the Royal Danish Ballet and very shortly afterwards he became a soloist with the London Festival Ballet, achieving international status before his twentieth birthday. He later became a danseur étoile with the Paris Opera and has appeared in major cities in Europe and the United States. He is a characteristic dancer of the Danish tradition with a brilliant technique and a superb lightness and delicacy. He appeared in both classical and modern roles and specialized in strongly, dramatic character parts. He is particularly famous for his performance in Roland Petit's *Le Loup*.

He assured his right to the leadership of one of the world's most important ballet companies by adding superb and original choreography to his list of achievements, when he created *The Lesson* in 1963, for Danish television. He was not yet 30 when he was appointed Artistic Director but, from the start, he had a very clear idea of his responsibilities.

He regards the company as being relatively small in comparision with the Bolshoi or Kirov companies, although, in fact, there are almost 90 dancers. He is conscious of the strong tradition and virtual monopoly of ballet the company has in Denmark. This places considerable demands on it to keep the classical tradition alive, especially the Bournonville repertoire. At the same time it is essential that the company does not stagnate or become a museum and Flemming Flindt has striven to achieve a balance between the old and the new. He has created a considerable number of works himself, including a second ballet based on a play by Ionesco, *The Triumph of Death*, based on *Jeux de Massacre*. The classical repertoire remains tremendously popular with the dancers and their audiences but, perhaps surprisingly, the new works by contemporary choreographers are achieving equal recognition, even Flemming Flindt's most avant-garde nude scenes. Many of the world's leading contemporary choreographers have been invited to create works for the company.

One of Flemming Flindt's first projects, when he took over the leadership of the Royal Danish Ballet, was to re-organize the school. The appointment of Vera Volkova had introduced order into the rather haphazard teaching methods applied before. However, although she was thoroughly experienced in the Vaganova system, she was not familiar with the Bournonville traditions of Denmark. Flemming Flindt decided to re-introduce the principles of Bournonville to the teaching, ensuring continuity from school to company. He has been interested more recently in establishing modern ballet classes and contemporary choreographers, such as Murray Louis, have been acting as guest teachers.

Another of Flemming Flindt's innovations was to increase considerably the company's touring schedule. He believes that it is important for the company to face the challenge of foreign audiences and standards. He feels that there is a danger in Denmark of becoming isolated and sterile and is very keen that the dancers should visit countries with very different dance traditions, such as the United States and the USSR. In fact, the Royal Danish Ballet's touring seasons have proved very popular and the unusual mixture of classical, Bournonville and modern ballet has been very well received.

Flemming Flindt did not find the problem of the lack of choreographic challenge as easy to solve. Although other ballet groups do exist in Denmark, none of them has the same stature as the Royal Danish Ballet and the stimulus of other choreographers is sorely missed. This is possibly one of the reasons which led to Flemming Flindt's decision in 1976 to resign his post as Artistic Director in 1978. He also points out that, by 1978, he will have been the Director for more than 12 years and he feels that both he and the company would benefit from a change and avoid becoming stale. He will leave behind him a company strengthened in style, training and repertoire.

The Company

Artistic Director:	Flemming Flindt (until 1978)
Assistant Director:	Henning Kronstam

Principal Dancers:			
	Ib Anderson	Mette Hønningen	Solveig Østergaard
	Fredbjørn Bjørnsson	Palle Jacobsen	Aage Poulsen
	Jonny Eliasen	Niels Kehlet	Flemming Ryberg
	Sorella Englund	Henning Kronstam	Inge Sand
	Flemming Flindt	Anna Laerkesen	Kirsten Simone
	Vivi Flindt	Niels Bjørn Larsen	
	Flemming Halby	Inge Olafsen	

The Repertoire

Apollo	Graduation Ball	Night Shadow	The Nutcracker
Aurora's wedding	Jardin aux Lilas	Pas De Quatre	The Prodigal Son
Carmen	Kermesse at Bruges	Pierrot Lunaire	The Life Guards of Amager
Cleopatra	La Fille Mal Gardée	Romeo and Juliet	The Three Musketeers
Coppélia	L'Arlèsienne	Swan Lake	Trio
Cyrano de Bergerac	La Sylphide	Tango Chicane	Triumph of Death
Etudes	La Ventana	The Blue Danube	Young Man Must Marry
Four Seasons	Le Loup	The Lady and the Fool	
Gala Performance	Miss Julie	The Lesson	
Giselle	Napoli	The Moon Reindeer	

Touring

The company has made several successful tours of major European and American cities.

FINLAND
The National Opera Ballet of Finland

In 1879, whilst Finland was still under Russian rule, the government built an opera house at Helsingfors, which had been the main city of the Duchy since the beginning of Russian domination in 1809. It was named the Alexander Theatre in honour of Czar Alexander II and very early in its career a ballet school was founded to supply dancers for the opera. It was not long before Finnish dancers were sufficiently well trained to replace the Russian dancers. During this time the Russian impresario Edvard Fazer was Director and in 1911 he organized a 'domestic opera' and also arranged for visits of Russian dancers from the Maryinksy Theatre in St Petersburg.

In 1917, following the Bolshevik revolution, Finland declared its independence and two years later, it officially became a republic and Helsingfors was renamed Helsinki. In the years which followed the ballet school developed and in 1921 George Gué, a native of St Petersburg but of Finnish extraction, became Ballet Master of the new official Finnish Opera Ballet Company. In February 1922 the first full-length ballet, *Swan Lake*, was premièred, with Marie Paischeff dancing the role of Odette-Odile.

For many years the Russian ballet tradition was faithfully preserved based on the model of the Maryinsky Theatre. George Gué remained Ballet Master and choreographer until the 1930s when he was replaced by the Russian dancer and teacher Alexander Saxelin who had, for many years been associated with the school. For over 50 years the strength of the company has been the productions of full-length works by Petipa and, even today, *Swan Lake*, first successfully created by Petipa and Ivanov, remains the most popular production of the National Opera Ballet. Other mainstays of the repertoire were the shorter ballets of Michel Fokine and almost all of these have been featured.

However, the company was never insular and has also been deeply influenced by major developments in dance in Western Europe. The leading companies of London and Paris profoundly affected the style of the Finnish Opera Ballet. The blending of eastern and western techniques has resulted in a characteristic Finnish ballet. Guest choreographers who have enriched the tradition have included Mary Skeaping who staged her version of the perennial favourite *Swan Lake*, and *The Sleeping Beauty*, Rotislav Zakharov who presented *The Fountain of Bakhchisarai*, Birgit Cullberg staged *Miss Julie*, and Harald Lander presented *Etudes*, *Aubade* and *Qarrtsiluni*. In addition, Nicholas Beriosoff, Lithuanian dancer and teacher, and father of the British ballerina Svetlana Beriosova, was Ballet Master of the National Opera Ballet from 1963 to 1964 and staged *The Sleeping Beauty*, *Swan Lake*, *Les Sylphides*, *Esmeralda* and *Le Sacre du Printemps* among other works. The company changed its name to the National Opera Ballet in 1956.

The first native Finnish choreographer was Irja Koskinen. In 1935 she staged a ballet to Jan Sibelius's *Scaramouche*. She remained the company's prima ballerina until she retired from the stage in 1959. She continued to teach in the school for some years and in 1965 she revived *Scaramouche*. The company has also been fortunate in the dancer, now teacher and choreographer, Elsa Sylvestersson. Since her choreographic debut with *Festivo* in 1966, she has created a number of works for the company including, in 1976, the first version of *Cinderella* staged by the company for 20 years. She also created the very

successful *Gayane* to the music of Khachaturian, achieving international recognition. Other principals who have since become choreographers include Maj-Lis Rajala, Heikki Värtsi and Doris Laine, who gained an international reputation during her career with the National Opera Ballet in the 1950s and frequent guest appearances abroad in the 1960s. The current repertoire consists mainly of works by Finnish trained dancers who reflect the truly national character of the company. In addition to mainstream ballet, the company has experimented with contemporary techniques and is particularly proud of the new work *Psykhe*, based on electronic music. It was particularly well received by audiences in Czechoslovakia and Leningrad where the company toured in 1976.

The company has been much restricted by the actual structure of the National Opera House. It is a small theatre with only one stage and 600 seats and is shared by the opera and ballet companies. The physical properties impose limitations on both companies in spite of renovations and repairs. There are plans to build a new theatre suited to the special requirements of opera and ballet. A site has been chosen and the design is being selected by means of open competition.

The company also makes regular national tours, attracting audiences as far north as Lapland. As the only professional company in Finland, it feels a special responsibility to provincial audiences as well as to those in Helsinki. At the same time, it aims at an international standard and helps to achieve this by touring abroad and by inviting foreign guests artists to Finland.

The Company

Choreographers:	Elsa Sylvestersson
	Heikki Värtsi
Repetiteurs:	Joan Blakeney
	Tuula Källström
	Virpi Laristo
Ballet Master:	Konstantin Damianov
Principal Dancers:	Ulrika Hallberg
	Marianna Rumjantseva
	Seija Silfverberg
	Arja Nieminen
	Tarja Ranta
	Aku Ahjolinna
	Seppo Koski
	Juhani Teräsvuori
	Martti Valtonen
	Heikki Värtsi
	Eero Huttunen
	Markku Heinonen
	Jarmo Rastas

The Repertoire

Cinderella (Sylvestersson)
Echo (Carlson)
Gayane (Sylvestersson)
Harlequin's Millions (Rajala)
Psykhe
Swan Lake (Shelest)
The Abduction of Kyllikki (Laine)
The Dark Sun (Värtsi)

Touring

Besides regular tours of Europe, the company has visited Latin America, the United States, Czecholsovakia and the USSR.

SWEDEN
The Royal Swedish Ballet

Ballet came to Sweden in the time-honoured, traditional way common to so many European countries. A French ballet master, Antoine Beaulieu, was engaged to create ballets for the royal family and the court, the first performance taking place in 1638. Ballets were presented at all the great festive occasions and the first professional dancers engaged went to Sweden in 1773, the year that King Gustav III founded the opera in Stockholm. Under the direction of another French teacher, Louis Gallodier, 24 dancers, a few of whom were Swedish, although most were French, made their debut in the opera *Thétis and Pelée*.

The company grew in size and popularity and Swedish dancers were sufficiently highly trained to become soloists. In 1781, Antoine Bournonville, whose son was later to contribute so much to the Royal Danish Ballet, joined the company. Bournonville was a pupil of Jean Georges Noverre, the famous French choreographer and ballet reformer. He brought about quite significant changes to ballet in Sweden and staged several of his own works. King Gustav III was a most cultured man with a deep love of the theatre and even appeared on the stage himself. He also wrote plays and operas, giving Swedish literature a distinct style known as Gustavian. He greatly admired dancers and manifested his appreciation by awarding scholarships to the most talented, enabling them to go to Paris and study with the best teachers in Europe. The ballerina Madame du Tillet was paid a higher salary than the leading singer of the opera – a reversal of the usual situation where the ballet was generally of secondary importance.

Charles Didelot was one of the dancers whose studies in Paris were financed by the King. Although he returned to Stockholm as premier danseur for three years, he left Sweden to embark on an international career working for many years as choreographer and head of the ballet school at the St Petersburg Imperial Ballet.

The Royal Swedish Ballet maintained its close association with the Paris Opera for many years after Gustav's death. French ballet masters went frequently to Stockholm and many successes of the Paris Opera were later presented in Sweden.

Premier danseur for a year and later a teacher of the Royal Swedish Ballet was Filippo Taglioni, father of the legendary Maria, who was born in Stockholm. Filippo Taglioni's chief contribution to the company was a complete re-designing of the costumes allowing much greater freedom of movement and permitting real elevation for the first time. It is hardly surprising that his daughter went on to free ballet from the artificiality and restraints of the eighteenth century and became one of the great romantic ballerinas. Maria Taglioni returned to Stockholm in 1841 after she had established her reputation in Paris, London and St Petersburg. She danced a suite from *La Sylphide* and *Le Lac des Fées* to a tumultuous reception. Her partner in *Le Lac des Fées* was one of the Royal Swedish Ballet's most talented young dancers, Christian Johansson, whom she persuaded to go to St Petersburg. He became premier danseur with the Imperial Ballet and later one of the greatest teachers in the history of the St Petersburg School. He was reputed never to have repeated a single enchaînement in his classes. In 1833, Anders Selinder became the first Swedish Ballet Master of the Royal Ballet. Selinder wanted to build up a national repertoire and introduce romantic ballet to Sweden in the same way as his contemporary, August Bournonville, was doing in

The Dying Swan, originally created by the incomparable Anna Pavlova in 1905, has proved a challenging role for ballerinas throughout the world. Mariane Orlando, for many years a leading dancer with the Royal Swedish Ballet, possesses an elegance of line, superb technique and classical purity, excellently suited to Michel Fokine's small masterpiece.

Denmark. Bournonville was, in fact, a guest choreographer of the Royal Swedish Ballet on a number of occasions and many of his ballets were staged in Stockholm. Selinder, like his more famous counterpart in Denmark, created many ballets about elves, fairies and sylphides but none of them has been preserved. He also made a collection of national folk dances which has proved invaluable to the company and to Swedish culture generally. He arranged some of these dances for a musical play entitled *Värmlänningarna* in 1846 and this forms part of the traditional Christmas programme of the Royal Swedish Ballet.

In spite of Anders Selinder's praiseworthy intentions and efforts, by 1860 the company had begun to decline. The management showed a marked preference for opera and little understanding of ballet and the needs of the ballet company. It was not until the beginning of the twentieth century that dance again became popular and public demand restored the full quota of dancers to the Royal Swedish Ballet. Two particular events stimulated public interest. In 1906 Isadora Duncan visited Stockholm and in 1908 Anna Pavlova gave her first performance outside Russia, in Sweden.

In 1913 Michel Fokine and his wife were invited as guest artists by the Royal Swedish Ballet. He presented several of his works with Vera and himself dancing the principal roles supported by Swedish dancers. He encouraged young dancers, selecting and helping those with special talent, particularly Jenny Hasselqvist, Carina Ari and Jean Börlin. After studying with Fokine, all three dancers had successful careers with the newly formed Les Ballets Suedois, although Carina Ari eventually went to Paris. Les Ballets Suedois was founded by an enthusiast, Rolf de Maré and acquired a number of the Royal Swedish Ballet's leading dancers during its brief existence from 1920 to 1925.

Fokine's occasional visits to Stockholm temporarily revived the spirit of the Royal Swedish Ballet but proper organization was lacking. The dancers were not trained to professional standards. There was no real technical skill and ballets and intermezzi in the operas were arranged with simple steps and degenerated into mere theatrical spectacle. The Swedish public was not prepared to accept this travesty of dance and turned its attention first to groups outside Sweden – Kurt Jooss' experimental company for example – and then to the new Swedish contemporary dance companies formed by Birgit Cullberg and Ivo Cramér.

In 1950 Antony Tudor became Director of the Royal Swedish Ballet and breathed new life into it. Nina and Albert Kozlovsky were appointed teachers for the younger students and introduced the Vaganova system to the school. The dancers were properly trained and in his brief stay in Stockholm, Antony Tudor brought great inspiration to the company. He staged *Giselle* and two of his own ballets, *Jardin aux Lilas* and *Gala Performance*.

Dance activity was reviving at the Royal Swedish Ballet when Mary Skeaping presented a full-length *Swan Lake* based on the version by Nicholas Sergeyev. This production was so stimulating to both dancers and the public that Mary Skeaping was invited to become Director of the Royal Swedish Ballet. She accepted and was faced with the formidable task of building up a proper company. There was no repertoire, as ballets were danced until interest waned and then they were abandoned and forgotten. Performances were most irregular because the opera took precedence.

Mary Skeaping built up a repertoire of classical works including her own particular productions of *Giselle* and *The Sleeping Beauty*. She also encouraged Swedish choreographers and most importantly she developed the dancers' technique by alternating the leading roles to give them a wide range of experience.

An exceptionally active and exciting period of activity followed in the

1950s. A national repertoire was created which gave the Royal Swedish Ballet its modern character and personality. Perhaps the most famous name associated with Swedish choreography is Birgit Cullberg. Her creation, *Miss Julie*, in 1950, introduced Elsa Marianne von Rosen to the Royal Swedish Ballet and a long association resulted from this. As well as dancing the roles Birgit Cullberg created for her, Elsa Marianne von Rosen frequently took the leading parts in the classics presented by the company. She, incidentally, was later to follow Mary Skeaping in building up a company and repertoire when she became Director of the Stora Theatre company in Gothenburg in 1970.

By 1961 the Royal Swedish Ballet's repertoire contained 12 ballets by Birgit Cullberg – *Miss Julie*, *Medea*, *Oscar's Ball*, *Ungersvennen och de Sex Prinsessorna*, *Pas de Coq*, *Romeo and Juliet*, *The Three Musketeers*, *Serenade*, *Moon Reindeer*, *Lady from the Sea*, *Odysseus* and *Eden*. In addition, Ivo Cramér had created *The Prodigal Son* and *The Linden Tree*. Contemporary dancer and choreographer, Birgit Åkesson, also created *Sisyphus*, *The Minotaur* and *Rites* for the Royal Swedish Ballet.

Since then, the Royal Swedish Ballet has consolidated its repertoire which contains an extensive range of mainstream ballets, many of them by world famous choreographers. Visits from major foreign companies, such as the New York City Ballet and the London Festival Ballet, have widened the dance experience of the company. The dancers have an expressive technical proficiency which has endeared the company to audiences both at home in Stockholm and on their tours abroad.

The repertoire of the Royal Swedish Ballet has maintained a careful balance between preserving mainstream traditional ballets and pioneering new contemporary works. Foremost among contemporary choreographers is Birgit Cullberg, who achieved international acclaim with Miss Julie *in 1950. Since then, she has created many major ballets for the company, including* Rapport, *shown here.*

179

The Gothenburg Ballet

The home of the ballet and opera companies in Gothenburg, the Stora, was opened in 1859. For some time it was very successful as a theatre for touring companies but gradually its popularity declined and in 1920 it was about to be sold as a cinema when it was rescued by a group of townspeople.

A resident ballet company was established and received some financial assistance from the city council. With a very few exceptions, the productions of this company were unremarkable and little notice was taken. 1949 was an important year in an otherwise uneventful period because the ballet school attached to the theatre was founded by the Finnish teacher Mila Gardemeister. In 1966 Conny Borg, formerly premier danseur of the Royal Swedish Ballet in Stockholm, was appointed Director. Full of youthful enthusiasm, he struggled to raise the status of the Gothenburg Ballet with his own productions and by invitations to internationally known choreographers from abroad. In spite of his efforts the company remained little known outside its own city. One notable legacy he left to the company, however, was the discovery of the young dancer Ulf Gadd's talent as a choreographer. Ulf Gadd is now the Director of the company and the repertoire includes a number of works created by him.

The Gothenburg Ballet's production of Orfeo *was created by Ulf Gadd in 1974 to music by Igor Stravinsky. The Maenads scene is shown here.*

The appointment of Elsa Marianne von Rosen as Director in 1970 was the turning point in the company's history. Elsa Marianne von Rosen had been the Royal Swedish Ballet's ballerina for eight years and had an international reputation as a choreographer. Her arrival infused the company with new enthusiasm and inspiration.

The company had no fixed repertoire. Generally, a production had continued until audiences lost interest and then it was abandoned and usually forgotten. Elsa Marianne von Rosen's first major production was Bournonville's *Napoli*. This was so successful that, by popular demand, it was repeated the following season and so established the practice of a regular repertoire for the company.

Another Bournonville classic, *La Sylphide*, followed the production of *Napoli* and Elsa Marianne von Rosen also produced her own versions of *Swan Lake* and *Romeo and Juliet*. New choreography is the life-blood of any ballet company and this aspect of the repertoire was not ignored. Elsa Marianne von Rosen presented her own ballet *Jenny von Westphalen* and also created *Pictures at an Exhibition*, to the interpretation of Mussorgsky's original music by the British pop group Emerson, Lake and Palmer. Works by Flemming Flindt were also included in the repertoire as well as ballets created by one of the company's own dancers, Ulf Gadd, including his own

version of the notorious, avant-garde *The Miraculous Mandarin*. In 1976 Elsa Marianne von Rosen left the company and Ulf Gadd was appointed Director and combines this responsibility with the busy life of a dancer and choreographer.

As well as an annual season at the Stora, the company also makes regular visits to schools. Successful seasons in Copenhagen, Stockholm and London have ensured the company's international status and distinguished guest artists include Gaye Fulton, Margot Miklosy, Claire Motte, Eva Evdokimova and Piers Beaumont.

Although a ballet company has existed in Gothenburg for over 50 years, the Gothenburg Ballet is essentially a young company. It has made such immense progress since 1970 that it looks with confidence towards an exciting and bright future.

In this scene from Elsa Marianne von Rosen's production of La Sylphide, *Eileen Jones dances the title role and Ulf Gadd is seen as James. A leading dancer with the company for several years and creator of a number of successful new works, Ulf Gadd is now Director of the company.*

The Company

Director:	Ulf Gadd
Ballet Mistress:	Margrethe Schultz
Ballet Master:	Tadeus Zlamal
Principal Dancers:	Jana Chalupa
	Nancy Clery
	Ulf Gadd
	Vilgot Gyllengran
	Christer Holgersson
	Eileen Jones
	Lillemor Jonsson
	Ivona Nordh
	Margrethe Schultz
	Taddeus Zlamal

The Repertoire

Apollon Musagète (Balanchine)
Aurora's Wedding (Petipa/Gadd)
Carmen (Petit)
Clowns (Jones)
Etudes (Lander)
Felix Luna (Flindt)
Gemini (Gadd)
Giselle (Skeaping)
Kalevala (Gadd)
La Sylphide (Bournonville)
Maison de Fous (Gadd)
Napoli (Bournonville)
Orfeo (Gadd)
Peter and the Wolf (Gyllengran)
Pictures at an Exhibition (von Rosen)
Prometeus (von Rosen)
Renard (Gadd)
Romeo and Juliet (von Rosen)
Swan Lake (von Rosen)
Symphony in C (Balanchine)
Tchaikovsky (Gadd after Petipa)
The Miraculous Mandarin (Gadd)
The Nutcracker (Petipa/Gadd)
Tratto (Gadd)

Touring

1973	Copenhagen
1974	Stockholm
1975	London

NORWAY
The Norwegian National Ballet

Giselle is one of the best loved classics and audiences therefore demand the highest standards of dramatic conviction and brilliant technique. In this scene from Act II, Viktor Róna, Leonie Leahy and Inge Johanne-Rütter dance the roles of Albrecht, Giselle and the Queen of the Wilis.

The story of the Norwegian National Ballet is a pleasing one of steady progress and growth from the time it was founded in November 1957 as part of the Norwegian Opera Ltd. Founded jointly by the State, the Municipality of Oslo and the Norwegian Opera Foundation, the new company was intended to present opera, operetta and ballet performances throughout Norway wherever it was practical.

To begin with, some anxiety was felt in dance circles that the ballet company would be of secondary importance to the opera company. To stress the importance of the ballet company, the first performance of the co-operative project was a ballet programme, consisting of *Carnaval, Coppélia Act II, Menuetto, The King's Fool, Pas de Deux from Giselle* and other divertissements. Furthermore, to emphasize that the companies were intended as a national enterprise and were not just confined to Oslo, this performance, on November 2, 1958, was given at a small town called Hamar. The company consisted of nine dancers under the direction of H. Algeranoff. With two guest artists, Anne Borg and Hanne Skram, and Birgit Cullberg as guest choreographer, six performances were given in Oslo during the first season. In addition the company toured southern Norway. Activity increased the following season and guest choreographers included Walter Gore and Ivo Cramér. H. Algeranoff left the company in September and the Latvian dancer Indris Lipkovskis took over the direction for the rest of the season. In 1960, Nicholas Orloff became Director and in the same year, Ivo Cramér created *The Nightmare of Count Bluebeard* for the company. This work has since been produced by the Royal Swedish Ballet and was very popular when the Norwegian National Ballet danced it on a tour at Gothenburg.

1961 marked considerable expansion. A corps de ballet of 10 dancers was added, who, with the ten soloists, made a total of 20 dancers. Joan Harris, former soloist of the Sadler's Wells Theatre Ballet and Ballet Mistress of the Bavarian State Opera, Munich, was appointed Director with Joan Mackeprang as assistant. Joan Harris worked hard to increase the company's repertoire. The first full-length production of *Coppélia* was performed and, during the next four years until she resigned from the directorship, Joan Harris added a number of works – Antony Tudor's *Jardin Aux Lilas* in 1962, Alan Carter's *The House of Shadows*, Birgit Cullberg's *Eden* and Brian Mcdonald's *Hymn* and *Counterpoint*, all staged by the choreographers, and *Swan Lake Act II* in 1963, Ian Carter's *The Miraculous Mandarin*, Walter Gore's *Street Games*, Ronald Frazier's *The Accused* and Gerd Kjølaas's *The Marquise* in 1964; *Giselle* staged by Doris Laine and Joan Harris and Walter Gore's version of *The Nutcracker*, as well as Birgit Cullberg's *Miss Julie*, Peter Wright's *Mirror Walkers*, Rita Tori's *Pas Gracieux* and Bill Earl's *Etudes de Degas*, plus a *Pas de Deux from Don Quixote* in 1965.

During these years the company continued to make national tours and appeared at the Bergen Festival. In June 1964, it made its debut abroad when it visited Kiel in Germany with a successful programme of *Counterpoint, The Moon Reindeer* and *The Miraculous Mandarin*. Under the inspired leadership of Joan Harris, the company continued to expand and develop a widely varied repertoire. By the time she resigned as Artistic Director in the spring of 1965, there were 30 dancers, including students.

In September, 1965, the company realized its early ambition of establishing a ballet school. Joan Harris took charge of the school and in only one year there were dancers trained to a sufficiently professional standard to join the corps de ballet. The school has also developed and expanded since its inception and has achieved a fine reputation in Europe.

In the autumn of 1966, the ballerina, Sonia Arova, was appointed Artistic Director of the Norwegian National Ballet and a further period of intense activity and expansion began. One of her major contributions to the repertoire was the introduction of works by George Balanchine beginning with *Apollon Musagète*, staged by Heinze Clauss. In the same season, guest choreographers presented various works – Job Sanders' *Bachianas Brasileiras*, Hans Brenaa staged *Napoli Act III*, Ivo Cramér created *Ski Ballet* – and Sonia Arova staged *Les Sylphides*, *Giselle* and *Le Corsair Pas de Deux*.

Developments continued uninterrupted in 1967. Rudolf Nureyev and Erik Bruhn appeared as guest artists. The appearance of such major international stars gave the company a tangible seal of approval. George Balanchine's *Symphony in C* and works by John Butler and Joseph Lazzini were added to the repertoire.

Sonia Arova was deeply interested in modern ballets and worked to

increase the already diverse repertoire in this direction. Birgit Cullberg's *The Moon Reindeer* was revived by Anne Marie Lagerborg. Walter Gore staged his own work *Eaters of Darkness* and Sonia Arova and Paul Podolski staged Act III of Rudolf Nureyev's version of *Raymonda*. Also in 1968, George Balanchine's *Four Temperaments* and Antony Tudor's *Dark Elegies* were presented and the company gave the world première of Job Sanders' *Summernight*, based upon the pictures of Edvard Munch, with music by Arnold Schönberg. Marten Molema, from the Nederlands Dans Theater, became Ballet Master in the autumn of 1969 and remained for a year. Then, Kenneth Tillson took on the responsibility of teaching and training. Guest artists, Jean-Pierre Bonnefous, Jeans Graff and Kirsten Simonsen appeared with the National Ballet. Terry Westmoreland staged Erik Bruhn's much acclaimed version of *La Sylphide*, Ray Powell presented *One in Five* and the Polish choreographer, Witold Borkowski, staged his version of *Romeo and Juliet*, which proved to be the most successful production of the season, to capacity audiences. Later the same year, guest choreographers Donye Feuer, Attilio Labis and Birgitte Thom staged *Aft Vemod*, *Arcade* and George Balanchine's *Serenade*, respectively.

By 1970, the company had expanded to 35 dancers and the repertoire contained a wide selection of full-length major classics and mainstream works by some of the world's leading contemporary choreographers, many of whom had staged the National Ballet's productions themselves. A number of changes took place in this year. The company began to give regular performances in a small theatre outside Oslo, while Sonia Arova was appointed Ballet Director of the Hamburg State Opera. She continued as Artistic Director of the Norwegian National Ballet for a further year, with Anne Borg, one of the leading soloists of the company, as her assistant in Oslo.

Doris Laine staged her version of *Cinderella* for the company, but for most of the year it was occupied with an extensive touring schedule. The company visited Italy, Finland, the major cities of Spain and also Trondheim and Stavanger. In 1971 Anne Borg took over the responsibilities of Artistic

Director completely. Poul Gnatt, previously a soloist with the Royal Danish Ballet and director of companies in New Zealand and Australia, was appointed Assistant Director. During that year, he staged his own ballet, *Prismatic Variations* and *Petrouchka*. Guest dancers included Jens Graff, Vivi and Flemming Flindt who also staged *Summerdances*. George Skibine staged his ballet, *The Prisoner of the Caucasus* and Anne Borg was particularly pleased to have Glen Tetley as guest choreographer when he staged *Mythical Hunters*. 1971 was an eventful year, for in addition to regular performances and the necessary rehearsals for incorporating new ballets into the repertoire, a workshop for young Norwegian choreographers was established. The works presented were *In All Eternity* by Kari Blakstad, *Light and Moments* by Jon Berle, *Ps. Sol Lonely Blooming* and *The Shadow* by Roger Lucas. This workshop experiment proved to be extremely successful and two of the ballets were later included in the company's regular repertoire.

During the spring of that year the company worked on a co-operative project with the National Television Company. For five weeks, specially created ballets were presented in the television studios, and a theatre performance was also televised. This enterprise was extremely successful and further projects have since been undertaken. A further diversification of activity was a children's programme devised by Anne Borg. The art of ballet is introduced and demonstrations include a class and excerpts from *Coppélia*, *Summerdances* and *Romeo and Juliet*.

George Skibine returned in 1972 to stage *Daphnis and Chloë* while Birgit Cullberg produced a new version of *Medea* and Walter Gore created *I am a Clown*. More importantly perhaps, a full-length Norwegian ballet, *Haugtussa*, was presented for the first time.

The next year of really intensive activity was 1974. Glen Tetley created a new ballet, *Strender*, for the company, in conjunction with the Norwegian composer Arne Nordheim. Other new ballets were Donya Feuer's *God is Alive and Well*, and Charles Czarny's *Haffner Symphony*. Further television productions were undertaken including a presentation of *The Moon Reindeer* and also the company made a six weeks' visit to the United States. The Hungarian dancer Viktor Róna joined the company in August 1974 as premier danseur and Ballet Master. The following year, he and Doris Laine staged a new production of *Giselle*, which was also seen on television. The 1975 workshop was particularly successful. The young choreographers Yngve Horn, Kjersti Alveberg, Wayne McKnight, Norman Shelburne and Alejandro Meza participated. All the ballets were subsequently incorporated into the company's repertoire. The 1975/6 season brought two world premières for the National Ballet – Karl Blakstad's *Johannes og Anima* to music by the Swedish composer Ralph Lundsten, and Henny Mürer's full-length work, *Pinocchio*, to music by Antonio Bibalo. Other new productions were Viktor Róna's stagings of *The Nutcracker* and Charles Czarny's *Concerto Grosso*. The association with Norwegian television was continued with a production of Glen Tetley's *Strender*.

Anne Borg had planned, for personal reasons, to resign from the direction of the company and the British dancer, teacher and director, David Blair, had been invited to become Artistic Director of the Norwegian National Ballet. His tragic and untimely death meant that Anne Borg continued for another season during which time she planned new additions to the repertoire – John Cranko's *Pineapple Poll*, George Balanchine's *Ballet Imperial*, a new ballet by Viktor Róna, Sir Frederick Ashton's *Les Patineurs*, Charles Czarny's *Sunny Day*, Wayne Soulant's *Kinderscenen* and a new ballet based on pop music by Yngve Horn. This last season is typical of Anne Borg's characteristically imaginative and comprehensive approach. When Brenda Last took over as

Artistic Director in August 1977, she came to a young and enthusiastic company with wide, international experience, a completely successful background, and a remarkably strong and varied repertoire.

The Company

Artistic Director: Brenda Last
Ballet Master: Viktor Róna
Choreologist: Britt Friberg

Principal Dancers: Ellen Kjellberg   Viktor Róna
Leonie Leahy   Inger-Johanne Rütter

Soloists:
Gøril Eie   Bridget Pugh   Terje Solberg
Antony Geeves   Gro Rakeng   Anne Merele Sundberg
Guri Pahle Glad   Kjersti Rødsten   Sissel Westnes
Frederic Konrad   Frederik Rütter
Stefan Petterson   Marle Saether

The Repertoire

Aft Vemod (Feuer)
Allegro Brillante (Balanchine)
Apollon Musagète (Balanchine)
Arcade (Labis)
Bach Brandenburg Three (Czarny)
Bachianas Brasileiras (Sanders)
Ballet Imperial (Balanchine)
Cappricio (Carter)
Cinderella (Laine)
Concerto (Lazzini)
Concerto Grosso (Czarny)
Coppélia (Ivanov/Sergeyev)
Counterpoint (Macdonald)
Dark Elegies (Tudor)
Daphnis and Chloë (Skibine)
Don Quixote Pas de Deux (Petipa)
Eaters of Darkness (Gore)
Eden (Cullberg)
Eight Days from KR.575 (McKnight)
Four Temperaments (Balanchine)
Giselle (Lavrovsky)
God is Alive and Well (Feuer)
Haffner Symphony (Czarny)
Haugtussa (Roger/Halle)
Hoops (Gore)
I am a Clown (Gore)
Imorgen? (Alveberg)
In All Eternity (Blakstad)
Jardin aux Lilas (Tudor)
Jeu de Cartes (Cranko)
Johannes og Anima (Blakstad)
Judgement of Paris (Tudor)
June and I (Horn)
Kinderscenen (Soulant)

La Sylphide (Bournonville)
Le Corsaire Pas de Deux (Petipa)
Les Patineurs (Ashton)
Les Sylphides (Fokine)
Let It Grow (Horn)
Medea (Cullberg)
Miss Julie (Cullberg)
Mythical Hunters (Tetley)
Napoli Act III (Bournonville)
One in Five (Powell)
Ophelia (Meza)
Pineapple Poll (Cranko)
Pinocchio (Mürer)
Prismatic Variations (Gnatt/Kerr)
Raymonda (Petipa/Nureyev)
Ritual (Butler)
Romeo and Juliet (Borkowski)
Serenade (Balanchine)
Street Games (Gore)
Strender (Tetley)
Summerdances (Flindt)
Summernight (Sanders)
Sunny Day (Czarny)
Swan Lake (Ivanov/Sergeyev)
Symphony in C (Balanchine)
Testament (Macdonald)
The Four Winds (Shelburne)
The Moon Reindeer (Cullberg)
The Nutcracker (Vainonen/Róna)
The Prisoner of the Caucasus (Skibine)
The Seven Deadly Sins (Schilling)
The Shadow (Lucas)
The Sleeping Beauty (Beriosoff)

Touring

Sweden, Finland, Germany, Spain, Italy, United States

WEST GERMANY
The Stuttgart Ballet

In 1760, Jean Georges Noverre, Parisian dancer, choreographer, creator of ballet d'action, revolutionary and reformer of dance, travelled to Stuttgart to take up his appointment as Ballet Master of the Württermberg Ducal Theatre. He remained there for six years, during which time he published his famous *Lettres sur la Dance et sur les Ballets*, created massive bills which eventually resulted in the dismissal of the company, and introduced the citizens of Stuttgart to the best and most exciting of contemporary dance activity. Such a happy situation was not to reoccur in Stuttgart for another 200 years.

In 1960, Walter Erich Schafer, administrator of the Württemberg Arts Complex and a man of extraordinary vision and imagination, invited John Cranko to Stuttgart as guest choreographer to stage *The Prince of the Pagodas*. This initiated one of the most remarkable associations in ballet history and marked the beginning of the Stuttgart Ballet's rise to the position it now holds as one of the most exciting and talented companies in the world.

John Cranko was born in South Africa where he began his training and created his first work, Stravinsky's *A Soldier's Tale*, for the Cape Town Ballet. He then went to London where he joined the Sadler's Wells Theatre Ballet for whom he created a number of works, firmly establishing his reputation as a choreographer of major importance with *Pineapple Poll* and *Harlequin in April*, in 1951. He was not an outstanding dancer but it was quickly realized that he was a most remarkable choreographer. He continued to create works for the Sadler's Wells companies, including *Lady and the Fool* and *The Prince of the Pagodas* and seemed destined to succeed Sir Frederick Ashton as Britain's foremost choreographer. He also created a number of ballets for other companies and many of his works are featured in the current repertoires of numerous international companies.

When John Cranko agreed to take up the leadership of the Stuttgart Ballet, it was a very minor company of little importance, firmly in second place behind the opera. In one way, at least, he was fortunate in that generous government funds relieved him of the worry of financial insecurity which so often inhibits the development of a company. Further, the large opera house is well equipped and set in beautiful surroundings, providing an environment which John Cranko found conducive to work.

Immediately he set about building up the company. He contacted Marcia Haydée, a superbly gifted dancer, who joined him as prima ballerina, has remained with the company since, and now heads it. The American dancer Richard Cragun also joined in the early days and has remained one of its principals throughout its spectacular history. The Danish dancer, Egon Madsen and the Rhodesian soloist, Judith Reyn, also responded to John Cranko's search for talent. German dancers were not ignored and Birgit Keil, Susanne Hanke, Heinz Clauss and Jan Stripling also joined the company.

Very soon after taking over the company, John Cranko founded the Ballet School and he continued to take a deep interest in this project. The British dancer and teacher Anne Woolliams joined the company in 1963. Trained by Vera Volkova, she was ideally suited to take on the direction of the newly formed school. This she did without relinquishing her other teaching responsibilities with the company itself. An exacting and gifted teacher, she has built up a school which, separately from the company, has established a

Kenneth MacMillan, Artistic Director of Britain's Royal Ballet, has a long history of association with the Stuttgart Ballet. In fact, his friendship with John Cranko began during their early days with the Sadler's Wells Theatre Ballet. Many of his works have been specially created for the German company. Requiem was premièred in 1976.

major reputation for itself. However, the school and the company have always been closely associated and students are trained to demanding, professional standards. In the early 1970s the school moved into a new building with excellent facilities for both dance and academic study and sufficient room for boarding pupils. The annual performances of the students fill the opera house, clearly demonstrating the school's reputation for being one of the finest in Europe.

John Cranko was an immensely gifted and prolific choreographer with the rare gift of flexibility of style. His technique was firmly rooted in the strong classical training of Dame Ninette de Valois, which derived, in turn, from the combined discipline and experiment of Diaghilev's Ballets Russes. John Cranko's impulse as a choreographer was basically emotional and he worked in a progression of images with a clear conviction that movement is the quintessence of ballet and should be capable of a valid existence independent of sets and costumes. This viewpoint enabled him to move easily from the great classics like *Swan Lake* or his famous story ballets like *Romeo and Juliet* to purely abstract works like *L'Estro Armonico*.

He showed wisdom when handling traditional ballets in that difficult choice of what to keep and what to discard of the so-called original choreography. In *Swan Lake*, for example, he retained most of Ivanov's choreography for Act II and restored the original Tchaikovsky score, discarding the additional Italian music introduced by Petipa. He introduced major changes of mood which he believed were closer to Tchaikovsky's original intentions than the versions popularly accepted. He saw the Prince as a rebel making the most of his last day without responsibilities, rather than as the sad and forlorn figure he often seems to be. His pursuit of the swans, rather than a hunt, was the result of a mysterious urge and this, undoubtedly, makes the Act II pas de deux with the Swan Queen more significant and convincing. The emphasis of Act III is on the national dances and John Cranko gave full scope to his remarkable ability with festive crowd scenes. Perhaps the most important change in his version comes in Act IV which ends tragically rather than with the happy outcome decreed by the Czar. Cranko maintained that Tchaikovsky intended *Swan Lake* to be a tragedy and that the lovers were never intended to 'live happily ever after' causing the feeling of anticlimax which so often permeates the final act in traditional versions. In his *Swan Lake*, the betrayal cannot be rectified – the magician is not killed, the lake overflows and drowns the prince and Odette remains a swan, doomed to continue her search for a true lover. This version is a combination of traditional and original elements giving a quality of freshness to the work. Certainly John Cranko showed masterly control of tragedy. His ballet *Onegin*, based on Pushkin's *Eugene Onegin* and often given that title by many authorities, including the Stuttgart Ballet itself, is acclaimed as one of the twentieth century's greatest creations. However, he was also capable of immensely humorous works and *The Taming of the Shrew* has been a constant delight to audiences since its première in 1969.

Initials R.B.M.E. has become something of a signature piece for the Stuttgart Ballet. It was inspired by the passionate feelings of friendship in Brahms' music and letters to Joseph Joachim and Robert and Clara Schumann. John Cranko created this abstract work to Brahms' Piano Concerto No 2 for four of his friends – Richard (Cragun), Birgit (Keil), Marcia (Haydée) and Egon (Madsen). This is indicative of another quality he brought to the Stuttgart Ballet. He developed a remarkable relationship with the company which has since been compared to a family. An extraordinary closeness existed between the dancers and their Director, giving the company a quality of warm enthusiasm which endeared it to audiences throughout the world. When John Cranko died suddenly in June 1973 on his return from the

company's third highly successful visit to the United States, it was a bitter blow, not only to the dancers, but to ballet lovers in general. Such was the affection he inspired that many ordinary citizens in Stuttgart felt a personal loss. The Stuttgart Ballet was so uniquely John Cranko's and the special family relationship he built up over 13 years made the question of a new director an especially difficult problem. It would have been forgiveably easy for the company to become a museum of John Cranko's works but the dancers themselves shared his tenacity and desire to experiment and develop.

In September 1974 the American choreographer Glen Tetley was appointed Artistic Director. His was a difficult task. John Cranko had died when only 46, at the peak of his career, leaving an extensive repertoire and a company acclaimed from the United States to the USSR. Unfavourable

John Cranko's Romeo and Juliet *has been widely acclaimed and is especially popular in Britain and the United States. As a choreographer, he possessed a unique ability to give animation and vitality to the scenes he created. This moving tragedy is especially well suited to a company which seems to possess an atmosphere of permanent youth.*

comparisons were inevitable and Glen Tetley's blend of classic and modern dance choreography and his aesthetic aims differed so radically from his predecessor's that many doubted the wisdom of his appointment.

Glen Tetley studied modern dance with Hanya Holm and Martha Graham, and classical ballet with Margaret Craske and Antony Tudor. He has been a member of several major companies, including the Martha Graham Dance Company, American Ballet Theatre, the José Limon Company and the Robert Joffrey Ballet. After his debut as a choreographer with *Pierrot Lunaire* in 1962, he joined the Nederlands Dans Theater for whom he created several major works. In 1965 he began a long and continuous association with the Ballet Rambert for whom he created *Embrace Tiger and Return to Mountain* and *Ziggurat*, among others.

Fortunately, the dancers of the Stuttgart Ballet under the leadership of the incomparable Marcia Haydée and Richard Cragun, accepted his direction with open minds. He, wisely, understood the necessity of keeping the Cranko repertoire alive whilst at the same time exploring new possibilities. His first major enterprise with the Stuttgart Ballet was *Voluntaries*, a valediction to John Cranko, set to Francis Poulenc's *Concerto for Organ, Strings and Percussion*. A beautiful ballet of intense poignancy, it reassured many who doubted the choice of Glen Tetley as Director. Earlier Tetley ballets, like *Pierrot Lunaire*, were included in the repertoire and he created several new works which received a mixed reception, such as the strangely stark and fluid *Greening* and *Daphnis and Chloë*.

During the time he directed the Stuttgart Ballet, the company had an opportunity to re-assess its aims and intentions. Birgit Keil and Richard Cragun, in particular, explored new possibilities within themselves and developed in new directions. However, Glen Tetley is really more suited to freelance choreography unlimited by the administrative responsibilities involved in directing a major company. Furthermore, his choreography is best confined to a few remarkable principals rather than a well-trained highly professional, full-sized company. The Stuttgart Ballet, of course, possesses the exceptional leading dancers Marcia Haydée, Birgit Keil, Richard Cragun and Egon Madsen but a rich fund of talent in the soloists and corps de ballet must also be fully used. Glen Tetley has now left the company and Marcia Haydée has taken over as Director. The company was once described as having 'John Cranko as its head, Marcia Haydée as its heart and Anne Woolliams as its backbone' and it is certainly difficult to think of anyone better suited than Marcia Haydée to lead it. The breathing space afforded by Glen Tetley's leadership and, equally important, the new directions suggested by him have been of great value to it.

One of the youngest major companies in the world, the Stuttgart Ballet inspires a special affection in the hearts of audiences in many different countries. Nevertheless, it does not rely on the memory of John Cranko or simply on the genius of his choreography and its survival, and present successes prove this.

The Company

Founder:	John Cranko	**Principal Dancers:**	Marcia Haydée
Director:	Marcia Haydée		Birgit Keil
Ballet Masters:	Alan Beale		Richard Cragun
	Alex Ursuliak		Egon Madsen
Choreologist:	Georgette Tsinguirides		
First Soloists:	Judith Reyn	Ruth Papendick	Barry Ingham
	Lucia Isenring	Vladimir Klos	Marcis Lesins
	Jean Allenby	Reid Anderson	

Soloists:

Gudrun Lechner	Mark A. Neal
Eileen Brady	Carl Morrow
Melinda Witham	Kurt Speker
Christian Fallanga	

The Repertoire

The Prince of the Pagodas (Cranko) 1960
Divertimento (Cranko) 1961
Family Album (Cranko) 1961
Solitaire (MacMillan) 1961
Intermezzo (Cranko) 1961
The Lady and the Fool (Cranko) 1961
Katalyse (Cranko) 1961
Antigone (Cranko) 1961
The Sleeping Beauty (after Petipa) 1961
Scènes de Ballet (Cranko) 1962
Coppélia (Cranko after Ivanov) 1962
The Seasons (Cranko) 1962
Nachtpfauenauge (Wright) 1962
Daphnis and Chloë (Cranko) 1962
Romeo and Juliet (Cranko) 1962
Les Sylphides (Wright after Fokine) 1963
L'Estro Armonico (Cranko) 1963
The Mirror Walkers (Wright) 1963
We Travel to Jerusalem (Cranko) 1963
House of Birds (MacMillan) 1963
Quintet (Wright) 1963
Variations (Cranko) 1963
Las Hermanas (MacMillan) 1963
Swan Lake (Cranko) 1963
Diversions (MacMillan) 1964
Design for Dancers (Wright) 1964
The Firebird (Cranko) 1964
Bouquet Garni (Cranko) 1963
Allegro Brillante (Balanchine) 1965
La Valse (Balanchine) 1965
Jeu de Cartes (Cranko) 1965
Onegin (Cranko) 1965
Opus I (Cranko) 1965
Song of the Earth (MacMillan) 1965
Danses Concertantes (MacMillan) 1965
Concerto for Flute and Harp (Cranko) 1966
Giselle (Wright from Coralli/Perrot) 1966
The Nutcracker (Cranko) 1966
Apollon Musagète (Balanchine) 1967
The Question (Cranko) 1967
Oiseaux Exotiques (Cranko) 1967
Quatre Images (Cranko) 1967
Holberg Suite Pas de Deux (Cranko) 1967
Namouna (Wright) 1967
Fragmente (Cranko) 1968
Présence (Cranko) 1968
Separate Journeys (Neumeier) 1968

Kyrie Eleison (Cranko) 1968
The Sphinx (MacMillan) 1968
Salade (Cranko) 1968
The Taming of the Shrew (Cranko) 1969
Brouillards (Cranko) 1970
Miss Julie (MacMillan) 1970
Poème de l'Extase (Cranko) 1970
Agon (Balanchine) 1970
Orpheus (Cranko) 1970
Paradox (Kylián) 1970
Cou, Coudres, Corps et Coeurs (Cranko) 1970
Adagio (Clauss) 1970
Raymonda Pas de Deux (Beale) 1970
Ballade (Cranko) 1970
Ebony Concerto (Cranko) 1970
Coming and Going (Kylián) 1970
Carmen (Cranko) 1971
Initials R.B.M.E. (Cranko) 1972
Legende (Cranko) 1972
Green (Cranko) 1973
Traces (Cranko) 1973
Concerto (MacMillan) 1973
Arena (Tetley) 1973
Voluntaries (Tetley) 1973
Blaue Haut (Kylián) 1974
Ritual Album (Berg) 1974
Pineapple Poll (Cranko) 1974
Les Noces (Nijinska) 1974
Gemini (Tetley) 1975
Mythical Hunters (Tetley) 1975
Laborintus (Tetley) 1975
Song of the Earth (MacMillan) 1975
Intermezzo (Feld)
Return from a Foreign Land (Kylián) 1975
Daphnis and Chloë (Tetley) 1975
Greening (Tetley) 1975
Pierrot Lunaire (Tetley) 1975
Alegrias (Tetley) 1975
Symphony in C (Balanchine) 1976
Anastasia (MacMillan) 1976
Le Sacre du Printemps (Tetley) 1976
Songs of a Traveller (Béjart) 1976
Pas de Deux (Ursuliak) 1976
Pavane (MacMillan) 1976
Nuages (Kylián) 1976
The Hamlet Case (Neumeier) 1976
Requiem (MacMillan) 1976

Touring

Regular tours to the United States and through Europe and a successful visit to the USSR.

The Hamburg State Opera Ballet

Ballet has always had an important and special place in the history of the Hamburg Opera. The first Hamburg Opera House was opened in 1678 and had the distinction of being the first in Germany. The opening performance was a typically spectacular baroque production and included a ballet intermezzo. Many subsequent operas included ballets and old theatre bills also advertised dance performances to music by the opera composers of the time – Lully, Keiser and Telemann. Pantomimes too featured dance at the Opera House.

By the middle of the eighteenth century Italian Opera had become very popular. These continued to include ballet and separate dance performances were often part of the evenings' programmes. Friedrich Ludwig Schröder, the opera principal, was himself trained as a dancer. In 1769 he took charge of the ballet company and began to create new works for which there was considerable public demand. His first ballet was *Don Juan*, probably derived from Christopher Willibald Gluck's dance drama created in 1761 for the Vienna Court Opera. By 1782 the company had a repertoire of 14 ballets of which it had given 74 performances, about one-third of the number of opera and play performances.

The nineteenth century brought the great developments of romantic ballet which spread across Europe from Italy and France. The Hamburg Opera presented ballets to the music of Wranitzky, Hérold, Milon and Auber. In 1838 the company, under the direction of two ballet masters, Teschner and Benoni, consisted of eight soloists, three women and five men, and a corps of 20 women, ten of whom were pupils. In that year, the celebrated Maria Taglioni visited Hamburg and appeared in the ballet *Le Dieu et la Bayadère*, created by her father, Filippo Taglioni, to music by Auber in 1830. Two months later Lucile Grahn, at that time prima ballerina of the Royal Danish Ballet, danced the same role at the Hamburg Opera House. It was the success of this visit, and an earlier one to Paris, that precipitated the quarrel with

August Bournonville which led to her departure from Denmark and her international career. She remained a great favourite in Germany and when she retired from the stage she became Ballet Mistress at the Leipzig State Theatre and, later, Munich Hofoper where she created many opera-ballets.

The distinguished list of guest artists at the Hamburg Opera included Fanny Cerrito and her equally famous husband Arthur Saint-Léon in 1840 appearing in *La Sylphide*. The cast also included Carlotta Grisi and the remarkable Price family. When Fanny Elssler appeared in 1845, Hamburg audiences could boast that they had seen the four greatest ballerinas of the time and this fact could not fail to stimulate public interest and serve as an inspiration for the company. Fanny Elssler later worked as a choreographer, preparing performances of *Giselle* and *Pas de Quatre* – a divertissement created by Jules Perrot and performed in London by the remarkable cast of Maria Taglioni, Fanny Cerrito, Lucile Grahn and Fanny Elssler. When she retired from the stage, Fanny Elssler continued to live, for many years, in the city where she enjoyed such triumph.

During this period, dance activity was at a peak in Hamburg. Afterwards the ballet company began to decline in importance although it never reached the very low level which characterized the opera-ballets of so many European countries at this time. From 1865 to 1930 the dancers were mainly incorporated into the opera repertoire and grand opera in particular made great demands on the ballet company. One or two evenings each season were devoted exclusively to ballet when works like *Die Puppenfee* and *Coppélia* were performed.

Olga Brandt-Knaack took over the leadership of the company, now called a dance group, after World War I. Under her direction the Hamburg Ballet became a centre for expressionist dance. In 1932, Helga Swedlund was appointed Ballet Mistress, and she immediately set about extending both the classical and contemporary repertoire – a notable success was *The Firebird*. She spent World War II in Vienna but returned to Hamburg in 1946 and staged *Noblissima Visione* (*St Francis*), *Rondo of the Golden Calf* and the Bavarian State Opera's version of *Hamlet*. In 1957 Gustav Blank became the Ballet Director. At this time Hamburg again became a dance centre in Germany and was visited by many international stars and major companies

John Neumeier was appointed Artistic Director of the Hamburg State Opera Ballet in 1973. He immediately set about producing new versions of the great ballet classics. Whilst retaining much of the essence of the originals, his approach is unusual and often controversial. Here, the company performs The Nutcracker *with Max Midinet as Ballet Master Drosselmeier.*

– The Bolshoi Theatre Ballet with Galina Ulanova, the Finnish Opera Ballet, the American Ballet Theatre with Nora Kaye and Erik Bruhn, Janine Charrat's Company, Britain's Royal Ballet and the London Festival Ballet.

In 1962 George Balanchine and the New York City Ballet visited Hamburg. To celebrate Igor Stravinsky's eightieth birthday, soloists of the New York City Ballet and members of the Hamburg Ballet gave a performance of *Apollon Musagète*. In the following year, the Hamburg Ballet incorporated a number of George Balanchine's works into its repertoire – *Concerto Barocco, Serenade, Four Temperaments, Symphony in C, Scotch Symphony, Orpheus, La Valse* and *Agon*.

Peter van Dyk became Ballet Director in 1962. From then until he left in 1970 he worked to extend the repertoire to include the major classics – *Swan Lake, Romeo and Juliet, Cinderella, Giselle*. He also presented *Pelleas and Melisande, Unfinished Symphony, Abraxas, Poème* and *Pinocchio*. The company also began to tour during this time, visting Spain, Italy, France and Switzerland. The soloists included Jacqueline Rayet, Dulce Anaya, Marilyn Burr, Christa Kempf, Nina Vyroubova, Maria Tallchief, Heinz Clauss, Rainer Köchermann and Peter van Dyk. Under Sonia Arova's leadership from 1971 to 1973, two of Glen Tetley's works were added to the repertoire – *Circles* and *Threshold*.

At the beginning of the 1973/4 season, John Neumeier was appointed Ballet Director and this marked a new period of dance activity for the Hamburg

John Neumeier has also developed contemporary abstract ballets. His work, The Third Symphony of Gustav Mahler *was premièred in June 1975.*

Ballet. Born in the United States, he completed his training at the Royal Ballet School in London. After he was seen in a class by Ray Barra, he was invited to join the Stuttgart Ballet – Ray Barra was, at that time a principal dancer with the Stuttgart Ballet. With the Noverre Society, a choreography workshop associated with the Stuttgart Ballet, John Neumeier was able to create new ballets under the guidance of John Cranko who hated *Haiku* but was very enthusiastic about *Separate Journeys*.

In 1968 he was invited by Lawrence Rhodes to create a new work for the Harkness Ballet and the result was *Stages and Reflections*. The success of this and of his work in Stuttgart prompted an invitation to become the Artistic Director of the Frankfurt Opera Ballet. He remained with the Frankfurt Ballet until 1973 building up a new repertoire and establishing the company in a way that compares with the early days of John Cranko's remarkable achievements at Stuttgart. Among the works he created at that time are his own controversial versions of *The Firebird*, *Invisible Frontiers*, *The Fairy's Kiss*, *Daphnis and Chloë* and *Romeo and Juliet*.

When he joined the Hamburg Opera Ballet he again set about building up a company with a firm basis in classical training. The great classics – *Romeo and Juliet*, *The Nutcracker* and *Swan Lake* – were newly staged. The development of new choreography is considered equally important. John Neumeier has instituted a series of matinées where members of the company can try out their own works. Also in his desire to establish a closer contact between the company and the public he has organized a workshop which aims to introduce the history of dance and give insight into the process of conceiving and preparing a new ballet performance.

In his first season at Hamburg he was called the 'Balletwunder von Hamburg', the ballet wonder of Hamburg. Once again, under John Neumeier's direction Hamburg has become a dance centre in Germany, giving 70 highly popular performances each season. It has also achieved considerable success abroad. A versatile and valuable repertoire has attracted a new and knowledgeable public which in turn stimulates further exciting developments in the company.

The Company
Artistic Director: John Neumeier

Principal Dancers:

Beatrice Cordua	Max Midinet
Eugen Ivanics	Persephone
François Klaus	Samaropoulo
Marianne Kruuse	Tanju Tüzer
Magali Messac	

The Repertoire

Romeo and Juliet (Neumeier)	*Le Sacre* (Neumeier)
The Nutcracker (Neumeier)	*Petrouchka Variations*
Swan Lake (Neumeier)	*Jeu de Cartes* (Cranko)
Meyerbeer/Schumann (Neumeier)	*Allegro Brillante* (Balanchine)
Third Symphony of Gustav Mahler (Neumeier)	*Divertimento No. 15* (Balanchine)
Ruckert-Lieder (Neumeier)	*Silence* (Neumeier)
Trauma (Neumeier)	*Agon* (Balanchine)
Rondo (Neumeier)	*Les Noces* (Robbins)
Daphnis and Chloë (Neumeier)	*Orpheus* (Howard)
Dämmern (Neumeier)	*Macrocosmos* (Neumeier)
Désir (Neumeier)	*Don Juan* (Neumeier)

Touring   Israel, Italy, Paris, Spain, France.

The Ballet of the German Berlin Opera

Until 1945 Berlin was the cultural focus of Germany, in ballet as in the other areas. Activities outside the capital were regarded as provincial and, perhaps unfairly, as inferior. In 1925, the teacher and choreographer, Tatiana Gsovska, trained both in Moscow and St Petersburg, went to Berlin. Four years later she opened a ballet school and several outstanding German dancers were trained by her – Gisela Deege, Maria Fris, Rainer Köcherman, Erwin Bredow and Peter van Dijk. The upheavals of World War II and the political complications which followed, disrupted the development of German ballet. Berlin continued to be central but the most important activities concerned the famous German State Opera Unter den Linden, in East Berlin, under the leadership of Tatiana Gsovska.

In West Berlin, the State Opera maintained a ballet company but, as is so often the case, it was only of secondary importance. Jens Keith and Gustav Blank were Ballet Masters from 1945 to 1949 and from 1949 to 1957 respectively. However, during this period, the status of the ballet company did not attract the most talented dancers and contemporary choreographers and consequently, growth and development were slight.

Tatiana Gsovska left the East German company in 1952 and, for a year, she was the Ballet Mistress at the Teatro Colón in Buenos Aires. She returned to Germany in 1953 and settled in West Berlin where she immediately began teaching. Shortly afterwards she founded the Berliner Ballett, a chamber company which rapidly established a major reputation. By the late 1950s it was making extensive and frequent tours throughout Europe and also visited both North and South America.

Tatiana Gsovska had also become associated with the State Opera Ballet. From 1954 she had acted as choreographer and later she became Ballet Mistress. In 1961 the Berliner Ballett and the State Opera company amalgamated and moved into a new building in the Bismarckstrasse. In 1962, Gert Reinholm, an exceptional dancer and close collaborator with Tatiana Gsovska in the Berliner Ballett, took over the leadership of the Ballet of the German Berlin Opera.

Tatiana Gsovska must take the credit for the direction and development which the company has followed. Firmly rooted in classicism, she pursued her own particular course and, at the same time, sought new material and new forms of expression. Even today her powerful influence extends over both the German and international dance scene. She is now the Director of the ballet school.

In 1966 she was succeeded as choreographer by the British Royal Ballet's Kenneth MacMillan who further extended the company's range, experience and tradition. In 1969, the leadership of the company returned to Gert Reinholm, assisted by John Taras from 1971 to 1972. A number of international figures were invited to Berlin as guest choreographers including Heinz Rosen, Erich Walter, Mary Wigman, David Lichine, Antony Tudor, Serge Lifar, Brian Macdonald, Dick Sanders, John Cranko, Sir Frederick Ashton and George Balanchine. Most recently the Dutch choreographers Hans van Manen and Rudi van Dantzig have worked with the company. Gert Reinholm has also invited foreign choreographers who have not yet achieved major international recognition to create new works for the company. These include László Seregi from Hungary, Nikolai Bojartschikow from the USSR, Conrad Drzewiecki from Poland and Ulf Gadd from Sweden. In addition, young German choreographers are encouraged.

Lilo Herbeth and guest star Eva Evdokimova are pictured in The Sleeping Beauty. *The ballet is by Kenneth MacMillan, Artistic Director of the Royal Ballet, London, who used much of Petipa's original choreography.*

The Ballet of the German Berlin Opera aims at a varied repertoire presenting a wide range of styles. It organizes its programmes, whenever possible, to present a combination of traditional ballets, works created especially for the company and the best of contemporary choreography. Undoubtedly the traditional repertoire is the most popular and includes *Giselle*, *The Sleeping Beauty*, *Swan Lake* and *Les Sylphides*. The work of George Balanchine is represented by such ballets as *Apollon Musagète*, *Symphony in C*, *Episodes* and *Serenade* and these too, have proved enormously popular. Great interest has been shown in the works of contemporary choreographers and particularly successful are Kenneth MacMillan's *Concerto*, *Anastasia* and *Cain and Abel*, John Cranko's *Firebird* and Ulf Gadd's *The Miraculous Mandarin*. The company has worked hard to build up a repertoire that would establish it as an important part of the international dance scene. At the same time the dancers have extended their range and developed a technical expertise enabling them to transfer effortlessly from the great romantic ballets of the nineteenth century to the extraordinary physical demands of modern dance. The range of dance vocabulary from Petipa to Murray Louis has given the Ballet of the German Berlin Opera its particular quality and its greatest strength, placing Berlin, once again, as a major cultural centre in the country.

Hans van Manen, the contemporary Dutch choreographer, was recently invited to Berlin to stage his ballet Adagio Hammerklavier *for the the Ballet of the German Berlin Opera. The dancers are Heidrun Schwaarz and Rheda Sheta, Dianne Bell and Klaus Beelitz and Eva Evdokimova and Lawrence Rhodes.*

The Company

Ballet Leader:	Gert Reinholm
Ballet Director:	Michael Heise
Ballet Mistress:	Gudrun Leben
Dance Teachers:	Cora Benador
	Gabriel Popescu

Principal Dancers:

Dianne Bell	Lilo Herbeth	Jeanne-Pierre Liégeois
Didi Carli	Rheda Sheta	Michael Tietz
Monika Radamm	Klaus Beelitz	Bernard Hourseau
Heidrun Schwaarz	Joan Lohan	
Hannelore Peters	Igor Kosak	

Coryphées:

Felicitas Binder	Maria Gisladottir	David Roland
Charlotte Butler	Julio Guinez	Jörge Schmalz
Lynda Forsythe	Alfonso Pinero	

The Repertoire

Adagio Hammerklavier (van Manen)
Apollon Musagète (Balanchine)
Bolero (Béjart)
Calligraph for Martyrs (Louis)
Concerto (MacMillan)
Coppélia (Pares)
Daphnis and Chloë (van Manen)
Death and the Maiden (Walter)
Episodes (Balanchine)
Four Temperaments (Balanchine)
Gala Performance (Tudor)
Giselle (Coralli/Tudor)
Kindertotenlieder (Casado)
La Bayadère (Memlies after Petipa)
Las Hermanas (MacMillan)
La Valse (Balanchine)
Metaphors (van Manen)

Monument for a Dead Boy (van Dantzig)
Opus I (Cranko)
Pelleas and Melisande (Walter)
Petrouchka (Taras)
Raymonda (Gsovska/Beriosoff)
Romeo and Juliet (Bojartschikow)
Serenade (Balanchine)
Swan Lake (MacMillan after Ivanov/Petipa)
Symphony in C (Balanchine)
The Firebird (Fokine/Cranko)
The Invitation (MacMillan)
The Miraculous Mandarin (Gadd)
The Moor of Venice (Drzewiecki)
The Nutcracker (Balanchine)
The Sleeping Beauty (Macmillan after Petipa)
The Wooden Prince (Seregi)
Three and Sixteen (Shortemeier/Baumann)

SOVIET RUSSIA

The Bolshoi Ballet is the largest company in the world and is as renowned in the West as it is in Soviet countries. It is well known for its splendid stagings of the great classics, such as Swan Lake, *shown here.* Many of these works were created in the days of Imperial Russia and were nearly lost forever in the years following the October Revolution in 1917.

Imperial traditions

There can be few people in the western world, even among those who have no special interest in dance, who have not heard of the Bolshoi Ballet or who are not familiar with the names, at least, of the great works of the Russian Ballet Masters, such as *Swan Lake*, *The Sleeping Beauty* and *The Nutcracker*. Most of the classical companies in the world feature some of these works in their repertoires and all owe an immense debt to the development of ballet in Russia. To understand how this came about and to appreciate the continuity and changes which have taken place in Soviet Ballet, it is essential to investigate dance activity in the days of Imperial Russia.

Russia has a long and continuing tradition of folk dance which, over the centuries, assimilated and adopted the styles of many foreign invaders, establishing a unique national quality. Even in the early folk tradition, the essence of Russian ballet, something quite separate from the French and Italian heritage, can be seen in the close musical structure and the use of the entire body as a dance instrument. Groups of professional dancers existed as early as the fourteenth century, sometimes itinerant and sometimes resident in the homes of the nobility. After an edict issued in 1551 by the church, a

Maria Petipa, daughter of Marius Petipa, created the role of the Lilac Fairy in the original version of The Sleeping Beauty, *with choreography by her father. She was not a particularly fine dancer but she was a talented and dramatic actress. She appears to have been dressed for the role in shoes with heels, a custom which had disappeared from the stage many years previously. This suggests that the original Lilac Fairy was not the lovely dance role it has now become in contemporary versions of this charming ballet.*

long period of persecution deprived many of them of their livelihood, although many princes still kept private theatres and companies of serf dancers.

The first Romanov emperor, Mikhail, set up an amusement room in his palace where he was entertained by acrobatics and dancing – an association which has figured importantly in the history of Russian and Soviet dance. In 1629, Ivan Lodigin, a 'German' dancer (in Imperial Russia, 'German' denoted any foreigner) was employed to teach children to perform and they, in turn, became court entertainers. This seems to be the earliest dance 'school'. The first record of a ballet performance is of *Orpheus and Eurydice*, ordered by Mikhail's son, Alexei. It took place in Preobrazhenskoye, a village near Moscow, on February 8, 1673. The ballet included singing and speech and was, apparently, danced in the French manner. As only one week was allowed for preparation, it seems likely that models were already in existence in Russia. The Czar was delighted, not leaving the performance for 10 hours and, as a result, ordered children to be trained.

With Alexei's death in 1676, theatrical activity came to an end until Peter the Great founded a theatre room in the Kremlin, which was used until the capital was moved to St Petersburg. Dancing masters were engaged at the court and also by noble families. Peter the Great was also interested in western social dancing and held magnificent assemblies which finally put an end to the exclusive association between dancing and the lower classes.

At this time, dancing was quite crude. The first professional court ballet took place on January 29, 1736 as part of the opera *La Forza dell'amore*. Over 100 dancers appeared and these were mainly Russian, the majority of whom were pupils at the military school, the Corps des Cadets. They had been trained for two years by dancing masters under the leadership of Jean Baptiste Landé who later founded the Imperial Ballet School at St Petersburg, which opened in 1738.

Jean Baptiste Landé requested permission to open a school and it began with 24 children of palace servants who were taught in two rooms in his house. It was later moved to a wing of the palace at St Petersburg. Landé reckoned that his pupils would require three years training before they could make court appearances. Many of the students made quick progress and were soon appearing beside Italian guest artists. Frequent ballet performances took place in St Petersburg and both comic ballets, derived from the Commedia dell'Arte, and serious works from classical mythology were presented.

Allegory was very popular. In 1742, as part of the celebrations for the coronation of Elisaveta in Moscow, two ballets were given, entitled *The Joy of the People on the Occasion of Astreia's Appearance on the Russian Horizon and the Re-Establishment of the Golden Age* and *The Golden Apple at the Feast of the Gods and the Judgement of Paris*. These were presented at a theatre erected specially for the occasion very near the site of the Bolshoi Theatre.

The Moscow Orphanage was founded in 1764 for children under the age of four. As they grew up, it was decided that they should be taught dancing in addition to crafts and their ordinary education. In 1773, the Italian dancing master, Filippo Beccari, was appointed to teach them. This proved very successful and one-third of the orphans became professional dancers in Moscow and St Petersburg.

It was about this time that the ideas of the reformer Jean Georges Noverre began to filter through to Russia. In 1759, the Austrian choreographer Franz Hilferding van Weven went to St Petersburg. Already famous for his abolition of masks on the Austrian stage, he was deeply interested in dramatic action and mime in the same way as Noverre. He created many ballets in Russia, some of which were based on mythology – *Cupid and Psyche, Apollo and Daphne* – and some comic – *The Lame Cavalier, The Isle of Fools*. In many of these he used folk dances, incorporating them into the action. The dancers were a mixture of Russians and foreign guests.

Franz Hilferding van Weven's successor was his pupil Gasparo Angiolini who went to St Petersburg from Vienna in 1776, at the request of the Empress Catherine II. His first work was a ballet pantomime in the opera *Didone Abbandonata*. This was very successful and was staged frequently at the ends of other operas. Angiolini mounted many ballets d'action in both St Petersburg and Moscow, including earlier works on which he had collaborated with Gluck in Vienna. He returned to Russia three times, finally leaving in 1786. He was a bitter opponent of Noverre, ridiculing the detailed programme notes of his story ballets. The controversy was personal rather than artistic, for the two men had much in common aesthetically.

His successor was Charles le Picq, Noverre's favourite pupil. He brought many of his teacher's ballets to Russia, although he often failed to credit his source. His own creations lacked Noverre's depth and he was more inclined towards spectacle, which was very popular.

In St Petersburg, ballets tended to be more serious than in Moscow where the atmosphere was less restricted because it was not under Court Ministry. Giovanni Locatelli had founded a theatre at St Petersburg where mythological and comic ballets and pantomime were performed. The theatre was open to the public and was very successful, particularly because great rivalry existed between the two leading dancers and their followings. Success at St Petersburg encouraged him to open a similar theatre in Moscow. Gradually interest waned and foreign dancers became the fashion. Locatelli returned to St Petersburg but interest had faded there too. Finally he returned to Moscow where he managed the University Ballet Company. Artistic circles in Moscow were much freer and more enlightened than in the capital. Moscow University had two ballet schools, one for the sons of nobles and the other for a mixture of social groups. The university theatre staged operas, comedies and dramas, mainly with the pupils of the second school. By 1757, women were invited to take part. In 1761 many of the best Moscow artists were transferred to St Petersburg, very nearly destroying the company.

The rising popularity of theatrical activity meant that many new theatres were built. In the 1770s, the Englishman, Michael Maddox, went to Moscow to demonstrate 'mechanical and physical wonders'. In conjunction with Prince Urusov he ran the Znamensky Theatre which, from 1776, gave regular ballet performances. As the direct descendant of this company, the Bolshoi Ballet dates its existence from 1776. In 1780 the Znamensky Theatre burned down, destroying the costumes and properties. Michael Maddox became a Russian citizen, changing his name to Mikhail Yegorovitch Maddox. He invested in a new theatre, called the Petrovsky, named after Petrovska Street which still runs beside the Bolshoi Theatre building. It was opened in 1780 and was one of the best in Europe until it was burned down in 1805. The repertoire was much to the taste of Moscow audiences. Much of it was by Russian authors and serious ballets were performed, although most of the repertoire was comic and based on Italian models, often interpreted in Russian folk dance. In 1784, the ballet school of the Orphanage was placed under Maddox's management and became a permanent school for theatrical training.

Serf dancers still existed, trained in private theatres and then frequently sold to the St Petersburg Theatre and other companies. These were highly trained professionals with foreign ballet masters. Serf dancers kept the folk tradition alive but their existences were extremely hard and they were often obliged to work in the fields as well as dancing. When the fashion for serf dancers ended in the nineteenth century, many were sold as ordinary labourers.

By the start of the nineteenth century, a Russian ballet was developing strongly. Ballet and opera were accessible for everyone who could afford a ticket and seats in the 'gods' (called *rayok*) were cheap. Theatres were no longer dependent on the private enterprise of such people as Maddox. Imperial theatres had been established by Catherine II in 1756, but these had remained primarily court entertainments in the eighteenth century. By the nineteenth century, however, more public city theatres were appearing. The Imperial Theatres of Moscow were founded in 1806. The new Bolshoi Petrovsky Theatre was even larger and better equipped than the one it replaced, which had burned down. Bolshoi, incidentally, means grand or big but not, as sometimes erroneously thought, great. Foreign artists were very fashionable and were paid more than Russians. Native artists were very badly treated and open to summary arrest if they offended the Director in any way.

In 1807, Ivan Valberkh was sent to Moscow as Ballet Master. He had danced in many of Le Picq's ballets and was familiar with ballet d'action. He carried the idea further with dramatic ballets and convincing characters based on history and literature. The works were still tied to eighteenth century conventions in that they were heavy and full of pantomime, but they were moving towards the future romanticism of the later part of the nineteenth century, in their feel and emotion, Ivan Valberkh was dancer, choreographer, Ballet Master and Ballet Inspector, a managerial post, for which he was paid a paltry salary considerably less than that of Canziani who was only the head of the school. He augmented his salary by translating French melodramas into Russian, incidentally discovering a rich source for plots for ballets, including a version of *Romeo and Juliet*. He also created contemporary tragic ballets and a number of patriotic works during the Napoleonic invasion. It was due to Ivan Valberkh's efforts that, when Charles Didelot arrived in St Petersburg, he found a highly-trained professional company and a well-organized school. Ivan Valberkh was appointed Director of the School and Inspector of the company at the St Petersburg Bolshoi Theatre in 1794. The Directorate of Imperial Theatres, whose main contribution to the development of ballet in Imperial Russia seems to have been unrelieved interference, attempted to introduce a policy whereby the ballet pupils should also learn to sing, paint sets and play in the orchestra. Ivan Valberkh fought strenuously for a long time to prevent this and eventually succeeded. When the Directorate of Moscow Theatres took over the Orphanage School, Valberkh was invited to organize it. He died of tuberculosis four months after his retirement in 1819.

Charles Didelot's ambitions were directed towards the Paris Opera but, although he made a successful debut there in 1788, feelings of envy and jealousy prevented him from becoming a permanent member. He accepted a three year contract with the St Petersburg company because it offered to pay him more than any other company, fully intending to return to Paris. He had been very successful in London, where he created several works, including *Flore et Zéphire*, but conditions had proved unsatisfactory and remuneration inadequate.

In St Petersburg he found the opera house well equipped with a deep stage suitable for the aerial flights for which his ballets were famed. Not only could the dancers 'fly' across the stage but they could also 'fly' from the front to the back. The Bolshoi Theatre in St Petersburg was built in 1783 as the Kamenny Theatre. It was rebuilt more grandly in 1802, but its classical style was retained. It was at this time, it acquired the name Bolshoi. It burned down in 1811, the year Charles Didelot completed his first visit to Russia, but was rebuilt in 1818 and so was available during his second visit, from 1816 to 1837. At first, all kinds of performances were given, including ballet,

opera and drama. After a further rebuilding in 1836, when the ceiling was raised to accommodate more machinery, it was used exclusively for opera and ballet. In 1889, it was declared unsafe and rebuilt by the Russian Musical Society. From 1889, all ballet performances took place at the Maryinsky Theatre only, which had been built in 1860.

The first works staged by Charles Didelot were based on familiar mythological subjects – *Apollo and Daphne* and *The Shepherd and The Hamadryads*. However, they were new in that he dispensed with court dress, wigs and buckled shoes for shepherds and dressed them, instead, in gauze tunics, their arms and shoulders bare and their feet in soft slippers. The poetic quality of the ballets and their lack of false opulence charmed the audiences of St Petersburg. He restaged his London success *Flore et Zéphire* as *Zéphire et Flore* with the virtuoso dancer Duport, famed for his spectacular elevation. The scope of the work was extended and the dance became central rather than the 'flying' cupids and so on mainly because of Duport's leaps.

Charles Didelot admired the ability of Russian dancers to project themselves into the character of the roles they danced. He repeatedly refused to encourage the Directorate in its determination to use guest artists in preference to Russian dancers. He also created many parts for children. There was a lot of youthful talent at the school but re-organization was essential before big ballets could be created. When Charles Didelot took over the school, he proved a strict teacher of technique and a thorough teacher of acting through facial and bodily expression.

On December 31, 1810, Charles Didelot suddenly left St Petersburg. His reason for going is not certain but it may have been because the Bolshoi Theatre had just burned down or because his salary was being paid in paper money rather than gold, thus reducing its value. He may just have decided to try his luck in Paris again. After leaving Russia, Charles Didelot spent two years in London and then he went to Paris where he still encountered hostility. In spite of Gardel, he managed to stage *Flore et Zéphire* which became a classic model with 189 performances and in which Maria Taglioni later danced. Disillusioned and frustrated by the Paris Opera, Charles Didelot returned to St Petersburg. This time, however, he could dictate his own terms.

During the next 15 years he revised a number of former successes and created new works. Several major dancers emerged during this period who firmly established the foundations of Russian ballet style. Charles Didelot revived *The Hungarian Hut* which had been very popular when it was originally staged in London. Although it contained a strong element of pantomime, it had dramatic conviction, mixing comedy and tragedy. This was followed by the major creation *Raoul de Créquis or The Return from the Crusades*. This was a tense, romantic drama which well demonstrated Didelot's mastery of theatrical effect. Although he always believed that music was of secondary importance to the choreography, he was an extremely musical choreographer and expected his dancers to be so too. His close collaboration with the composer Catarino Cavos was a contributory factor in the success of this work.

Another very popular trend in the ballets of this period was towards the oriental. Within this genre Didelot created *The Prisoner of the Caucasus*, and vastly extended the range of 'eastern' ballets. The work was based on a poem by Alexander Pushkin and, in fact, appeared only four and a half months after its publication. It differed from the poem in several ways – it was set in ninth century Russia and the story was given a happy ending. However, the romantic spirit of the poem was retained and Pushkin, who had, by this time, been exiled, expressed deep interest in the ballet. The role of the Circassian girl was danced by Ardotia Istomina, and both she and Charles Didelot were immortalized in Pushkin's famous work *Eugene Onegin*.

The Prisoner of the Caucasus was Charles Didelot's last major work and its creation was followed by a period of intense persecution by the Directorate of the Imperial Theatres. It has been suggested by Russian ballet historians that this was the result of Didelot's identification with Russian cultural life at a time when foreign artists alone were appreciated by the court. Prince Gagarin, in particular, led the offensive against Charles Didelot, characterized by petty insults and constant interference. Pupils trained by Didelot were sent to work in dramatic theatres and the school's training programme was altered giving ballet a far more subordinate position. Eventually Charles Didelot was arrested for refusing to obey an order to shorten the interval during a performance of *Thésée et Arianne*. This final insult was followed by more than a year's argument and fuss, yet Charles Didelot retained his immense popularity with both the public and the dancers. In 1833, after a revival of *The Hungarian Hut*, which received a 15 minute ovation, the dancers paid tribute to Charles Didelot in spite of the wrath of the Directorate. After this he led a life of enforced retirement, which he hated, and died in 1837.

The next major figure to emerge and a true heir to Charles Didelot was Adam Gluszkowski. He graduated from the school in St Petersburg in 1809 and joined the company. Three years later he was sent to Moscow where, with unassuming modesty and great industry, he worked until 1839, creating many divertissements based on the Russian folk heritage. Premier danseur, head of the school and principal Ballet Master at the Bolshoi Theatre, he never lost his admiration for Charles Didelot, many of whose ballets he revived and staged in Moscow.

By this time, the fundamental principles of romantic ballet had become established in Russia. Partly this was due to the composer Glinka, whose developments with symphonic form and interest in dance had formed a link to romantic ballet. He was however, ahead of his time and generally suffered from inadequate choreography. In 1837, Maria Taglioni visited St Petersburg, where she danced *La Sylphide* to public acclaim, but some critical doubts. Audiences missed the dramatic quality to which Didelot had accustomed them, and content has always been of major importance in the development of Russian ballet. After her initial visit, Maria Taglioni returned for five seasons from September to Lent, giving 200 performances on alternate days. However, she never visited Moscow. The purity of her movement and the delicate blending of principals and corps de ballet in Filippo Taglioni's choreography appealed to Russian audiences. By 1842, her popularity had declined and, although she wished to remain in St Petersburg as a teacher, she left Russia permanently.

Meanwhile, Russian ballerinas benefited from the influence of European romanticism. Yelena Andreyanova, who had been singled out by Maria Taglioni as particularly promising, danced *Giselle* in 1842, reproduced from the Paris Opera version. She was a very popular and extremely gifted dancer, managing with ease the difficult transition in mood from Act I to Act II. She created many romantic roles in Russia including the title role of *La Péri* and Bertha in *Le Diable à Quatre*. In 1847, she partnered Petipa in *Paquita* for his St Petersburg debut and she also visited Moscow, Paris and London.

In 1848, Fanny Elssler visited Moscow and St Petersburg, dancing *La Esmeralda* and *La Fille Mal Gardée*, as well as an unsuccessful performance of *Giselle* to which she was not really suited. She was especially popular in Moscow and introduced to Russia the other aspect of romantic ballet, the warm and emotional aspect rather than the lyrical and ethereal. Russia also had a ballerina comparable to Fanny Elssler in Yekaterina Sanskovskaya, a deeply moving dancer who was adored by the public.

Jules Perrot worked with the St Petersburg company during the 1850s where he also found the opportunity to dance character roles. He produced his version of *Giselle*, not in partnership with Coralli, during this time. Carlotta Grisi gave a magnificent performance of this in 1850, but the public missed the drama of Yelena Andreyanova's interpretation of the role. Jules Perrot was forced to retire in 1859.

By this time there was a complete lack of artistic freedom and the Directorate expected ballet masters to produce spectacles to order. In 1859, Arthur Saint-Léon offered his services as Ballet Master and was quite willing to stage a continuous supply of new ballets, many of which were, in fact, old ones renovated. Most of his works were protracted divertissements and he was quite hopeless at creating dances for large groups and the corps de ballet. Jules Perrot had been dependent on inspiration, but Saint-Léon created ballets to order. It would be wrong to suppose he lacked talent but he was forced to work at a tremendous rate and consequently, he borrowed freely from every available source, including national dances. His main concern and that of the Directorate was to present a succession of new tricks. The superficiality of his work did not appeal to Moscow audiences and even in St Petersburg the lack of content provoked criticism. During this time major social and literary changes were taking place and cultural circles found much to despise in ballet and lost interest in it.

One of Saint-Léon's chief works was the awful *The Hump-Backed Horse*. Strangely, it became very popular and remained in the repertoire for many years. Constant changes and revisions improved it, particularly those of Petipa in 1895 and Gorsky in 1901. It was the Bolshoi company which finally turned it into a Russian ballet, insisting that the emphasis should be on the male role, which was danced by an exceptional dancer with a tremendous talent for mime, Vassily Geltser. In addition to constant revisions of the choreography of *The Hump-Backed Horse*, more music was added and finally 18 composers were represented in the work. Although Saint-Léon was not responsible for the decline of ballet in Russia at this time, he certainly contributed to it. That he did not lack talent or imagination can be seen from his most famous work, *Coppélia*, which he created in Paris after leaving Russia. The idiocy of the Directorate and the absence of any outstanding choreographers almost destroyed Russian ballet, but the tenacity of the dancers and the excellent foundations of the schools, particularly in Moscow which was further from official interference, provided an element of continuity. The Bolshoi company, however, did suffer from having to perform the St Petersburg repertoire.

Blasis went to Moscow where he stayed from 1861 to 1864 but his creative powers were already declining. Although the ballets he staged were unremarkable, his teaching was valuable and he assisted in the designing of the new school building which opened in 1866. In the following years some remarkable dancers, such as Sergei Sokolov, emerged but no outstanding choreographers.

In 1878, Tchaikovsky began work on *Swan Lake*, based on a theme common in Russian folklore and which he had had in mind for many years. Rehearsals began in March 1876 at the Bolshoi Theatre in Moscow. Tickets for the première on February 20, 1877 were completely sold out. However, the Ballet Master, Wenzel Reisinger, was quite incapable of the choreography. With the exception of two national dances, probably created by a member of the company, the choreography was disastrous and the work was a catastrophic failure. The ballet continued to endure appalling choreography well into the 1880s.

The great name of Russian ballet in the last half of the nineteenth century was Marius Petipa. He was the grand master, although he never learnt a word of the language. He began his career, young and unknown, in St Petersburg and became premier danseur, making his debut in *Paquita*. He was versatile, good at mime and acting, and a completely reliable partner—he partnered Fanny Elssler when she visited Russia. He acted as assistant to Jules Perrot and staged *Giselle* for Carlotta Grisi under his guidance, although he created some original additions to Act II. He later came under the influence of Saint-Léon and the trend towards strings of divertissements. However, Petipa's divertissements were extraordinarily spectacular including the Grand Pas he added to *Paquita*, using new music by Minkus and a mazurka for 80 pupils, still remembered but no longer performed. Throughout his life, Petipa's work was characterized by the conflict between his search for dramatic material and three-dimensional characters and the exceptionally banal. His first important creation was *Pharoah's Daughter* in 1862. It took six weeks to complete and the music was composed simultaneously. The ballet consisted of strong dramatic scenes interspersed with divertissements and rapidly became very popular. Arthur Saint-Léon was still Ballet Master at this time and seems to have been anxious about Petipa's advancing career. In 1867, he was nearly transferred to Moscow, probably at Saint-Léon's instigation, but financial problems prevented this taking place.

In 1854 he married Maria Surovshchikova shortly after her graduation from the St Petersburg school. As well as a revival of *Pharoah's Daughter*, he created many ballets for her, including *The Blue Dahlia* and *The Beauty of Lebanon*. She had very weak pointes, so he created most of her roles on demi-pointe. Great rivalry existed between her and the ballerina Muravieva. She and Petipa separated in 1869 and her popularity declined rapidly afterwards. In 1882, she died and Marius Petipa regularized his union with the Moscow dancer Savitskaya.

However, earlier in the 1860s, Petipa created *King Candaules* in his search for new, exciting material. The ballet was novel because it ended tragically when the heroine went mad at the sight of her murdered husband's ghost. The première was at Moscow, although a number of St Petersburg fans travelled there especially for it. The ballet provided continuous spectacle, a classical Petipa grand pas, and great demonstrations of virtuosity, including five pirouettes sur la pointe, considered, at that time, a remarkable achievement. It also provided a strange mixture of good and poor taste.

Shortly after *King Candaules*, Saint-Léon left Russia. However, before Petipa could return to St Petersburg and take over the vacant position of Ballet Master, he was required to produce one more major work in Moscow. He created *Don Quixote* to music by Minkus. He knew Moscow audiences well and supplied a logical plot, three-dimensional characters and plenty of colourful dances. The version he staged in St Petersburg, two years later, was quite different. A fifth act was added and the robust comedy scenes were deleted. The remaining scenes were blended together with an academic quality that became characteristic of Petipa's choreography and a valuable development in Russian ballet. By this time Petipa was Ballet Master of the St Petersburg company. He never left any aspect of his choreography to chance but worked out the movements, using models, before rehearsals began. One of Petipa's great strengths was that he constantly created new enchaînments, using an immense classical vocabulary, enabling him to vary mood, tempo and dance quality with apparent ease. He had great skill at handling groups of dancers contrasting or harmonizing dance phrases to create a symphonic form.

Several remarkable dancers were associated with Petipa including the ballerinas Yekaterina Vazem and Yevgenia Sokolova. Both began in the days of Saint-Léon but became true Petipa dancers. He created several ballets for them and they were frequently invited to appear abroad. Yekaterina Vazem later taught Anna Pavlova and Agrippina Vaganova. On her

Marius Petipa is seen here with his son and daughter. He was a primary force in the development of ballet in Imperial Russia and was responsible for the creation of such major works as The Sleeping Beauty *and* Swan Lake, *in conjunction with Lev Ivanov. In spite of his dedication and genius, his final years were spent without honour or recognition by the Directorate of the Imperial Theatres.*

retirement from the stage, Yevgenia Sokolova became Ballet Mistress at the Maryinsky Theatre and taught both Anna Pavlova and Tamara Karsavina. Petipa also created many parts for the Ivanov-trained dancer, Varvara Nikitina, who was a wonderfully lyrical dancer well suited to dramatic roles. She created the role of Princess Florine in the *Bluebird Pas de Deux* with Enrico Cecchetti. She never received the honours due to her because the Directorate vastly underestimated native talent and was besotted with Italian guest artists. Petipa's own daughter, Maria, was also a member of the company. An indifferent dancer, but a splendid character actress, she created the original and majestic Lilac Fairy.

Unquestionably, the leading male dancer was Pavel Gerdt. Of German origin, he graduated from the Theatre school in 1864. He was an extremely expressive and noble dancer and made a splendid partner. Petipa's interest was really centred on ballerinas and Pavel Gerdt spent much of the early part of his career as an attractive and supporting background against which the virtuosity of the ballerinas was displayed. It was customary, at that time, for two male dancers to perform different aspects of the same role. In *La Bayadère*, for example, Ivanov, who was older, less athletic but more experienced, performed the mime and the younger Pavel Gerdt danced the same role, when required. He established a tradition of elegance which still characterizes Leningrad's Kirov Ballet. He continued to teach until 1904 and among his pupils were Anna Pavlova, Tamara Karsavina and Michel Fokine.

Another great teacher was Christian Johansson, a Swede who went to Russia from the Royal Danish Ballet. He was a virile dancer and an even better teacher, for whom Petipa had enormous respect. His classes at St Petersburg were well organized and in his entire life, he never repeated a single enchaînment.

Ivan Vsevolojsky was appointed Director of the Imperial Theatres in 1881 and he had the idea of creating *The Sleeping Beauty* as a gala spectacular. The score was commissioned from Tchaikovsky who was immensely enthusiastic. The richness of Tchaikovsky's music gave magnificent scope for the creation of roles and dances. Petipa himself admitted that the creation of *The Sleeping Beauty* was a huge task of great difficulty. The choreography matches the music following the development and growing maturity of the young princess. Petipa created the role of Princess Aurora with the young Italian guest dancer, Carlotta Brianza, in mind. He also created a wealth of roles for the company's own talented soloists – the six good fairies, the four precious stones, the Cat and Puss in Boots, Little Red Riding Hood and the Wolf, Cinderella and Prince Fortune and the incomparable Bluebirds. The evil fairy, Carabosse, was mimed by Enrico Cecchetti who also created the Bluebird. The new Prince Désiré was danced by Pavel Gerdt. Surprisingly, *The Sleeping Beauty* was not an immediate success. Petipa was accused of creating a court ballet about foreign fairy tales and it was some time before the truly Russian character of the work was recognized and appreciated. The dancers loved the ballet and it is now a favourite with audiences throughout the world.

Petipa created one further important work after this, *Raymonda*, to a superb score by Glazunov. After this achievement Petipa continued to work, producing small and adequate ballets, but nothing spectacular. His final attempt at a great work was *The Magic Mirror* which proved a disastrous failure.

The other great name of this period was Lev Ivanov. He joined the Bolshoi Theatre Company in St Petersburg, as a member of the corps, in 1852. For the first two years he danced only in other theatres in minor works, although he was greatly in demand as a partner to several promising ballerinas including Maria Surovshchikova and Marfa Muravieva. He received a number of

small promotions and in 1858 he began teaching. He was extraordinarily musical and, in fact, composed a number of pieces. He was one of the 18 composers whose works finally comprised *The Hump-Backed Horse*. His scrupulous attendance at rehearsals and performances made him so familiar with the repertoire that he was able to take on leading roles at short notice and this encouraged the Directorate to exploit him. Finally in 1869 he was promoted to premier danseur when Petipa replaced Saint-Léon. His inclination was towards romantic roles but Pavel Gerdt was a vastly superior classical dancer. However, he excelled in character roles and was magnificent at mime. He became the company's regisseur in 1882 and, although he was rather weak-willed he was very popular with the dancers. In 1885 he was appointed second Ballet Master. Under the leadership of Petipa, the scope for original choreography was limited and he was mainly concerned with staging revivals and divertissements in operas, including the *Polovetsian Dances from Prince Igor* which profoundly influenced Fokine when he created his much acclaimed version 20 years later.

Ivanov's greatest choreography grew directly out of music and conse-

Yekaterina Geltser and Vasily Tikhomirov were major forces at Moscow's Bolshoi Theatre, both before and after the 1917 revolution. This photograph, taken in 1903, shows them in Alexander Gorsky's Goldfish.

215

quently his association with Tchaikovsky was particularly successful. He assisted with the choreography and preparations of *The Sleeping Beauty* and was probably responsible for the vision scene, although he received no credit from Petipa. In 1892 he was given the opportunity to create his own full-length Tchaikovsky ballet, *The Nutcracker*, owing to a sudden illness which prevented Petipa from working on it. With the waltz of the Snowflakes, Lev Ivanov had full opportunity to create a small symphonic work. The rest of *The Nutcracker* was created along more conventional lines. The ballet has remained a perennial favourite, especially with young audiences, and often features in the Christmas programmes of many of the world's major classical companies.

Lev Ivanov's greatest work was in *Swan Lake*. It is possible that, in his capacity as second Ballet Master, he had staged Act II for a performance at the Czar's private theatre. Certainly he was responsible for a performance of this act at the Maryinsky Theatre in 1894 at a gala concert dedicated to the memory of Tchaikovsky. When Petipa later set about producing a full-length version, he left Ivanov's Act II unaltered. Petipa concentrated on the spectacular crowd scenes and Ivanov handled Act IV. Once again his influence on Fokine is apparent for the famous *Dying Swan* owes much to Ivanov's Odette. Since its creation, the dual role of Odette and Odile has provided a vast range of interpretative scope for ballerinas across the world as well as many of the great names of Soviet ballet such as Semenova and Ulanova.

After his *Swan Lake*, Ivanov created only minor one-act ballets with the exception of a suite of character dances for Olga Preobrajenskaya in a performance of *The Hump-Backed Horse* in 1900. He died the following year and it is only since his death that his achievements as a choreographer have been truly appreciated.

During this period at the end of the nineteenth century, the Bolshoi Theatre in Moscow was less fortunate than the Maryinsky in St Petersburg and there was little worthwhile activity. The Belgian choreographer Joseph Hansen was appointed Ballet Master in 1879, but he lacked originality and imagination. The lack of content and real choreography in the ballets he staged displeased the demanding Moscow audiences. When he left Russia in 1882, Russian officials under the leadership of Pchelnikov, not an artistic but a military man, decided to reform Moscow ballet. Pchelnikov was unpopular with the dancers and had little interest in ballet. The size of the company was reduced by 92 and many of the leading dancers were transferred to St Petersburg. The status of ballet was reduced to providing divertissements for operas and the Theatre school was in danger of being closed. For almost one year the company was without a Ballet Master. In 1883, Alexei Bogdanov was appointed. He completely lacked the real talents required of a Ballet Master, but he did re-introduce regular classes and rehearsals. He staged a number of revivals from the St Petersburg repertoire but these were not of sufficiently high standard to rescue Moscow ballet. He was then replaced by the Spanish Ballet Master José Mendez, also known as Joseph Mendes, who had studied with both Carlo Blasis and Paul Taglioni. He spent almost 10 years in Moscow and his most valuable work was with the pupils of the school. His style was, however, quite out of character with that of Russian dancers and his most promising pupils usually completed their training at St Petersburg. His activities with the company were less successful and the glittering spectacle of European ballet did not find favour with Moscow audiences. Talented dancers, such as Lydia Geiten, found little scope and many of them travelled abroad and eventually transferred to St Petersburg. Lydia Geiten eventually formed a small company of her own to tour the provinces and was in many ways, responsible for maintaining traditions which would otherwise have been lost.

The replacement of Pchelnikov as Director, by Teliakovsky began a revival of ballet in Moscow. Although a retired cavalry officer, he was deeply interested in the arts. However, the real rescuer was Alexander Gorsky. He entered the Theatre School in St Petersburg in 1880, more or less by chance. After his graduation he joined the corps at the Maryinsky Theatre. He was a very versatile dancer and exceptionally good at mime. He became a close friend of Vladimir Stepanov who developed a form of dance notation, which Gorsky learned thoroughly. At one time he requested assistance and payment from the Directorate to record *The Sleeping Beauty* in Stepanov notation. He was refused both of these but still recorded it and, in 1898, he mounted a production at the Bolshoi Theatre in Moscow from his own record, in three weeks. He found Moscow very different from St Petersburg and quickly became familiar with the artistic changes taking place through Stanislavsky's Art Theatre, the Mamontov Opera, the Maly Theatre and the University.

In 1900 he was promoted to soloist at St Petersburg and shortly afterwards accepted the post of regisseur at Moscow, which had left a profound impression on him. Gorsky continued to develop his interest in the broad cultural life of Moscow, visiting Chekhov and attending art exhibitions. His first task in the revival of ballet at the Bolshoi, was a revival of Petipa's *Don Quixote*. In true Stanislavsky tradition, he treated the corps de ballet as a real crowd, giving each dancer a particular activity, such as selling fruit, rather than forming rigid lines and patterns. The sets designed by Korovine and Golovine showed a realistic inn or village square and the costumes matched the period. This revolution was not effected without opposition but the younger dancers readily appreciated it.

In 1901, he presented a new version of *Swan Lake*, although everyone thought he was mad, as all earlier versions had been disastrous. However, it proved extremely successful and he gave a total of five productions during his life. He retained the outline of the St Petersburg version but treated scenes like the Prince's birthday party in the same way as he had treated *Don Quixote*, giving the crowd a new quality of liveliness and reality.

He staged more ballets in the same sort of way, including *The Hump-Backed Horse*, and his activities attracted the attention of the Directorate who appointed him official Ballet Master in 1902. At the same time, his version of *Don Quixote* was transferred to St Petersburg, amidst far greater hostility and uproar than it had encountered in Moscow.

Meanwhile Gorsky wished to create a new work, rather than simply revive old ones. He planned that it would be based on Victor Hugo's novel, *Notre Dame de Paris*, and in order to distinguish it from *La Esmeralda*, he called it *Gudule's Daughter*. The part of Esmeralda was created for Sophia Fedorova who was a superb actress as well as a brilliant dancer. Gorsky created the ballet along the lines he had followed previously and the acrobatic quality of the execution scene was years ahead of its time. The ballet was premièred in November 1902 to a most indignant reception. Nevertheless, Gorsky regarded *Gudule's Daughter* as one of his most important works.

His other really major work was *Salammbô*, based on Flaubert's novel. He carried his feeling for realism further than ever before, dispensing with conventional divertissements and variations, and the corps de ballet was dressed in long robes and sandals. The leading roles were created by the famous dancers Yekaterina Geltser and Mikhail Mordkin, a true Gorsky dancer.

Gorsky created other works and his importance to the development of Russian ballet was enormous. He was the first choreographer with a definite artistic direction. He led the Bolshoi Theatre company to a new maturity raising it to the level of the company in St Petersburg.

The early years of the twentieth century saw unrest throughout Russia as well as in the small world of the St Petersburg ballet company. There were strong dancers and a good repertoire, but there was no real sense of future direction or powerful leadership, once Petipa was gone. In 1905 unrest among the dancers resulted in a strike for more artistic freedom and an increased salary. Among the dancers involved were Olga Preobrajenskaya, Anna Pavlova, Michel Fokine, Tamara Karsavina and Sergei Legat. In comparison with the feelings of disquiet permeating the country, this was a small affair, but it greatly disturbed the Directorate and the leaders were not forgotten.

To all intents and purposes, the company was without a Ballet Master, for although Petipa still received his salary, he was not allowed to work. A number of very minor figures staged several indifferent works and Teliakovsky contemplated transferring Gorsky from Moscow. Nicolai Sergeyev planned to put himself into a position of authority, although officially he was only the regisseur. He was a dictator and many soloists resigned. His unpleasant behaviour during the 1905 strike, earned him Fokine's undying contempt. However, Sergeyev was a benefactor of quite another ballet company and of ballet generally in the West. He stole the records of *Coppélia*, *Giselle*, *Swan Lake*, *The Nutcracker* and *The Sleeping Beauty* from the files at the Maryinsky Theatre and these eventually found their way to the Vic-Wells Ballet in London, which eventually became Britain's Royal Ballet.

Michel Fokine graduated in 1898, and was immediately given leading roles. He was extremely irritated by the silliness of the St Petersburg ballet and quite early he developed plans for reforming it. In 1904 he began teaching a girl's class which enabled him to put some of his ideas into practice. In the same year he sent a memorandum to the Directorate outlining a two-act ballet and the principles of production. The Directorate ignored it. The main idea of the memorandum was to suggest that dances, music and costumes should be appropriate in style to the situation and period they were supposed to represent. He also objected to the dancers stopping and bowing during the course of performances. When he did get the opportunity to create ballets, he insisted that the dancers fully understood the nature of the characters they were representing.

He revived Ivanov's ballet *Acis and Galatea* for a school graduation performance. He created a special solo for a young dancer who seemed particularly promising, although he still had two more years training left. The young man was Vaslav Nijinsky. Fokine's methods of working deeply impressed the young dancers, but he was not able to put his ideas completely into practice, even when he later collaborated on *Le Pavillon d'Armide* with Alexandre Benois.

Meanwhile Serge Diaghilev arrived in St Petersburg from Perm. He quickly became part of a circle of young painters and musicians, although he later abandoned his own musical studies. He hoped to become Director of the Imperial Theatres and although he made every effort to achieve this, he was never appointed and, in fact, he was dismissed or forced to resign from the Imperial Theatres in 1907. After this he set about organizing a permanent touring company with Nijinsky as its head. Nijinsky's career with the Imperial Theatres came to an abrupt halt after a quarrel with the stage manager when he had appeared in *Giselle* without the customary shorts covering his tights.

Fokine had already created *Les Sylphides*, known as *Chopiniana* in Russia, and a version of *Carnaval*, as well as the famous *Dying Swan* for Anna Pavlova, when he began his association with Diaghilev. Paris was amazed by the virility of Fokine's *Polovetsian Dances from Prince Igor* and by the

brilliance of Sophia Fedorova. The second season in Paris included *Carnaval* and *Scheherazade* and the third season brought *Narcisse*, *Le Spectre de la Rose* and *Petrouchka*. By the fourth season changes began to occur. Fokine returned to Russia and Diaghilev began to move in a new artistic direction with Nijinsky's *L'Après-Midi d'un Faune*. They rejoined for a short time in 1914 and for a while Fokine also worked with Anna Pavlova but her small touring company was too limiting.

Eventually he returned to the Imperial Theatres and was made Ballet Master. The works he created were less exciting than his first period with the Maryinsky, but the influence of his ideas remained strong.

Anna Pavlova was a weak child and when she entered the Theatre School in 1891, her teacher, Yekaterina Vazem, was doubtful about her future. Both Pavel Gerdt and Christian Johansson noticed her talent and so did Petipa. In a school performance in 1898 she danced with Fokine, beginning an association which lasted while she remained in Russia. She was accepted into the Maryinsky Theatre as a soloist and frequently danced major roles. One of her earliest achievements was in *The Awakening of Flora*, in which she danced with Fokine. As well as being an extraordinarily lyrical and ethereal dancer as in *Giselle*, she was also a talented character dancer, as in *The Hump-Backed Horse*. She was totally dedicated, constantly working to improve her technique. The Directorate never forgot her part in the 1905 strike and she often suffered from being cast in inadequate roles. Although she danced in Russia for 10 years, when her contract expired it was not renewed and she began to travel abroad and eventually settled in Ivy House in England in 1913.

In 1917 the October Revolution disrupted all Russian life including the Imperial Theatres. The Soviet Ballet companies which eventually emerged were based on the solid foundations of the companies of Imperial Russia which stretched back through the centuries, but in 1917, the future seemed very doubtful.

Varvara Nikitina was trained by Lev Ivanov and appears in his masterpiece The Nutcracker *at the Maryinsky Theatre, St Petersburg in 1892. She is partnered by Pavel Gerdt, a dancer renowned for his unassuming elegance and grace*

The Kirov Ballet

The Maryinsky theatre in St Petersburg had been, for many years, the ballet centre of Imperial Russia. However, when the October Revolution took place in 1917, the company was already in a critical condition. Many leading figures, dissatisfied with the lack of artistic freedom, had left Russia. Anna Pavlova, for example, settled in England in 1913. Michel Fokine was one of the few major artists still remaining. Ballet had again become a source of entertainment for the privileged few and the organization of the Imperial Theatres was such that the changes so evidently required at the Maryinsky, could not occur internally. When the revolution came it brought to ballet the radical changes it brought to the entire country.

It is fortunate that the first Soviet Commissar of Education was Anatoly Lunacharsky. He was a man who greatly valued national traditions and was deeply interested in maintaining quality. From the start he thought in terms of developing a new Soviet ballet growing from the strong foundations of Russian ballet.

However, at that time, the very right of ballet to exist was being questioned. The Proletkult wanted to invent completely new forms of art and revolutionize opera and ballet. Free tickets to the theatre were issued for ballets which seemed worth preserving because of the value of their music. *King Candaules* was revived, with a new plot concerning an uprising against a tyrannical king. Most of Petipa's choreography was retained but the music was re-orchestrated. It did not survive long. The choreography was adapted to the new plot by Leonid Leontiev. He had danced with the Diaghilev company in its first seasons and, although not a strong classical dancer, he was good at mime. After the revolution, he became head of the theatre school from 1918 to 1920, and manager of the company from 1922 to 1925. During this time he produced a number of adequate ballets and with some dancers of the former Maryinsky – Lopukhov, Monakhov, Shiryaev and Chekrygin – he endeavoured to maintain normal life for the company after about 40 per cent of the members had left and the future looked bleak.

The continued activities of the company began to gain popularity. Food was scarce and heating non-existent, but the dancers tried to preserve the traditions of technique and elegance for which the Maryinsky had been famous. For the first years, all the leading ballerina roles were taken by Yelizaveta Gerdt, who inherited her beauty and graceful line from her illustrious father. She had been taught by Anna Johansson and Michel Fokine and had danced with Nijinsky. She danced her first ballerina role in February 1917. After the revolution, most of the leading ballerinas left the country and so Yelizaveta Gerdt took on about 15 major roles from Odette-Odile to the first Soviet ballet, *The Red Whirlwind*, created by Lopukhov in 1924.

Fortunately the Proletkult did not flourish for long and had more or less ceased to exist by 1922. Lenin felt that proletarian culture could not be imposed but must grow out of what had preceded it. Ballet had a national heritage, developed by generations of choreographers, teachers and dancers and the company which remained at the former Maryinsky could now set about preserving it in earnest. In 1922, Fedor Lopukhov revived *The Sleeping Beauty*, using the complete Petipa choreography. This gave the dancers an opportunity to perfect their classical technique. The part of Aurora was first danced by Olga Spesivtseva and, after she left it was danced alternately by Yelizaveta Gerdt and Yelena Lucom. Yelena Lucom was a particularly interesting dancer because she was the last Russian, and first, truly Soviet ballerina. She trained and danced with the old Maryinsky company but developed a new acrobatic technique with the innovations of Soviet ballet.

Leonid Yacobson created a number of works for the Kirov Ballet. The most important of these was Spartacus *which demonstrated the full range of his very plastic, classically based style.*

She remained the leading Leningrad ballerina until she was superseded by Marina Semenova, the first Soviet trained ballerina.

The school also survived in spite of attempts by the Proletkult to abolish it and difficulties with leadership. The company lacked leadership following the revolution, and after Fokine left for Sweden and, eventually, the United States, Nicolai Legat and Nicolai Sergeyev attempted to gain control. The dancers remembered their pre-revolutionary activities, particularly Sergeyev's, and were horrified. Nicolai Legat was a good teacher but an indifferent choreographer. Eventually he was appointed second Ballet Master and Mime Teacher and attempted to arrange for the critic, Akim Volynsky, who had supported his claims, to be made head of the school. This resulted in great resentment, and further indignation was caused by Legat's and Volynsky's efforts to get Sergeyev appointed Director.

Fortunately, not long after this, Agrippina Vaganova came to the school. She had been a pupil of Yekaterina Vazem and Nicolai Legat and absorbed much of their teaching technique. She had also observed the classes of Enrico Cecchetti and his pupil Olga Preobrajenskaya. As a dancer she was remarkable for her beats and elevation but, although she danced many leading roles, she was not given ballerina status until 1915, shortly before she retired from the stage. She did not start teaching immediately, but after the revolution there was a great need for teachers. From 1919 to 1921 she taught at Akim Volynsky's School of Russian Ballet and then she was invited to the Leningrad Choreographic Technikum, the former Maryinsky school, where she eventually became the leading teacher. In her first years, she taught pupils of all stages and was developing her new methods by trying them out on actual students. She trained both Natalia Kamkova and Marina Semenova from their earliest years. Later she taught only advanced students in their last two years when they were perfecting their technique.

In many ways, Agrippina Vaganova was responsible for what is now considered the Soviet style. It was founded on Russian tradition but she introduced a greater fluidity to arm movements, greater strength of line and increased elevation. The Vaganova style also extended to male dancers and, in particular, they acquired her characteristic back, dancing from the trunk. This gave them greater muscular manoeuvrability, especially with leaps, and tremendous elevation which are now considered characteristic of Soviet male dancers. As Vaganova developed her style, choreographers began to create works for the dancers she trained and she responded by studying them and refining her methods further.

Vaganova was opposed to the idea that the classical repertoire should be entirely replaced but she was interested in the possibilities of Soviet choreography. She devised special warming up and acrobatic exercises for the company's classes because acrobatic lifts were beginning to appear in works at this time.

The first, daring piece of new choreography was Lopukhov's *Tanzsymphonia* in 1923. Lopukhov conceived the idea in 1916 but was prevented from developing it until after the revolution. Eighteen people gave up their summer holidays to prepare the production. These included George Balanchine, Leonid Lavrovsky and Alexandra Danilova. The ballet, to Beethoven's Fourth Symphony, presented the cycle of life in the universe. It was perhaps a naive concept but the symphonic form was a valuable achievement. Lopukhov studied the score thoroughly before he began work. This was relatively uncommon among choreographers, with the specific exceptions of Ivanov and Fokine. Even Petipa, who was capable of superb correspondence between music and dance, was not always familiar with the whole score and produced some extremely inappropriate pieces of choreography. With *Tanzsymphonia*, Lopukhov, who believed passionately in symphonic ballet, linked totally dance movement and musical movement. In the early 1920s this was an extremely progressive approach. The ballet had a very mixed reception. Certainly the theme was obscurely complex and, possibly, the choice of that particular symphony was not very wise.

In 1927, the unusual ballet, *Ice Maiden*, was presented. The abrupt, non-lyrical choreography created the cold character of the title role. It was performed more than 60 times and remained in the repertoire for several years. Some odd results came out of these early experiments. A new version of *The Firebird*, with a complicated, allegorical plot having no relevance to the fairy story, was hissed throughout. A deliberately controversial version of *The Nutcracker* was presented in 1929. Works at the opposite end of the spectrum were also prepared, such as *Serf Ballerina*, which took realism to an extreme degree, completely lacked unity and was not a success.

There were a number of major Soviet dancers emerging at this time. Marina Semenova was a Vaganova pupil and graduated in 1925, when still only 17 years old. She joined the State Academic Theatre, the former Maryinsky Theatre, taking on the role of Aurora. As well as displaying an excellent technique, she had an exhilarating quality to her dancing. She was most renowned for her performances as Odette-Odile. In 1930, she became the prima ballerina at the Bolshoi Theatre where she remained until she retired to teach in 1952.

The first male dancer with the active, energetic, heroic style of contemporary Soviet ballet was Alexei Yermolayev. He entered the Leningrad school in 1924, when aged 14, and graduated with honours, two years later. He danced all the leading male roles in Leningrad and was instrumental in introducing the idea that a premier danseur was an integral, active part of the ballet and not merely a porteur. Both he and Marina Semenova pre-dated the style which finally became established in the 1930s.

After the developments of the 1920s, choreographers began to seek deeper and more serious subjects for Soviet ballet. Theatre and ballet have always been closely linked in Russia and, during the 1930s, this association became more direct. The first suitable subject for the new ballet was found in a story about the French Revolution. It was called *The Flames of Paris* and was a synthesis of music, singing and dance. The music was composed by Boris Asafiev and was his first monumental ballet work. It was partly a montage of songs and music from the French Revolution and partly new music composed in the style and character of the period. The aim of the choreography was to extend beyond the plot and present the theme by means of dramatic expression. The march of the dancers to *Ça Ira*, transformed into a symphonic piece by Asafiev, was extraordinarily impressive and was presented during the celebrations of the fifteenth anniversary of the revolution, in October 1932. The complete ballet was performed the following day and the next June it was performed at the Bolshoi Theatre.

The Flames of Paris enabled many young dancers to show their talents. The leading Marseillais was created by Vakhtang Chaboukiani, who invested the character with immense pathos. The virtuoso dancer, Feya Balabina, who later became Artistic Director of the school, was the first Jeanne. Also interesting was Nina Anisimova, as character dancers were not usually given very active roles. She created the role of Thérèse, who, because of her portrayal, became one of the principal heroines. She later created the role of Nastia in another of Vainonen's ballets, *Partisan's Days*. She showed real talent for characterization and later she became one of the first, female, Soviet choreographers.

Vainonen trained at the Maryinsky School and graduated into the company in 1919, later becoming a character soloist. His first work was *Moskovski Waltz*, created for the Young Ballet Group and still famed for its acrobatic lifts. Gradually, he ceased to dance and concentrated on choreography. His first major work, *The Age of Gold*, with music by Shostakovich, presented remarkable choreography and cardboard characters. Real success came with *The Flames of Paris*, two years later, with interesting characters, good scenery and artistic unity. He staged a number of ballets, including a version of *The Nutcracker* which remained in the repertoires of the Kirov and the Budapest Opera for many years. In 1950 he assisted in the revival of Hungarian ballet.

The new demands of human feelings and emotions of Soviet ballets in the 1930s required new ways of acting and dancing. Choreographers began to introduce powerful leaps and broad movements in attempts to realize the new extensiveness of the heroes. The crisp technique and extreme expressiveness of the new ballerinas required the complete freedom of the stage.

Choreographers began to look to literature as a source of new ballets – Pushkin, Lermontov, Gogol, Shakespeare and Lope de Vega. Pushkin's poem, *The Fountain of Bakhchisarai*, had already provided inspiration for opera, and Filippo Taglioni had planned a ballet based on it, especially for St Petersburg, after his visit in 1838. Some other attempts were made but all missed the quintessence of the poem.

Nicolai Volkov wrote the new scenario, presenting the psychological conflict of the characters, within a plot which linked the visualization of Pushkin's poetic ideas. The music was composed by Boris Asafiev, who employed the same technique as he had used for *The Flames of Paris*, using musical material from Pushkin's lifetime. He made use of the romantic *To the Fountain of the Bakhchisarai Palace*, by Alexander Gurilyov to begin and end the ballet, and also John Field's very popular music as a lietmotiv for Maria, one of the principal characters.

The choreographer was Rotislav Zakharov. He followed his training at the Leningrad school, from 1920 to 1925, with a brief dancing career before concentrating on choreography. He studied all aspects of theatre because, at that time, no choreographic school existed. He later founded the Choreographer's Faculty of the State Theatre Institute in Moscow in 1946. His approach to choreography was undoubtedly influenced by the activities of Stanislavsky in the theatre. He began by holding a conference with the leading dancers to enable them to understand the emotion and psychology of the roles. This revolutionary approach caused considerable comment. Zhakarov also spent many hours studying in museums to find the essence of the imagery. The roles of Zarema and Maria were created by Olga Jordan and Galina Ulanova and the difficult choreography demanded the full professional training of Soviet schools. With Galina Ulanova, Zhakarov had the ideal Maria. She was the embodiment of the aspirations of Soviet ballet with agile perfection and spiritual beauty. She began her training with her mother and entered the theatre school in 1919, much against her will, because she was far more interested in boyish pursuits than in dancing. Considering what a lyrical dancer she became, this is difficult to believe. For the last four years of her training she was taught by Agrippina Vaganova and, in 1928, after graduation, she joined the company. Her distinct personal style and brilliant characterization were quickly noticed. The role of Maria in *The Fountain of Bakhchisarai* was a turning point in her career. She approached the character from within and, in fact, continued to work at the part for many years. She was truly a thinking dancer as well as being the greatest exponent of the fluid Soviet style. She later created leading roles in three Prokoviev ballets, *Romeo and Juliet*, *Cinderella* and *The Stone Flower* and her interpretation of Giselle at the Bolshoi Theatre, where she was prima ballerina for 20 years, was an unforgettable experience.

Zhakarov also created other ballets based on the work of Pushkin – *The*

Prisoner in the Caucasus, Mistress into Maid and *The Bronze Horseman*. None of these was as good as *The Fountain of Bakhchisarai*. The first two ballets were to music by Boris Asafiev and the third was by Reinhold Glière.

After *The Flames of Paris*, it became necessary to find a contemporary theme for Soviet ballet. The Bolshoi Theatre had little success with the *Bright Stream* and attention was again focused on the Leningrad theatre, which had been re-named the Kirov in 1935. Vainonen began work on *Partisans' Days*, which portrayed the struggle of partisans in the North Caucasus against White Cossacks. The music was composed by Boris Asafiev and the first performance took place on May 16, 1937. Vainonen had travelled to the Caucasus to study national dances and these were skilfully used in the ballet as a means of characterization. This innovation was later taken up by other Soviet choreographers. *Partisans' Days* was also the first ballet danced completely off pointe in character shoes, the principal role of Nastia being taken by the character dancer Nina Anisimova. Audiences were deeply moved by the plot and Act I was very well conceived, but the rest of the work was rather disjointed with too much theatre and too little dance.

The problems of Soviet social realism in ballet were manifold. The significant episodes had to be portrayed through mime rather than through dance. A lack of really imaginative choreographers and the predominant political climate meant that there were few works as forceful as *Partisans' Days*. However, to some choreographers this challenge provided a vital stimulus.

Vakhtang Chaboukiani was from Tbilisi, previously Tiflis, and discovered ballet whilst still a child. He acquired some basic training and finally went to Leningrad to learn more, in 1926. He was far too old for the school but managed to gain admission to the evening classes. Within two years, he was transferred to the main class and then graduated into the State Academic Ballet. His superb classical technique soon raised him to the rank of premier danseur. He did much to establish a really worthwhile Soviet technique. A vigorous dancer, with magnificent elevation, he developed many new movements and transformed old ones. He danced many danseur noble and leading classical roles including Prince Siegfried in *Swan Lake*, Basil in *Don Quixote*, Albrecht in *Giselle*, the Bluebird in *The Sleeping Beauty* and the grand pas in *Raymonda*. He was also of primary importance in creating many leading roles in Soviet ballets, such as the Sportsman in the *Age of Gold*.

He quickly became dissatisfied with the emphasis on mime, and began to think about creating ballets himself. His first major work was *The Heart of the Hills*, in 1938. Although the story was historical, the ideals it presented were contemporary, concerning an uprising against oppression. Again folk dance played an important part and the choreography depicted character through an ingenious interweaving of classical and folk movements and steps. The music by Andrei Balanchivadze was well suited to the ballet.

The Heart of the Hills was followed by *Laurencia*, based on Lope de Vega's very popular and much admired play *Fuente Ovejuna*. The leading role was danced by Natalia Dudinskaya, an excellent dancer with sound technique, whose passionate acting contributed enormously to the ballet's success. However, the real heroes of the story were the 'masses' and the real achievement of the choreography was in the artistic unity of the corps de ballet. *Laurencia* was featured for many years in the repertoires of both the Kirov and the Bolshoi theatres, with the incomparable Maya Plisetskaya gaining great renown in the leading role of the latter.

Another leading choreographer was Leonid Lavrovsky, later named People's Artist of the USSR. He danced many leading classical roles at the Kirov Theatre and was, at the same time, a member of the Young Ballet, founded by George Balanchine and Vladimir Dmitriev. He also appeared in contemporary experimental ballets, such as Fedor Lopukhov's *Tanzsymphonia*. His first attempt at choreography was a graduation piece, much acclaimed critically. His first major creation was *Fadette*, based on a work by George Sand. In this he established the foundation of his creative technique, using classical dance as a means of characterization. In 1935 he created *Katerina*, a work about serf ballet presenting 'a ballet within a ballet', a time-honoured theatrical technique but new in the world of dance. Act III, in particular, was exceptionally moving with extremely plastic mime. From 1936 to 1937 he was Artistic Director at the Maly Opera and then he returned to head the Kirov company.

His next major project was *Romeo and Juliet*. The ballet had been conceived by Sergei Radlov, in 1934, and he had originally approached Rotislav Zakharov about the choreography, with the intention of presenting the ballet at the Bolshoi Theatre. The scenario was written by Sergei Radlov in conjunction with Adrian Piotrovsky, with advice from Rotislav Zakharov. This resulted in considerable mutilation of the original story, including the interpolation of Moorish dances. The chief offence perpetrated was that the story was given a happy ending, when Friar Laurence prevented Romeo from killing himself and the lovers and their families were cheerfully united. Four acts and nine scenes were prepared, but the total lack of tragic tension decided the Bolshoi Theatre against continuing with the project. In 1936, the Kirov approached Sergei Prokoviev about staging the ballet, but he was doubtful after his experiences with the Bolshoi Theatre. Furthermore, he had never heard of Leonid Lavrovsky. He agreed to discuss the matter, but at the same time, he received an offer from the Czechoslovakian State Theatre at Brno. In December 1936, the first performance of Prokoviev's *Romeo and Juliet* was given at Brno. It appears that during the intervening months the composer had re-written the ending and the final tragedy had been re-introduced.

In 1938, the Kirov and Prokoviev re-opened negotiations. The composer and choreographer argued endlessly about changes to the score, as Lavrovsky was keen to return to the central tragic core and Prokoviev was tired of constant re-writing. Finally, Prokoviev refused to countenance any more alterations, but Lavrovsky was still not satisfied. He introduced Prokoviev's Second Piano Sonata into the ballet and a tempestuous scene resulted at the next rehearsal. However, Prokoviev wrote a new piece of music exactly matching the rhythms and phrasing of the piano sonata and, after this incident, the collaboration was much calmer.

Romeo and Juliet was finally staged at the Kirov on January 11, 1940 and its impact was staggering. Even Shakespearean scholars were impressed. In the USSR, Lavrovsky's choreography is considered the definitive version of the ballet, and it has been widely acclaimed abroad. Romeo was danced by Sergeyev and the extraordinarily demanding role of Juliet was created by Galina Ulanova. She claimed it was one of the most difficult roles she had ever undertaken, but her performance enchanted audiences everywhere and the part has become identified with her.

In the years preceding World War II, Soviet ballet established its identity. Ballet had become humanized from the ethereal world of sylphs and fairies. In the years since then, all that had been learned about dramatic characterization has been put to more artistic use, with less overt emphasis on social realism. After Lavrovsky's transference to the Bolshoi Theatre, the Kirov's leading choreographer was Konstantin Sergeyev His ballet, *The Path of Thunder* was based on the South African novel about the conflict of love and racial discrimination, by Peter Abrahams. The score was composed by Kara Karayev who had made a study of African music. It was created as a series of dance suites with four duets as the central thematic core. The feeling of African dance, rather than actual steps or movements, was presented within a classical framework. Sergeyev was not as talented as Lavrovsky at handling the minor roles, but the main characters especially Sarie, the white girl, were well developed and fully three-dimensional. At the première, on 31 December, 1957, Sergeyev himself undertook the role of Lenny, the ill-fated black boy.

He created a new and controversial version of *Cinderella* in 1964, a ballet he had first worked on in 1946. The choreography was based on classical technique, but none of the traditional elements was retained. The Prince was presented as heroic and virile and was danced alternately by Vladilen Semenov and Yuri Soloviev. The charming and lively Cinderella was created by Irina Kolpakova, one of Vaganova's last pupils before her death in 1951. Cinderella became one of Kolpakova's leading roles.

One of the Kirov's most interesting choreographers at this time was Leonid Yacobson. His work has always been firmly rooted in classical technique, but he is inclined towards, free, plastic movement. He created his first works when he was quite young, including *Till Eulenspiegel* in 1933, and part of the *Age of Gold*. His first major work was *Shuraleh* for the State Theatre in 1941. This was then performed at the Kirov in 1950 and the Bolshoi in 1955. Once again, national dance was featured, and Tartar and classical steps were interwoven into a symphonic form.

His most famous ballet was *Spartacus* to the magnificent music of Khachaturian. The scenario was by Nicolas Volkov and was founded on the true story of the slave Spartacus, but new characters were invented to give dramatic form to the ballet. These included Crassus' mistress Aegina as a counterbalance to Spartacus' wife, called Phrygia in this version of the story, and Garmodius, a morally feeble Thracian, who finally betrays Spartacus. The style of the work evokes memories of Michel Fokine. The entire ballet was dèsigned to be danced off pointe, rather against the company's wishes, since it was felt that this undermined the dancers' status. However, it was soon realized that the choreography demanded the highest technical expertise and the solos of Phrygia and Aegina, in particular, on three-quarter pointe, were challenging for even the most virtuoso ballerinas. The story was presented almost as a series of friezes, rather than as an episodic narrative. There were many exciting and impressive scenes, such as the slave market, the uprising and Phyrgia's valediction to her dead husband. The first Spartacus at Leningrad was Askold Makarov, an extremely heroic dancer who was excellently suited to the role, and Alla Shelest created an unforgettable Aegina. *Spartacus* remained in the Kirov's repertoire for many years and was also danced at the Bolshoi Theatre. Although a new version by Yuri Grigorovich has now achieved international acclaim, *Spartacus* was unquestionably Yacobson's most important work.

Yuri Grigorovich, who now heads the Bolshoi Theatre Ballet, began his career at the Kirov after he graduated from the Leningrad school, in 1946. He quickly became a leading demi-caractère soloist and showed an early talent for choreography. For a graduation performance in 1956 he created Glinka's *Valse-Fantasia* and a year later he started work on a new version of *The Stone Flower*, with some friends. It was conceived as a succession of dance suites with a total integration of dance and mime. The choreography, particularly for the Mistress of the Copper Mountain, was very acrobatic and this has characterized his later work also. The work proved immensely successful and was later included in the repertoires of the Bolshoi Ballet and several State companies.

The Kirov has had an unfortunate history with many of its most promising dancers. In the 1920s, the trend of previous centuries was reversed and many of Leningrad's leading dancers were transferred to the new capital, Moscow. In 1958, the young dancer, Rudolf Nureyev, joined the company and it seems likely that he would have been one of the greatest danseurs nobles of

the USSR, epitomizing the strength and elegance which particularly characterize the Kirov dancers. However, in 1961, when the company visited Paris he sought political asylum because he was frustrated by the lack of opportunities in the rigid hierarchy and inflexible repertoire at Leningrad. The position which might have been Nureyev's – Sergeyev was training him to take over his roles – became Yuri Soloviev's, a fine dancer with great purity of line and outstanding elevation.

Two other male dancers, who seemed to have promising careers with the Kirov, have also since left the USSR and are furthering their careers in the less rigid artistic atmosphere of the West. These are Mikhail Baryshnikov whose technical expertise has found freer expression with American Ballet Theatre, and the fine dancer Valery Panov, who is currently associated with the San Francisco Ballet. Furthermore, the Kirov lost its most radiant ballerina, Natalia Makarova, when she too left the company, while on a European tour in 1970.

With the reported death of Yuri Soloviev in January 1977, the Kirov Ballet became even more deprived of leading dancers. The artistic atmosphere of Leningrad has always been more restricted than that of Moscow and it is becoming increasingly apparent that a greater freedom is essential for the full realization of the potential of the dancers and the company itself.

The Bolshoi Ballet

Maris Liepa is one of the Bolshoi Ballet's most exciting dancers. He is one of the finest exponents of the spectacular elevation now considered characteristic of Soviet dancing, appearing to fly through the air with no apparent effort and landing with great control and lightness. Here, he is dancing in Les Sylphides, *known as* Chopiniana *in the USSR.*

The Bolshoi Ballet, although it could hardly remain unaffected by the October Revolution, did not undergo, to the same extent, the tribulations which characterized the years following 1917 at the Maryinsky Theatre. Alexander Gorsky had done much to revitalize the Bolshoi after a long period of decline in the late nineteenth century. Consequently, although affected by the political upheavals of 1917, the Bolshoi was in a far more stable state and not suffering the internal crises permeating the Maryinsky company.

Although the company was in a relatively better position to maintain its artistic unity, nevertheless it endured enormous hardships with no food, fuel or transport. The school was turned into a hospital for tending the wounded and, as the theatre was almost impossible to heat, plans were made on several occasions to close it. These suggestions were opposed personally by Lenin on each occasion. As in Petrograd, free tickets to the theatres were issued. So many people travelled to Moscow, that the Bolshoi and the former Zimin Opera had to increase the number of performances.

The influence of the Proletkult was felt in Moscow and, as late as 1925, articles were still being written defending the ballet company's right to exist. In November 1917, the Council of People's Commissars placed theatres under the jurisdiction of the Commissariat for Education and the following year a special Theatre Department was organized. In 1919, all artists were commissioned to serve in special units of the Red Army and performances in all Moscow theatres, including the Bolshoi, were given for soldiers.

In the 1920s, activities at the Bolshoi began to resume a degree of normality. The classical repertoire and the traditions of Moscow ballet were carefully preserved by the dancers, headed by Alexander Gorsky until he died in 1924, and then by Vassily Tikhomirov. The Bolshoi company was fortunate too, in that fewer dancers fled from Russia, although some talented soloists, such as Mikhail Mordkin and Sophia Fedorova, were lost. However, Yekaterina Geltser remained as prima ballerina and a strong group of soloists included Victorina Kreiger, Leonid Zhukov, Anastasia Abramova and Nina Podgoretskaya.

The school was re-opened in 1920 and by 1925, 53 dancers had graduated. Several other ballet schools existed in Moscow at this time and their most talented pupils transferred to the Bolshoi School. Asaf Messerer, who graduated from the Bolshoi School into the company, was one such student.

The general feeling of political and social reform could not fail to penetrate the ballet company. The young dancers began to feel frustrated by their masters and a desire for something new and different in the world of dance, began to form. It seemed that the artistic atmosphere was claustrophobic and still imprisoned in the days of Imperial Russia. In an attempt to present scenes of popular protest against tyranny, Gorsky had created *Stenka Rasin*. The crowd scenes impressed audiences at the première on the first anniversary of the October Revolution but, otherwise, it was quickly forgotten. In 1922, he created a ballet for children, entitled *Ever Fresh Flowers*. He created it in collaboration with the composer Boris Asafiev to music by Tchaikovsky. Alexander Gorsky was the first choreographer to work closely with Boris Asafiev, who later composed a number of ballets for the Kirov company, including *The Flames of Paris* and *The Fountain of Bakhchisarai*. Apart from these two indifferent works, Gorsky concentrated on preserving the classical repertoire, continuing his earlier policy of completely re-working the choreography. This policy is still allowed to dominate the Bolshoi's approach to classical ballet today. In 1919, he revised *The Nutcracker*, presenting the story in the form of Masha's fantasies. The little girl, called Clara in the West, is known as Masha in the USSR. The Sugar Plum Variation was given to Masha but these changes did not survive in later Soviet versions. The transformation of the Nutcracker Prince, however, has continued in other versions both inside and outside the USSR. The use of overt fantasy in this ballet did not re-occur until 1976 when Ronald Hynd created a new version for the London Festival Ballet introducing a new character – the older sister – who also performs the Sugar Plum Variation.

In 1920, Gorsky presented his fourth staging of *Swan Lake*. He collaborated with Vladimir Nemirovich Danchenko in order to introduce the Stanislavsky method of acting into ballet. None of the original Ivanov choreography was retained. Deliberately controversial in his approach, Gorsky dressed the dancers in tunics rather than tutus. Odette and Odile were danced by different dancers and the black swans who accompanied Odile, appeared in Act II. Two years later he produced his final version of this ballet, which was far more traditional in approach. Most of Ivanov's original choreography was restored and one ballerina danced the dual role of Odette-Odile. Moreover, he made use of his experience as a choreographer by introducing a new vitality and realism into Act I. Prince Siegfried was danced by Asaf Messerer shortly after his graduation. He replaced the outdated mime with expressive acting and performed many new steps and enchaînments and his elevation was particularly spectacular. During his career as a dancer he built up a wide ranging repertoire, not only as a danseur noble, but also including many demi-caractère roles. He started teaching as early as 1923 and from 1942 he taught a class for perfecting the technique of advanced students. He was the first Soviet dancer to tour abroad.

After Alexander Gorsky's death in 1924, Vassily Tikhomirov took over the leadership of the Bolshoi Ballet. The younger dancers were not impressed by his appointment and some of them, led by Igor Moiseyev left the company, although they returned one week later. The new generation of dancers did approve of Kasyan Goleizovsky, however. He had begun his training in Moscow and then transferred to St Petersburg, graduating into the Maryinsky company. Whilst in St Petersburg, he studied the work of Michel Fokine and when he returned to Moscow he was closely associated with Alexander Gorsky. He greatly admired and was deeply influenced by both these major dance reformers. He founded his own company – The Chamber Ballet – after the October Revolution, while still remaining a member of the Bolshoi. He had many innovative, choreographic ideas and was influential in both Moscow and Leningrad. Although a fully-trained professional dancer, he maintained that classical steps and movements were only relevant to subjects concerning the periods when they were developed, and that new times demanded new forms. His insistence on dispensing with the daily class angered Agrippina Vaganova, Yekaterina Gelster and Vassily Tikhomirov, who were all fully occupied in trying to preserve classical technique. Goleizovsky's choreography was a mixture of very acrobatic movement and posing rather than dance. Although, for a short time, he had a reasonable sized following at the Bolshoi Theatre, he angered many people with his overt eroticism. In an effort to create a work in harmony with the times and to demonstrate his theories about dance, he presented *Whirlwind* in 1927. This was an allegory about the proletariat, which was represented by dancers waving hammers and sickles, and capitalists, who performed the foxtrot. The audience walked out of the theatre during the first performance and it was never shown again. After this catastrophe, he completely lost his following and left the Bolshoi company.

Meanwhile, Vassily Tikhomirov set about reviving some of the more neglected ballets of the classical repertoire, including *The Sleeping Beauty*, in which he preserved the best pieces of Petipa's original choreography. He did however, recognize the need to create contemporary ballets and used a new staging of *Esmeralda* as a compromise until a satisfactory theme could be found. New music was commissioned, the emphasis on anti-clericism was strengthened and the work was treated as popular drama. However, a happy ending was introduced in which Esmeralda was rescued from the scaffold by the rising populace and then pardoned. In spite of this rather odd variation in the plot, this version of *Esmeralda* was a step towards the creation of Soviet ballet.

The Red Poppy was a very important development in the history of Soviet ballet. It put an end to the quarrels between the 'new' and 'classical' factions and introduced the heroic theme to ballet in Moscow, which has characterized many of the Bolshoi's most successful productions since, including Yuri Grigorovich's much acclaimed *Spartacus*.

The method of creation of this ballet is also interesting. The original idea was conceived by the dancer Mikhail Kurilko, after reading about events in China. He discussed it with Yekaterina Geltser who was very interested in the role of Tao-Hoa, the tea-house dancer. A detailed plan of the ballet was then worked out by Tikhomirov in close collaboration with the composer Reinhold Glière. The responsibility for the choreography for the character dances was given to Tikhomirov's assistant, Lev Lashchilin, who was more experienced with this idiom.

The Red Poppy was premièred on 14 June, 1927. Yekaterina Geltser created the role of Tao-Hoa, which offered tremendous scope for her remarkable dramatic abilities. Vassily Tikhomirov undertook the role of the Soviet captain and the divertissements of the Acrobat with a Ribbon and the Golden Acrobat, both created by Asaf Messerer, were spectacular displays of virtuosity. The new ballet was very successful and, during the next 10 years, over 300 performances took place at the Bolshoi Theatre. It was also included in the repertoires of other companies all over the country, although it did not appear in its original form at Leningrad.

The Red Poppy did not escape criticism entirely. Political extremists failed to recognize the innnovation of the ballet and its essentially Soviet quality. Nevertheless, it developed ballet in new directions leading up to the dramatic works of the 1930s.

As the capital had been transferred back to Moscow, the status of the Bolshoi Ballet was, naturally, a concern. It was considered to be of greater importance than the Kirov. Many leading dancers and teachers were transferred from Leningrad to Moscow during the 1920s and 1930s. Also many of the Kirov's most successful creations were transferred and were often staged by their original choreographers. One of the first of these was *The Flames of Paris* created by Vassily Vainonen. Act III was performed at the Bolshoi Theatre on the same day as the full-length ballet was given in Leningrad, in November 1932. The complete work was performed in Moscow in the following June. *The Flames of Paris* afforded the opportunity for the young dancers in both Leningrad and Moscow to show their talents. The slight differences in interpretation of the leading roles at the two companies are interesting to compare. In Moscow, the leading Marseillais was created by Alexei Yermolayev, who emphasized the heroic determination of the character through his vigorous, virile style of dancing. Nadezhada Kapustina created the role of Thérèse in Moscow, and her interpretation had almost as much an impact as Anisimova's in Leningrad. Sulamith Messerer created the role of Jeanne, but it became identified with Olga Lepeshinskaya.

Olga Lepeshinskaya was accepted into the Bolshoi School in 1925 and danced her first role, Cupid in *Don Quixote*, the following year. Even before her graduation in 1933, she had been noticed as being especially talented and her natural abilities combined with her perfectionism and hard working personality, promised a valuable career as a ballerina. She appeared in *The Nutcracker* while still studying and when she joined the company she undertook major roles from the start. *The Flames of Paris* was her first Soviet ballet and the exuberance with which she attacked the role of Jeanne made it uniquely her own. Her virtuoso technique was really ahead of her time and *The Flames of Paris* provided a rare opportunity for her to display it. She excelled, too, in the classical repertoire, giving great charm to her interpretation of Kitri in *Don Quixote* and an attractive flirtatiousness to Aurora in the Rose Adagio in *The Sleeping Beauty*. In 1951 she was given the title People's Artist of the USSR. After her retirement she spent two years in Budapest as Ballet Mistress and advisor and was an invaluable help when the Hungarian company staged *The Flames of Paris*, in 1965.

Although the Bolshoi Theatre benefited from the new choreography taking place at the Kirov, the company was not merely content to reproduce Leningrad's successes. However, the problems of finding and interpretating suitable contemporary themes remained immense. Fedor Lopukhov created *The Bright Stream* to music by Shostakovich. The ballet was first performed at the

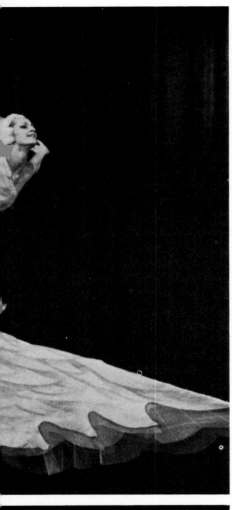

Maly Opera in June 1935 and then presented at the Bolshoi the following November. The plot was quite extraordinarily awful, involving a group of dancers visiting a collective farm. One of the workers becomes enamoured of the ballerina and the others, including his wife, decide to punish him. By co-incidence, the wife, who had studied ballet, knew the ballerina and enlists her co-operation to make an assignation with the husband. The.engagement is kept by the wife in disguise, the husband repents and everybody rejoices. Apart from this singularly dreadful story, the choreography bore no relevance to the period in which it was set and the national dances were totally unconvincing. The plot proved completely incomprehensible to the audience and the music was a series of isolated interludes so that the work lacked any unity. One of the severest critics of *The Bright Stream* was Agrippina Vaganova, who felt that the work discredited both contemporary and classical ballet. It compared very unfavourably with *The Flames of Paris* and with the Kirov's other great achievement of the period, the superb *The Fountain of Bakhchisarai*.

The Bolshoi company continued its search for the right story and the appropriate idiom to express it. In 1937, three dancers, Alexander Radunsky, Lev Pospekhin and Nicolai Popko made their debut as choreographers with *The Baby Stork*, for a school graduation performance. It was a fairy story involving several animals and children, particularly one Soviet and one negro. The children saved the baby stork and this rescue has a parallel in the stork's later rescue of the orphaned negro child from Africa. Much of the ballet was presented in the form of divertissements and lacked thorough characterization, but several scenes, such as that when the children teach the young bird to fly, were well thought out. However, it gave greater scope than any previous Bolshoi choreography, for developing realism. The part of the cat was created by Maya Plisetskaya while she was still a pupil. Although *The Baby Stork* was not precisely what was required at this stage of the company's development, it was, nevertheless, very popular and remained in the repertoire for a number of years and was regularly performed at the company's second theatre.

Having gained experience with *The Baby Stork*, the same group of dancers created *Svetlana*, two years later. The story of the sacrifice of a Soviet heroine proved very popular. The title role was created by Olga Lepeshinskaya and much of the ballet's success was due to her performance. The choreographers had insufficient experience to present the characterization through dance and, consequently, too much mime fragmented the work. However, the main characters were well-conceived and provided some strong roles. *Svetlana* remained in the repertoire for several years.

During the years before World War II, a Soviet style of ballet was established in both Leningrad and Moscow. The times demanded dramatic ballets with a clear plot and strong characterization, rather than great depth of thought or feeling. This had created a new kind of dancer who, in addition to tremendous physical strength and control, was very expressionistic and capable of combining mime and dance, based on a virtuoso technique regarded as a matter of course.

Above left *Contemporary technique in the USSR has become a notable blending of classicism and acrobatics. The strong muscular back and athletic approach, developed through the teachings of Agrippina Vaganova, have resulted in impressive lifts such as this, demonstrated here by Stanislav Vlasov and Ludmilla Vlasova in* The Doves.

Left *Maya Plisetskaya, for many years prima ballerina at the Bolshoi Theatre, pictured in* The Dying Swan, *immortalized by Anna Pavlova.*

Spartacus, *with choreography by Yuri Grigorovich, is a tremendously dramatic ballet which has been triumphantly received both in Moscow and in many major cities visited by the Bolshoi Ballet. Maris Liepa's remarkable performance as Crassus has made the role uniquely his own.*

In 1944, the Bolshoi Theatre gained two major figures from the Kirov, Leonid Lavrovsky and Galina Ulanova. To mark the centenary of the first production of *Giselle* in Russia, Lavrovsky revived it at the Bolshoi with Ulanova in the title role. Her superb technique, wonderful acting and poetic interpretation have never been matched. This production has been acclaimed throughout the world and the incomparable Ulanova continued to enchant international audiences and inspire other ballerinas with her lyrical and youthful portrayal of the role, until she retired from the stage in 1962, aged 52. She continued her association with the Bolshoi Ballet, coaching young dancers in her most important roles, particularly assisting Yekaterina Maximova in preparing the role of Giselle. She was appointed People's Artist of the USSR, was the winner of the Lenin prize in 1957, and was the first Soviet prima ballerina assoluta.

In 1946, Lavrovsky staged his *Romeo and Juliet* for the Bolshoi company, making a few changes to the original. The tradition of powerful acting had always been strong in Moscow and this ballet was excellently suited to the company's particular talents. Galina Ulanova undertook the role of Juliet which she had so successfully created in Leningrad, and this remained one of her main roles for nearly 20 years.

In the freer artistic atmosphere of the Bolshoi Theatre, and with the cultural changes of post-war years, the styles of new ballets moved away from the drama and mime of earlier ones. Lavrovsky continued to create works motivated primarily by the force of the music. In 1953, he created his first version of *The Stone Flower* and five years later he revised *The Red Poppy*, giving it the new title, *The Red Flower*. In April 1960, he presented *Paganini* set to Rachmaninov's well-known *Rhapsody on a Theme of Paganini*. He created his own scenario, which was quite different from that devised by Michel Fokine in 1939. Lavrovsky's version presented Paganini as a creative artist and portrayed the conquest of art over death. The scenario was not episodic but rather, Lavrovsky attempted to present Paganini's inner life. There were no props and the effects were produced by means of subtle lighting on a draped stage. The choreography was a complete blending of mime and dance and the corps de ballet was an integral part of the action. The title role was exceptionally exhausting and was brilliantly created by Vladimir Vasiliev, with Yekaterina Maximova as the Muse.

Lavrovsky's last major creation was *Night City*, a new version of Béla Bartók's *The Miraculous Mandarin*. The new scenario caused considerable controversy, because Bartók had been very specific about the action in his footnotes to the score. The first scene was more or less the same, but the plot continued as a love story in which the young girl tries to defend the victim, a repair-man, from the thugs. He is eventually killed and everything, except the girl's confused feelings, returns to the way it was at the beginning. The tone of the choreography was contemporary but firmly rooted in classical technique. Nina Timofeyeva gave a surprisingly strong performance as the girl. She had previously seemed a rather academic dancer but revealed unexpected powers of acting and mime. After *Night City*, Lavrovsky continued his exploration of the symphonic style with Ravel's *Bolero* and *La Valse*. In 1964, he was appointed Director of the Moscow Academic Choreographic School, previously called the Moscow Bolshoi School of Ballet. In 1965, he was named People's Artist of the USSR.

Leonid Yacobson created his version of *Spartacus* at the Kirov in 1956. Igor Moiseyev had negotiated with Nicolai Volkov as early as 1933, and had had the ballet in mind for many years. On 11 March 1958, he staged his version at the Bolshoi Theatre. His circus scenes were more dramatic than Yacobson's and his 25 years experience with his own folk dance group was very useful. The ballet was danced on pointe, unlike Yacobson's version, but it lacked continuity and did not last long in the repertoire. In 1962, Yacobson staged his version of *Spartacus* at the Bolshoi Theatre. He reduced the length of the ballet to three acts and so, completely lost the character of Garmodius and abbreviated the role of Aegina. As a result, Phrygia became increasingly important and the role was danced by prima ballerina Maya Plisetskaya.

A very typical Soviet dancer, she graduated into the Bolshoi company in 1943 and undertook solo roles immediately. She was promoted to ballerina status in 1945 and achieved considerable renown for the plastic and expressionistic vitality of her body. She was interested in the challenge of Yacobson's choreography, with the use of the three-quarter pointe, and its very plastic quality. She was especially admired for her moving portrayal of Phrygia mourning for her dead husband. The role did not afford sufficient opportunity for Plisetskaya to display her virtuoso technique as her main scenes as Phrygia were quite far apart. Consequently, Yacobson's *Spartacus* did not remain in the Bolshoi's repertoire very long, although Maya Plisetskaya did include a section of the ballet in her programme when she was nominated for the Lenin Prize in 1964.

It is interesting to note that when Moiseyev staged his version of the ballet, Maya Plisetskaya danced the opposite role of Aegina. Some fans suggested that, if the timing of the ballet permitted it, she should dance both Aegina and Phrygia. She is particularly famed for her powerful and highly individual interpretation of Odette–Odile.

Maya Plisetskaya's regular partner was Nicolai Fadeyechev, premier danseur at the Bolshoi. An elegant dancer with a perfect technique, he is an excellent partner. During the 1950s he oftened partnered Ulanova, particularly in *Giselle*. When the British Royal Ballet dancer, Nadia Nerina visited Moscow in 1961, she particularly asked him to partner her in *Swan Lake*.

When Lavrovsky became head of the School he was replaced as choreographer by Yuri Grigorovich. He was trained in Leningrad and created his first ballet for the Kirov company. Since he transferred to the Bolshoi he has created a number of works, including a highly-acclaimed version of *Spartacus*. He is firmly committed to a policy of pure dance, expressing action through it and not by means of mime. However, his choreography is very simple and unimaginative. It is particularly weak when he is creating for groups of dancers, although he shows rather more invention when dealing with solos and duets. Much of the success of *Spartacus* can be attributed to the actual performances of the dancers themselves, in particular the muscular elevation of Maris Liepa as Crassus.

More recently, Grigorovich created *Ivan The Terrible* and in 1976 he was invited to stage the work for the Paris Opera. The plot of the ballet suffers from the problems that has characterized Soviet Ballet for many years, that is, extreme banality. It is unquestionably very spectacular with several, fine dramatic roles such as Ivan, Prince Kurbsky and Anastasia. The score is fragmented and consists of parts of works by Prokofiev assembled inexpertly by Mikhail Chulaki. This, naturally, does not assist in attaining any kind of unity within the ballet. Once again, the impression on the audience is brought about by the sheer merit of the dancers, including Grigorovich's wife, Natalia Bessmertnova's acrobatic and breath-taking Anastasia.

The Bolshoi Ballet is the biggest company in the world and can boast of some of the finest dancers. It has the use of two theatres in Moscow and has visited many of the world's major cities. Ballet lovers in many countries have been deeply impressed by the dramatic power and magnificent technique of the dancers. As with all Soviet companies, its greatest weakness is in the choreography. However, it is possible that soon a choreographer will emerge from the present generation of dancers who can use these talents to their fullest extent and realize the company's true potential.

Prima ballerina assoluta and People's Artist of the USSR, Galina Ulanova was probably the best known and most loved dancer of her generation. Her grace, beauty and perfect technique delighted audiences throughout the world. She was an exquisite Giselle and even when she was about to retire, she captured the youthful carefree loveliness of the role in Act I and the tragic beauty of Act II, making the transition with professional ease.

Ballet in the Soviet Republics

Besides the famous companies at the Bolshoi and the Kirov, there are about 30 ballet companies in the Soviet Union. Many of the major cities in the Soviet Republics have opera houses and ballet companies of variable standards.

One of the best known and most important of these 'lesser' companies, is the Maly Ballet. The Maly Opera was founded in the early 1930s, at the former Mikhailovsky French Theatre in Leningrad by Fedor Lopukhov. It was intended to offer an alternative to the traditional Maryinsky repertoire and to present comic ballets. Fedor Lopukhov began by reviving Drigo's *Harlequinade* which had originally been presented in 1900 with choreography by Petipa. This was followed by a production of *Coppélia* with a new plot, based very loosely on the original, concerning a travelling circus, a talking doll and a soldier who quarrels with his sweetheart. Not only is this typical of the period but such an attitude towards the classics has been characteristic of the Maly throughout its history.

However, the company also presented dramatic ballets. Leonid Lavrovsky was appointed Artistic Leader in 1935 and he quickly began to stage more serious works. These were often based on literary themes and included *The Prisoner in the Caucasus*, considered more successful than the Zakharov version at the Bolshoi Theatre in 1938. A second successful ballet derived from the works of Pushkin, *The Tale of the Priest and his Workman Balda*, was staged in 1940. An important addition to the company at this time was Boris Fenster who joined in 1936 after his graduation from the Leningrad Ballet School. As well as dancing many solo roles, he was appointed Assistant Ballet Master under Lavrovsky. He was the first choreographer who began his career at the Maly and not only did he absorb the traditions during his formative period as a choreographer, but he was present as these traditions were being created. From 1945 to 1953 he was chief choreographer and created several major works during this time, such as *The False Bridegroom*. This was a remarkably successful period in the history of the Maly for artistic collaboration. The author of the scenario was the writer, Yuri Slonimsky and the composer was Mikhail Chulaki, both of whom have a long and close association with the company. Furthermore, several exceptional dancers were members of the company, Nicolai Zubkovsky, Galina Isayeva and Svetlana Sheina.

During the 1950s the company revived several ballets from the classical repertoire. Among these were the *Grand Pas from Paquita* and *Swan Lake*, in, as far as possible, their original forms. Their rather old-fashioned quality had a mixed reception but did give the dancers the opportunity to explore the demands of classical dance and for young dancers to learn. One particularly promising young man was Valery Panov whose performance in the 1961 revival of *Petrouchka* was especially notable. A versatile dancer, his dramatic ability suited the realistic style of the Maly superbly. He created a number of leading roles before he was invited, in 1963, to join the Kirov Ballet where he became one of its premiers danseurs. He has since left the USSR. From 1960 to 1962, the Maly Opera Ballet was led by Pyotr Gusev who was mainly responsible for raising the company's standards to international status. He was greatly interested in classical ballet and an inspired teacher. By this time too, the company was attracting fully-trained professional dancers. The present Director is Oleg Vinogradov and under his leadership the company has continued to develop its reputation for innova-

Nikita Dolgushin staged his ballet Clytemnestra *at the Leningrad Maly Opera and Ballet Theatre. Originally, the work was part of Gluck's opera* Iphigenie en Aulide Tauride *and Nikita Dolgushin has tried to present an eighteenth century production, involving an emphasis on mime not normally seen today.*

238

The Perm Opera and Ballet Theatre has achieved an important reputation in the USSR. Shown here are two leading soloists, Lubov Fominykh and Yuri Petukhov in a pas de deux from The Sleeping Beauty.

tion and energy, certainly justified within the USSR, although perhaps not so true in the freer cultural atmosphere of western countries. Oleg Vinogradov has followed a policy of presenting a mixture of the classics, on which he aims to shed new light, and new works by contemporary choreographers. For example, his version of *Romeo and Juliet* is a stylized commentary on young love. He has dispensed with everything that seemed to him, incidental – flamboyant costumes, crowd scenes, many of the minor events and even some characters, including the Nurse and Benvolio. The ballet has been refined down to the essentials and is arranged in two, rather than the more usual three, acts. Particularly interesting is his treatment of the lovers' deaths. After the hands of Juliet, already secretly married to Romeo, and Paris are ceremoniously joined by her father, she is left alone on the stage. She removes the loose dress which she wears over a plain leotard and tights, a costume worn by most of the characters. She places the dress on the only piece of furniture on the stage, which has represented in turn, a chair, altar and tomb. After stabbing it with a dagger she leaves the stage. Similarly, Romeo, after expressing his grief removes his tunic, stabs it and walks off the stage. Intermingled with this kind of symbolism is the quality of robust realism characteristic of the Maly company. The duel between Romeo and Tybalt, for example, is thoroughly nasty. Opinion of this work is mixed but it is unquestionably interesting and suggests that the company is moving in an exciting direction.

Moscow's second ballet company at the Nemirovich-Danchenko Theatre, grew out of a small group of dancers who, dissatisfied by the lack of scope in the Bolshoi's repertoire, formed a small company which toured the country around Moscow and also performed in the city. In 1927 it presented its own version of *Scheherazade* called *In the Chains of the Harem*. In 1928, it began to expand and Viktorina Kreiger, a Gorsky ballerina, became the Artistic Director of the group.

With the extreme enthusiasm of youth, the company adopted the ideals of realism. Classical dance was only permitted if the action justified it. The dancers created their own ballets, including a new version of *La Fille Mal Gardée*, called *The Rivals*, portraying the conflict between a rich and a poor girl for the love of Colas. Several other works were created on these principles, but they were never artistically convincing, although they achieved some success.

These ideas became somewhat modified by the mid-1930s. Rotislav Zakharov was invited to stage *The Fountain of Bakhchisarai*, which was produced about eight months before the Bolshoi Theatre. The company gained a considerable reputation for its dramatic abilities, particularly with ballets based on works by Pushkin, It was at this time that it was invited to become the permanent company at the Nemirovich-Danchenko Theatre.

At this time the choreographer, Vladimir Bourmeister began his association with the company. He had graduated from the Lunacharsky Theatre School in 1929 and made his debut as a choreographer with a new version of *Le Corsaire*, two years later. Since then, his works have constituted the major part of the company's repertoire, for example *The Merry Wives of Windsor*, *Scheherazade*, *Jeanne d'Arc* and a widely acclaimed version of *Swan Lake*, which he also staged for the Paris Opera. Another choreographer whose work has featured in the repertoire is Fedor Lopukhov, who was invited to create a ballet to Mussorsgky's *Pictures at an Exhibition* in 1963.

Outside the main ballet centres of Leningrad and Moscow, there are several notable companies who perform outside the USSR. One of the most interesting of these is the Novosibirsk Theatre of Opera and Ballet. It began as a more or less amateur company and several dancers trained there later joined the leading Soviet companies. This trend has now been reversed and dancers from the major companies have transferred to Novosibirsk. The company opened its own ballet school and dancers are trained to high professional standards.

The repertoire is large and varied, based on mainstream traditional ballets. For some time Oleg Vinogradov, now director of the Maly Opera Ballet, was associated with the company. He staged a number of works including a version of *Swan Lake*, when still only a student, and the original rendering of *Romeo and Juliet* currently featured in the Maly company's repertoire. In 1964, the Novosibirsk Opera was awarded the title 'Academic' giving it the same status as the Bolshoi, Kirov and Maly. Since then the ballet company has performed regularly in Moscow and also visited Western Europe.

Other companies of high standard, which are more rarely seen outside the USSR include the Perm Opera Ballet, the Kiev Ballet, Ukraine and the Tbilisi Ballet, Georgia. Each of these is well supplied with professionally trained dancers from their excellent schools. The Kiev Ballet School was founded by Galina Berezova who was a pupil of Agrippina Vaganova and the high standard of teaching is a valuable and carefully preserved tradition. The professionalism of these companies and others in Estonia and Lithuania, for example, is indicative of the serious artistic value placed on ballet in the USSR. Technically superb, the main lack in Soviet ballet, both in these smaller companies and the more illustrious world-famous ones, is real choreographic talent. Companies outside the USSR have benefited greatly from their opportunities to observe Soviet dancers and it is to be hoped that this will eventually become a two-way process and that Soviet companies will learn from and develop the experiments in choreography which have taken place in Western ballet companies.

EAST GERMANY
Ballet of the German State Opera

The Ballet of the German State Opera has a long history, stretching back some 230 years, always closely associated with the famous opera house Unter den Linden. From its earliest years, major figures in the world of ballet have been associated with the company, including the famous eighteenth century reformer Jean Georges Noverre and the twentieth century theoretician Rudolf von Laban and many illustrious dancers from Isadora Duncan to the present stars of the Bolshoi ballet.

Since the political re-organization of Germany which followed World War II, the Ballet of the German State Opera has adopted the techniques of Soviet teaching. It is the largest company in the German Democratic Republic with approximately 70 dancers, 20 of whom are soloists. In addition to giving regular ballet performances, it frequently appears in opera intermezzi.

During the last twenty years it has concentrated on the presentation of the great classical and traditional ballets. Some of these, *Swan Lake*, *Giselle*, *The Sleeping Beauty*, *Les Sylphides* and *The Nutcracker*, for example, are still performed with a considerable amount of the original choreography. Besides the classics, some of the major mainstream ballets of the twentieth century are also featured in the repertoire. Among these are *Spartacus*, *Le Sacre du Printemps* and *The Miraculous Mandarin*. Furthermore, the company has a special responsibility to young people, both juvenile audiences and student dancers. A number of programmes are staged regularly to introduce children to the art of ballet. Apart from the perennially popular *The Nutcracker*, performances of *Peter and the Wolf* and *The Emperor's New Clothes* are given. Close co-operation exists between the company and the State Ballet School, Berlin and pupils and students participate in several ballet evenings each year. The students are thus given the opportunity for practical stage experience.

On the first night of a new season, the company usually presents a full-length work from the regular repertoire. This can be one of the classical ballets, a dramatic work or a ballet specially commissioned for the company.

The second evening is usually devoted to experiment. Short ballets by well-known contemporary choreographers and new works are performed. In the last few years, these have included Tilo Medek's *David and Goliath*, Hans Dieter Hosall's *Bernarda Alba's House* and Wilhelm Neef's *How Much Earth Does Man Require*. This pairing of evenings continues throughout the season.

In addition, a choreographic workshop is included in the company's activities. Young choreographers from throughout the Republic are invited to present short works, usually to taped music. The best of these are taken into the regular repertoire and performed during chamber evenings both at home and abroad. Some of the most successful experiments of the workshop are *Oedipus and the Sphinx* by Grita Kräkte, *Bird Flight*, *Pas de Deux between a Dancer and a Spotlight* and *An Old Theme with Variations* by Dietmar Seyffert, *Freedom for Angela* by Lothar Hanff and *Two* by Harald Wandtke.

In recent years, a number of guest choreographers have worked with the company. These have included Natalia Kassatkina and Vladimir Wassiljow with *Le Sacre du Printemps*. Lázló Seregi with *Spartacus*, Tom Schilling with *Coppélia*, Conrad Drzewiecki with *The Miraculous Mandarin*, Dimitrije Parlic with *Joan von Zarissa* and Alberto Alonso with *Carmen Suite*. Most recently, Brigitte Thom staged George Blanchine's *Symphony in C*. The differing personalities and artistic approaches of these choreographers proved immensely stimulating for the company and it hopes to co-operate

George Balanchine is probably the biggest single influence in the world of classical ballet today. His works seem to be included in the repertoires of major companies in almost every country in the world. Monika Lubitz and J. Hanus Sklenar dance in Symphony in C.

with more guests from a wide variety of countries in future.

As well as regular seasons at the opera house Unter den Linden, the company visits many large provincial cities, particularly those with adequate theatre facilities but no ballet companies of their own. This also gives the company greater opportunity to develop individual works fully which may not have been possible otherwise because of demands on performing time at the opera house in Berlin.

During the last few years, regular festival weeks have been organized. Many international guest soloists have been invited to appear with the company and this has both encouraged audiences and enabled the dancers to discover new ideas and keep in touch with developments taking place throughout the world. Guest artists from the leading Soviet ballet companies, including the Bolshoi, as well as from London, Amsterdam, Paris and Helsinki have appeared with the Ballet of the German State Opera.

The company enjoys tremendous popularity at home and has made several very successful visits abroad. It is the leading company of the German Democratic Republic and maintains a strong sense of tradition with an open mind receptive to the best new ideas and outside influences.

Monika Lubitz and Bernd Dreyer dance the roles of Princess Marie and Prince Nutcracker in Vasily Vainonen's and Konstantin Schatilow's version of this tremendously popular ballet.

The Company

Prima Ballerina:	Monika Lubitz	**First Soloists:**	Gisela Ambros
Principal Dancers:	Bernd Dreyer		Peter Berger
	Roland Gawlik		
Soloists:	Ursula Fischer	Brigitte Preuss	Wilfried Jahn
	Ramona Gierth	Helga Schiele	Stefan Lux
	Annelies Kiontke	Doris Töpel	Winfried Mank
	Margot Leupold	Pedro Hebenstreit	J. Hans Sklenar
First Coryphées:	Ines Dalchau	Frank Bade	Hans Vogelreuter
	Anita Tank	Karl Maschwitz	
Second Coryphées:	Elke Beyer	Elke Stehr	Klaus Galler
	Stefanie Büttner	Ute Wisznawitzki	Harry Müller
	Sonja Gaubies	Dieter Bisch	Jürgen Nass
	Kristina Rouvel	Christian Eschrich	Klaus Sehmisch
	Gerlinde Specht	Egon Fischer	Alexander Winkler

The Repertoire

An Old Theme with Variations (Seyffert)
Bernada Alba's House (Krätke)
Bird Flight (Seyffert)
Carmen Suite (Alonso)
Coppélia (Schilling)
Giselle (Perrot/Coralli)
Grand Pas Classique (Gsovsky)
Grand Pas from Don Quixote (Gorsky)
Grand Pas from Useless Precautions (Petipa)
How much Earth does man require (Hanff/Reinthaller)
Invitation to the Waltz (Bischoff)
Joan von Zarissa (Parlic)
Le Sacre du Printemps (Kassatkina/Wassiljow)
Les Sylphides (Fokine)
Match (Schilling)
Oedipus and the Sphinx (Krätke)

Pas de Deux from Romeo and Juliet (Corelli)
Pas de Deux from the Firebird (Krätke)
Pas de Deux from the Flower Festival at Genzano (Bournonville)
Pas de Quatre (Perrot)
Peter and the Wolf (Hanff)
Petrouchka (Krätke)
Spartacus (Seregi)
Swan Lake (Gruber/Petipa/Ivanov)
Symphony in C (Balanchine)
The Dying Swan (Fokine)
The Emperor's New Clothes (Seyffert)
The Miraculous Mandarin (Drzewiecki)
The Nutcracker (Vainonen/Schatilo)
The Temptation of St Anthony (Lux)
The Three Musketeers (Seyffert)
Two (Wandtke)

HUNGARY
The Hungarian State Ballet

The story of ballet in Hungary is a strange one for, although it appeared in the eighteenth century, new developments did not begin until 200 years later. It seems astonishing that when Fokine's *Les Sylphides* (known as *Chopiniana* in Soviet countries) was staged at the Opera House in Budapest in 1965, it was the first time it had been seen in Hungary.

In the eighteenth century, astute theatre managers staged ballet performances based on those taking place in Western Europe. Ballet masters, however, quickly became interested in Hungarian folk dance. In fact, the famous dancer, choreographer and teacher Salvatare Vigano, staged the *Verbunk*, a Hungarian folk dance, in 1794 after he had toured Central Europe. The vitality of the folk idiom remained a strong influence on Hungarian ballet – sometimes positive and creative and at others, limiting and tiresome.

By the early nineteenth century, travelling theatre companies had become established. These groups moved from town to town and performed musical plays, dramas, pantomimes and ballets. Comic pantomimes were especially popular and often included dancing, either as part of the main action or in the form of interludes between plays. It is interesting that one of the most popular seems to have been a version of *Joko, the Brazilian Ape*.

Classical ballet was popular in the early part of the nineteenth century. However, foreign ballet masters were expensive and only the major companies could afford them. Generally, companies presented a combination of folk dance, ballet and pantomime, often on topical themes reflecting the strong nationalist feeling of the time. One particularly interesting example of this was a performance of a work about the battle of Fehértemplom on 20 November, 1848, during the War of Independence. The actual battle did not take place until 10 days later and happily confirmed the choreographer's predictions of victory.

Opportunities for development were presented when the Opera House in Budapest was opened in 1884. A succession of ballet masters from Italy was invited to train the dancers and Hungarian ballet has been greatly influenced by Italian teaching methods. As well as acting as teacher, these masters, including Pini, Smeraldi and Mazzantini danced principal roles in the performances. The last of these figures was the remarkable Nicola Guerra one of Europe's most influential teachers. He went to Hungary in 1902 and remained until 1914. He introduced a concentrated version of the techniques of Carlo Blasis whose teaching methods are still fundamental to classical ballet. Guerra trained a number of dancers to a very high standard, including Ferenc Nadasi who later studied with Enrico Cecchetti at St Petersburg.

Although, at this time, the Budapest Opera could boast of dancers trained to a high standard, some of whom were known internationally – Emilia Nirschy, Anna Pallay and Ferenc Nádasy – the company suffered from a lack of competent choreographers and creativity. This lack became even more apparent when Diaghilev's Ballets Russes visited Budapest in 1927. Undoubtedly the Ballets Russes' vitality and innovation was an inspiration to the ballet company and a delight to Hungary's most famous composer, Béla Bartók. Bartók had already composed two ballets – *The Wooden Prince* and *The Miraculous Mandarin*.

Ede Brada, the first native ballet master of the Budapest Opera was invited

The character of the Hungarian State Ballet has evolved from the fusion of diverse dance styles. This variety can be seen clearly in the repertoire which includes a wide range of choreographers. Here Imre Dózsa, Vera Szumrák, Mária Kékesi, Lilla Pártay and Katalin Czarnóy appear in a scene from Béjart's Serait-ce la Mort?

to create *The Wooden Prince* in 1917. He was not, however, a gifted choreographer and had no real experience or tradition to assist him in this difficult
task. His ballet failed dismally to match the standard of Bartók's score, which
in turn, was not really understood or appreciated by Hungarian audiences.
The Miraculous Mandarin was not staged at that time and suffered numerous
setbacks before it was seen in Hungary. In fact the first production was in
Cologne in 1926 where it was banned on the grounds of immorality. Béla
Bartók himself had already been accused of immorality in composing *The
Miraculous Mandarin* after the fall of the Hungarian Council Republic and
production of the ballet was prevented.

During the 1920s there was no real development in ballet in Hungary.
Politics interfered with art and policy insisted on the conservative and
nationalistic. It is significant that Rudolf von Laban, whose work provided
the basis for modern dance both in Europe and the United States, found no
outlet for his talents in Hungary. He worked for many years in Germany and
later in England, developing his theories of rhythm and movement, training
dancers like Kurt Jooss and inventing a system of dance notation, sometimes called Labanotation.

It was during the 1930s that ballet in Hungary began to develop and take
on a truly national character. The collecting of and research into folk music
by Béla Bartók and Zoltán Kodály acted as a considerable stimulus. Two new
Hungarian Ballet Masters were appointed to the Opera House, Ferenc
Nádasy and Gyula Harangozó. Ferenc Nádasy had a wide variety of experience as a dancer throughout Europe and was most interested in teaching.
Gyula Harangozó was a brilliant character principal and concentrated on
choreography.

Harangozó created many works for the company. The first of these was a

one-act ballet, *Scene in the Csarda*, based on a Hungarian folk tale. Fifteen years later, he based his first full-length work, *Kerchief*, on the same theme. Excerpts from *Kerchief* still feature in the repertoire. Harangozó's work is characterized by a skilful blending of classical ballet and traditional folk elements. In 1939 he staged a new version of *The Wooden Prince* rising to the challenge of Bartók's music. He continued work on this for many years, developing and extending his original choreography, completing his final version in 1958. He frequently danced the leading character-roles in his own ballets and gave a remarkable performance as the grotesque, puppet-like Wooden Prince.

Other choreographers were also given opportunities. The Polish choreographer, Jan Cieplinsky worked in Budapest for nearly 20 years creating *Joseph's Legends*, *Bolero* and *Hungarian Dreams*, in particular. The young Hungarian choreographer, Aurel Milloss also created a number of works for the Opera Ballet – *Prometheus*, *Petrouchka* and *Carnival*. These were not well received in Hungary and Aurel Milloss left to work in Rome, Cologne and Vienna.

Whatever other effects the political events following 1945 may have had in Hungary, they certainly opened up enormous possibilities for ballet. The influence of Soviet Russia was phenomenal, creating new and freer possibilities. In 1950, the State Ballet Institute was opened. Training dancers became the responsibility of the state, eliminating the problems of finance which so often prohibited the full development of a school. The Institute gives a general education as well as training dancers to a professional standard. Continuity has been maintained, however, as many of the teachers were themselves pupils of Ferenc Nádasy. The courses at the Institute have become so

Harald Lander's Etudes *is a fine opportunity for a classical company to display its technique. Fernec Havas, Adél Orosz and Imre Dózsa lead the company of the Hungarian State Ballet.*

popular that a programme of establishing schools in towns and villages was begun during the 1960s.

The corps de ballet was vastly increased in size and technique and a large theatre staff was organized. The company, now known as the Hungarian State Opera Ballet, added a whole new generation of young, talented and professionally trained dancers – Gabriella Lakatos, Zsuzsu Kun, Adél Orosz, Imré Dósza, Ferenc Havas and Viktor Róna. At the same time, the leading dancers of the old company continued with renewed enthusiasm and encouragement – Karola Szalay, Melinda Ottrubay, Zoltán Sallay and Gyula Harangozó.

When Hungary became part of the Eastern bloc, it had its first opportunity to become acquainted with the achievements of Soviet ballet and the traditions of Russian ballet preserved in the USSR. The Soviet ballet masters Vainonen, Messerer and Lavrovsky trained the dancers of the State Opera House and directed performances of the great Russian interpretations of the classics – *The Nutcracker* (1950), *Swan Lake* (1951), *Giselle* (1958), *The Sleeping Beauty* (1967).

As well as the classics, the Soviet teachers brought more contemporary creations from the USSR to Budapest. *The Flames of Paris* with choreography by Vainonen was produced in 1950. The stylized French folk dances and the dramatic action of a people in revolt accorded well with the traditions of Hungarian ballet. Other Soviet ballets included in the repertoire at this time were *The Fountain of Bakhchisarai*, based on a dramatic poem by Pushkin in 1952, the colourful oriental ballet *Gayane* to the music of Khachaturian with choreography by Anisimova who also directed the Budapest performance in 1959, and Lavrovsky's version of Sergei Prokofiev's *Romeo and Juliet* in 1962. As well as the direct Soviet contributions to ballet in Budapest, Hungarian choreographers continued to work with the State Opera, notably Gyula Harangazó. Besides *Mischievous Students* in 1949 which gave him an opportunity to blend the characteristic elements of Hungarian dance, *Kerchief*, a full-length, deeper and richer development of *Scene in the Csarda*, and the less successful *Mattie the Gooseboy*, Harangazó also, at last, presented *The Miraculous Mandarin*. As with *The Wooden Prince*, he constantly revised *The Miraculous Mandarin*, each time getting closer to Bartók's original conception, producing his final version in 1956. Besides the creation of new works, he also staged versions of *The Polovetsian Dances from Prince Igor*, *Promenade Concert* and *Scheherazade*.

Other Hungarian choreographers working in Budapest at this time included Ernó Vashegyi who created *Bihari's Song* and György Lórinc who created *The Maiden of the Sea*. Viktor Fülöp and Zsuzsu Kun, inspired by Thomas Mann, created *Mario and the Magician* in 1964, a one-act ballet combining classical and modern styles. László Sergi began work in Budapest at this time, creating a number of intermezzi for such operas as *Faust* and *Tannhäuser*.

The Firebird, *Petrouchka* and *Chopiniana* (*Les Sylphides*) were staged in their original forms. Ravel's *Daphnis and Chloë* and *Le Sacre du Printemps* were also presented in an exciting new interpretation by Imre Eck. He had already established a reputation for experiment with *Csonger and Tünde* in 1957, and later created the expressionistic *Music for Strings, Percussion and Celesta*, to music by Bartók, and *Miner's Ballad*. In 1960 Imre Eck left Budapest to found his own company, Ballet Sopianae, at Pécs in south-west Hungary. His philosophical approach and vigorous introspective creations have continued to exercise considerable influence on ballet in Budapest.

The single most important choreographer at the State Opera now is László Seregi and many of his short ballets are frequently featured in the repertoire. A strong folk tradition is apparent in works like *Spinning Room* but Seregi is a versatile choreographer and his abilities extend to an ambitious blending of ballet and jazz in the film *The Girl Danced Into Life* and a challenging presentation of *Walpurgisnacht*. His primary inspiration is musical and he displays great musicality as well as rich inventiveness and sensitivity.

In 1968 he created *Spartacus* to Khachaturian's score and this was triumphantly received in Hungary. The production combines all the elements which fused to produce the national character of Hungarian ballet – national dance-plays, Soviet ballet drama, classicism, folk-dance and contemporary dance. Each act presents a different point of view – that of Spartacus, that of Crassus, the Roman general, and that of Spartacus's wife, Flavia. Exciting, dramatic and deeply moving, *Spartacus* marks a new maturity and artistic autonomy in the history of the Hungarian State Opera Ballet.

Since *Spartacus*, Seregi has created a number of works for the company and the current repertoire includes his versions of *The Wooden Prince* and *The Miraculous Mandarin*. Also ballets from western European choreographers are featured bringing yet another strand of development into this varied and versatile company.

The Company
Principal dancers:

Katalin Csarnóy	Márta Metzger	Imre Dózsa	Zoltán Nagy
Erzsébet Dvorszky	Adél Orosz	József Forgách	Gábor Keveházi
Ildikó Kaszás	Lilla Pártay	Viktor Fülöp	Sándor Erdélyi
Zsuzsu Kun	Maria Kékesi	Ferenc Havas	Sandor Perlusz
Gabriella Lakatos	Vera Szumrák	Levente Sipeki	
Jacqueline Menyhárt	Ildikó Pongor	László Sterbinszky	

The Repertoire

The Fountain of Bakhchisarai (Zakharov)
Coppélia (Harangozó)
The Miraculous Mandarin (Seregi)
The Nutcracker (Vainonen)
Etudes (Lander)
The Wooden Prince (Seregi)
Giselle (Lavrovsky)
Violin Concerto in E Major (Fodor)
Opus 5 (Béjart)
Pas de Quatre (Dolin)
La Fille Mal Gardée (Ashton)
Spartacus (Seregi)
La Sylphide (Bournonville/Brenaa)
Sylvia (Seregi)

Le Sacre du Printemps (Béjart)
The Firebird (Béjart)
The Cedar (Seregi)
Mischievous Students (Harangozó)
Scheherazade (Harangozó)
Serait-ce la Mort? (Béjart)
Le Spectre de la Rose (Fokine)
Metamorphosis (Fodor)
Polovetsian Dances from Prince Igor (Harangozó)
The Sleeping Beauty (Petipa/Gusev)
The Creation of the World (Kasatkina/Vasiljov)
Grand pas The Kingdom of shades from La Baydére (Petipa)

Touring

1936	Bayreuth	1964	Helsinki, Stockholm, Cairo
1938	Florence		
1953	Bucharest (World Youth Festival)	1965	Moscow, Monte Carlo
		1966	Zagreb, Belgrade, Sofia
1957	Prague, Brno, Bratislava	1967	Vienna
		1968	Wiesbaden, Helsinki, Bergen, Berlin
1959	Bucharest		
1960	Warsaw, Poznan, Wroclaw	1969	Baalbek, Paris, Le Havre
1961	Turin, Berlin, Dresden	1970	Bologna, Bucharest
1962	Helsinki	1971	Dortmund
1963	Edinburgh, Paris	1975	Warsaw

DEVELOPMENTS ACROSS THE WORLD~ MEXICO

Ballet Folklorico de Mexico

Not one, but several companies, the multi-faceted Ballet Folklorico de Mexico is a national institution with an international reputation. Its development is entirely due to the imagination and broad intellect of Amalia Hernandez, the company's Director. At the age of eight she decided to become a dancer and persuaded her father, a wealthy businessman and public figure, to allow her to have lessons. He agreed on condition that she would never dance in public, a promise which she later broke to the great benefit of Mexican culture. He provided her with a private studio and the best teachers available.

Amalia Hernandez then became a teacher and choreographer at the National Institute of Fine Arts in Mexico City but she was satisfied with neither classical nor modern ballet. One of her early teachers had been Luis Felipe Obregon, an expert and researcher in Mexican folklore, and she had been deeply influenced by him. Her interest in the dances of Mexico developed during her adolescence and continued to increase. In 1952, she founded her own company in order to present folklore ballets created and directed by herself. Eight students from the National Institute joined her. In conjunction with Emilio Azcarraga, Director of a Mexican television network, the Hernandez Company presented a series of folklore programmes.

The series was so successful, the Mexican Government sponsored further productions and on the strength of this, the number of dancers was increased to 20. By 1954, 67 such programmes had been presented and a small regular following was established. At this time, the Department of Tourism invited the Hernandez Company to become an official cultural representative of Mexico, and as a result, it visited Canada, Cuba and Los Angeles.

In 1959 President Lopez Mateos asked the company to prepare and perform a special programme for the Pan American Games in Chicago. By this time, the size had increased to about 50 dancers and musicians. The com-

pany's visit to Chicago was a triumphant success and, on its return to Mexico, the President requested Celestino Gorostiza, Director of the Fine Arts Institute, to help organize the Hernandez Company as a national group. As the Ballet Folklorico de Mexico, it occupies this position still.

In May 1961, the government sent the company to the Théâtre des Nations Festival in Paris. It was well aware of the competition it faced, for many of the world's leading companies and dancers were present and the arrival of the Ballet Folklorico aroused little interest at such a major international gathering. The company's delight was unimaginable when it was awarded first prize and so achieved international recognition more or less overnight.

By this time the Ballet Folklorico had grown to include 400 people and five companies. One company performed regularly in Mexico City and another was more or less permanently on tour. A large circus tent had been presented by the government enabling over 4000 performances to be given in towns and villages throughout the countryside. The administrative demands of such an enterprise were immense. In addition, Amalia Hernandez continued her researches into folk tradition and was creating new ballets. Moreover, the Department of Tourism was making increasing demands on the company's time in Mexico City thus lessening the scope for tours abroad. It was decided, therefore, to establish a resident company at the Palace of Fine Arts in Mexico City. Amalia Hernandez appointed her daughter, Norma Lopez Hernandez as Director and she has proved a tremendously capable administrator. She had danced with the company but had always wanted to direct. There were 110 performers in the resident company and 90 in the touring company which Amalia Hernandez continues to direct. These 200 dancers also perform in the other three companies – the First and Second Companies of the Ballet of the Americas and the Classical Company. Norma Lopez Hernandez now assists with the direction of both main companies.

This new arrangement enabled Amalia Hernandez greater freedom to tackle the problem of new talent and professional training. The School of the Ballet Folklorico was founded in 1968 and there are approximately 150 students, some of whom have been awarded scholarships financed by the company's box office. Members of the company teach the unique style of the Ballet Folklorico and classical and modern ballet is taught by guests from all over the world. The government is interested in establishing another company in Mexico City and, if this project goes ahead, its members will be drawn from students at the school.

Amalia Hernandez already leads an exceptionally busy life, but she has found time to extend her interest in Mexican traditions even further. As Mexico becomes increasingly urbanized and industrialized, many aspects of village life are disappearing, in particular the musical and dance heritage. Amalia Hernandez has instituted a programme of documenting village folk dances on film in order to preserve a record of them. These films are, of course, useful in the preparation of new ballets but also provide a unique

Ballet is spreading across the world and becoming very popular in a number of countries where the dance tradition is quite different. The Tokyo Ballet Company is a particularly successful and attractive manifestation of this worldwide development.

anthropological library.

The process of creating new works for the Ballet Folklorico is arduous. Creation must be preceded by painstaking historical research. Amalia Hernandez travels throughout Mexico as well as being a constant visitor to museums to study sculpture, murals and paintings for information about myths and legends of the past. She also studies extant dances, rituals and cermonies to provide the basic source for her final dramatic creation. Only when all this has been completed, does she select a theme and begin work on the dance.

Similar detailed research is involved in the design of the magnificent and colourful costumes for which the Ballet Folklorico is particularly renowned. Mexico has a rich diversity of national costumes because of the variety of nationalities which have affected the country throughout its history. Similarly, scenery and properties are as authentic as possible.

This careful attention to detail results in a final spectacle of unique magnificence. No other dance company in the world combines such a variety of elements drawn from so rich a cultural heritage.

The Ballet Folklorico de Mexico is especially famous for its colourful and authentic stagings. Boda en el Istmo de Tehuantepec *is a series of three dances of love, courtship and marriage derived from the south of Mexico.*

The Company

Director General and Choreographer:	Amalia Hernandez	Director:	Norma Lopa Hernandez

Dancers:

Martha Garcia	Humberto Treviño	Evangelina Pola	Carlos Ochoa
Azucena Jimenez	Raul Valdez	Argel Alvarado	Francisco Perez
Roseyra Marenco	Eduardo Velazquez	Leticia Cazares	Victor Nolasco
Maria Elena Gonzalez	Emilio Ceron	Maria Teresa Lugo	Carlos Rios
Guillermina Lopez	Fidel Herrera	Celia Davila	Cesar Gomez
Alma Rosa Martinez	Efren Tello	Thelma Gandarilla	Mario Mejia
Enriqueta Amaya	Carlos Casados	Socorro Sumano	Roberto Vidaña
Sonia Ornelas	Juan Jose Gasca	Olga Ruiz	Efren Flores
Isabel Corona	Everardo Hernandez	Concepcion Morales	Guillermo Acuña
Laura Lojo	Haydee Maldonado	Violeta Jimenez	Nestor Castelan
Evelia Beristain	Ana Maria Tapia	Juan Medellin	Armando Pecero
Maria Esther Vizcarra	Maria Luisa Gonzalez	Jose Santacruz	Alfonso Rivera
Carmen Molina	Marcia Cravioto	Pedro Rodriguez	Guillermo Pensado
Mercedes Loza	Teresa Padilla	Francisco Cruz	Alfredo Espinoza
Gloria Rocio Torres	Elsa Garcia	Rolando Miguel Cano	Juan De Dios Gomez
Rosalinda Torres	Rosa Elena Jimenez	Antonio Lizaola	Kleber Garcia
Jose Villaneuva	Maria Elia Macias	Enrique Martinez	Jose Eduardo
Dante Palomino	Aida Polanco	Jorge Garduño	Fernandez
Ricardo Higuera	Josefina Maldonado	Ramon Dominguez	Jesus Carreon

The Repertoire

Boda en el Istmo de Tehuantepec	*Los Dioses*
Boda en la Huasteca	*Los Mayas*
Chiapas	*Los Olmecas de Tabasco*
Danza del Venado	*Los Tarascos*
Guelaguetza	*Misa Chamula*
Jalisco	*Serenata*
La Revolucion	*Sones de Michoacan*
La Vida es Juego	*Tonanzintla*
La Zafra en Tamaulipas	*Veracruz*

Touring

Canada, United States, Germany, Belgium, Italy, France, Latin America.

ARGENTINA
Teatro Colón

When the prestigous Teatro Colón in Buenos Aires was opened on 25 May 1908, it was already evident that it would be essential to build up companies of performing artists who would be able to use the splendid new facilities fully. A small ballet group was already in existence and work began immediately to develop a full-size company with these dancers as its core. Initially, professional Italian dancers were contracted to provide a stimulus for native talent and for public interest. Generally, lyrical works only were presented but major international stars were invited to appear as guest artists.

In 1925 it became possible to establish permanent performing companies at the theatre and among these was a ballet company. It consisted of both Argentinian dancers and foreign artists resident in the country. The first Director of the company was Adolf Bolm who had trained at St Petersburg and later became a soloist at the Maryinsky Theatre. He appeared with Diaghilev's touring company in its early seasons and later resigned from the Maryinsky company to become premier danseur, choreographer and ballet master with the Ballets Russes, travelling through Europe and North and South America. He remained in the United States where he gained some valuable experience in establishing new ballet companies.

Georges Kyascht was appointed Ballet Master and Adolf Bolm obtained the services of a number of international ballerinas such as Ruth Page, Anna Ludmila and Aimée Abraanova. Later, it became possible for Argentinian artists to alternate with foreign dancers in the leading roles. In 1929, the first Argentinian ballet was premièred. *La Flor del Irupe*, with choreography by Constantino Gaito, was the first ballet totally conceived, including plot and scenery, for the Teatro Colón.

By the 1930s, a number of outstanding Argentinian dancers had emerged. These included Dora del Grande, Leticia de la Vega, Lida Martinolli, María and Angeles Ruanova, Estela Deporte, Angel Eleta and Beatrice and Victor Ferrari. In addition, the company benefitted from two resident foreign dancers, Michel Borovsky and Jorge Tomin, born George Fostikoff. A talented dancer, Jorge Tomin partnered Olga Spessivtzeva in *The Bluebird Pas de Deux* and *Elegie*, when she visited Buenos Aires in 1937. In 1939 he joined the Original Ballet Russe for a tour of the United States and then returned to the Teatro Colón as premier danseur. He acquired a sizeable repertoire and for many years was Ballet Master and choreographer.

By the mid-1940s the company had established a major reputation. Its form had been completely revised. Talented soloists had emerged from the corps de ballet and were able to undertake many principal roles and new dancers were graduating into the corps to replace them. Furthermore, new ballets created in Argentina were gradually being added to the repertoire. The company has continued to invite world-famous guest artists and choreographers to Buenos Aires. Among these were major figures such as Bronislava Nijinska, Boris Romanov, Michel Fokine, Margaret Walmann, Tatiana Gsovska, Tamara Grigorieva, Nicholas Zverev and Antony Tudor.

The repertoire has featured works by many of the world's greatest choreographers including George Balanchine, Leonide Massine, Elsa Marianne von Rosen, John Taras, William Dollar, Jack Carter, Serge Lifar, Aurel Milloss, Rudolf Nureyev, George Skibine and Pierre Lacotte. In addition, works by the Argentinian choreographers Oscar Araiz, Antonio Truyol, Nestor Roigt and Miguel Miranda have achieved international recognition and are also

Swan Lake is an essential item in the repertoire of any large classical company. The Teatro Colón is especially proud of its version. The disciplined technique of the corps de ballet is evident from this photograph.

257

included in the repertoire.

The stimulus and encouragement of visiting foreign dancers has been extremely valuable to the company. It has been exposed to influences from all over the world and has benefitted from experiments and developments taking place in all the leading companies. The artistic force of the Bolshoi Ballet was particularly impressive and a number of visits from the London Festival Ballet profoundly affected the style of the Argentinian dancers. As a result of such visits the company has acquired a wide classical repertoire, a varied dance vocabulary and a polished and dramatic technique. Other ballet companies which have appeared at the Teatro Colón include the Original Ballet Russe, the Ballet of the Paris Opera, la Compania de Alicia Alonso, the Marquis de Cuevas company, Ballet du XXème Siecle, Ballet of the German Berlin Opera, the Australian Ballet, the National Opera Ballet of Finland and the Nikolais Dance Theatre.

The company regularly makes national tours and in the 1960s, it appeared outside Argentina for the first time. In 1968, José Neglia won an award at the Paris Festival. He became a member of the company at an early age and was quickly promoted to a soloist, creating the role of Roderick in Massine's *Usher* in 1955. He was further promoted to premier danseur the following year and his wide repertoire included *Swan Lake, The Three-Cornered Hat, Apollon Musagète, La Flor del Irupe* and *Pillar of Fire*. He had consolidated his position as Argentina's leading male dancer when, in the early 1970s, he and eight other soloists, including the ballerina Norma Fontenia, were tragically killed in an air accident. This was a sad blow to the company and it was some years before it regained its full strength.

All companies depend for their future on the solid foundation of a school where new dancers can be trained to professional standards and the Teatro Colón has not neglected this aspect. In 1922 the Institute of Superior Arts was founded and academies of singing and dancing were established. This has gradually expanded and in 1958 and 1959, it was re-structured and extended to include dance, singing, stage direction, scenery design and the technique of preparing operatic music. On graduation, the students are absorbed where possible, into the performing companies.

In 1976, Antonio Truyol was appointed Artistic Director and he continues the tradition established by his predecessors of presenting a wide range of mainstream ballet. The directors of the company have almost always been closely involved with the daily activities of the dancers, frequently continuing to perform principal roles and creating new works. The previous Director was María Ruanova, ballerina at the Teatro Colón for many years and for whom George Balanchine created *Mozart Concerto*. She was much admired by the many guest choreographers who worked with the Teatro Colón and when she retired from the stage she took on the combined responsibilities of Artistic Director and Ballet Mistress until her death in June 1976.

The Ballet of the Teatro Colón has fulfilled more than adequately the original hopes of establishing a company worthy of the splendid theatre. A broad artistic and cultural background has created a company of international repute and yet, by developing native talent, it has acquired a unique national character.

The Company

Artistic Director:	Antonio Truyol		
Choreographer:	Olga Ferri		
Principal Dancers:	Esmeralda Agoglia	Nancy Lopez	Gustavo Mollajoli
	Olga Ferri	Enrique Lommi	Antonio Truyol
Soloists:	Estela Deporte	Beatriz Moscheni	Ruben Chayan
	María Garcia	Lydia Segni	Patricio Guiloff
	Violeta Janiero	Mercedes Serrano	Leandro Regueiro
	Ada Kristel	Vera Stankaitis	
	Esther Lisogorsky	Paula Svagel	
Coryphées:	Beatriz Chaiquin	Rodolfo Fontan	Eliseo Pinto

The Repertoire

Annabel Lee (Skibine)
Apollon Musagète (Balanchine)
Bolero (Milloss)
Carmen (Alonso)
Cinderella (Skibine)
Concert Variations (Taras)
Constantia (Dollar)
Daphnis and Chloë (Sibine/Lozano)
Divertimento (Dollar)
Don Quixote Pas de Deux (Petipa/Nureyev)
Dream of a Girl (Lichine)
Gaîté Parisienne (Massine)
Giselle (Coralli)
Hallo (Araiz)
Interplay (Lambrinos)
Juan de Zarissa (Gsovska)
La Sylphide (Lacotte)
La Tragedia de Salomé (Andrade)
La Valse (Bolender)
Le Sacre du Printemps (Araiz)
Le Spectre de la Rose (Fokine)
Les Sylphides (Fokine)
Mekhano (Andrade)
Orfeo (Andrade)

Pillar of Fire (Tudor)
Pulsaciones (Biaggi)
Raymonda (Petipa)
Romeo and Juliet (Skibine)
Sebastian (Dollar)
Seventh Symphony (Biaggi)
Siegfried's Idyll (Biaggi)
Spiritu Tuo (Truyol)
Suite de Danses (Petroff)
Suite en Blanc (Lifar)
Swan Lake (Carter)
Swan Lake – 'Black Swan' Pas de Deux (Petipa/Nureyev)
The Firebird (Skibine)
The Miraculous Mandarin (Araiz)
The Nutcracker (Nureyev)
The Polovetsian Dances from Prince Igor (Fokine)
The Prisoner of the Caucasus (Skibine)
The Sleeping Beauty (Carter)
The Sorcerer's Apprentice (Carter)
The Three-Cornered Hat (Pericet)
Usher (Massine)
Vitrales (Andrade)

Touring

Lima, Mexico, Santo Domingo, Curaçao, Brazil, Paris.

CUBA
The National Ballet of Cuba

The first professional Cuban ballet company, the Ballet Alicia Alonso, was founded in Havana in October 1948, under the direction of Alicia and Fernando Alonso, with the collaboration of the choreographer Alberto Alonso. In 1955, the company's name was changed to the Ballet de Cuba. Following the political revolution of 1959, it achieved the true national identity which it had sought.

Since its inception in the pre-revolutionary period of Cuba's history, the company has struggled to extend its art beyond the false limits of an apparent cultural and intellectual elite. It has been a constant aim to bring ballet to audiences drawn from all sectors of the population and to encourage talent wherever it can be found. With this in mind, the company used its limited financial resources until 1956, to offer scholarships to its school, which had been founded in 1950. Many performances were given in public places, such as parks and town squares, throughout the country. During this period, seven foreign tours were also made, establishing an early reputation abroad.

From 1950, the company had received financial assistance from the Government. However, by 1956, the political situation in Cuba was becoming increasingly chaotic and anxiety lest the company should become an instrument of propaganda led to a refusal of further state aid. Political activists regarded this as a triumphant act of cultural revolution and the issue became a subject for major debate. Whatever the political value of the gesture, it was an unfortunate development artistically and the company went into a rapid decline. This was exacerbated by the refusal of Alicia Alonso to perform in Cuba while the unpopular Batista régime remained in power.

It was not until the years which followed the 1959 revolution that the company believed it had gained the artistic and creative freedom it really required. Almost immediately, it became involved in a period of intense activity, holding seminars in work centres and military and student establishments. It re-asserted the importance of its original aim to enrich the artistic and cultural life of the entire Cuban community. The quality and frequency of performances rapidly increased and a distinct national style evolved, recognized internationally as well as in Cuba.

It is praiseworthy that in this atmosphere of fundamental change, the National Ballet of Cuba deliberately concentrated on the rich international heritage of its art. The broad experience of its founders and senior members proved invaluable in the establishment of an extensive repertoire, which was planned to provide an integrated mixture of classical and romantic ballets and contemporary works by major choreographers of different styles and nationalities.

The National Ballet continues to maintain the importance of development an evolution in ballet, believing that all art is an expression of contemporary concern. However, it also regards continuity as an important part of this process and the company's style is firmly based on a thorough training in the classical technique.

National tours continue to feature in the company's schedule and, in addition it has made many visits to countries in North and South America, Europe and Asia. Furthermore, the International Festival of Ballet, held in Havana, is acquiring a considerable international reputation.

Alicia Alonso has been a frequent guest artist with American Ballet Theatre. Other members of the National Ballet of Cuba have also been invited to appear abroad and here she is partnered by Jorge Esquival in a gala performance in 1975.

The Company

Director:	Alicia Alonso
Deputy Director:	Isobel Rodríguez
Choreographers:	Alberto Alonso
	Alicia Alonso
	Gustavo Herrera
	Alberto Méndez
	José Parés
	Iván Tenorio
Ballet Masters:	Laura Alonso
	Joaquín Banegas
	Silvia Marichal
	Keremia Moreno
	Aldolfo Roval
Prima Ballerina:	Alicia Alonso
First Principals:	Loipa Araujo
	Aurora Bosch
	Marta García
	María Elena Llorente
	Josefina Méndez
	Mirta Plá
	Lázaro Carreño
	Jorge Esquivel
	Orlando Salgado
Second Principals:	Cristina Alvarez
	Sonia Calero
	Mirta García
	Pablo Moré
	Andrés Williams
	José Zamorano
First Soloists:	Amparo Brito
	Clara Carranco
	Ofelia González
	Caridad Martínez
	Rosario Súarez
	Raúl Bustabad
	Hugo Guffanti
	Fernando Jhones

The National Ballet's version of Carmen *has been acclaimed on their foreign tours and has been featured in the repertoires of several major companies, including the Bolshoi Ballet. Here, prima ballerina Alicia Alonso dances the title role, partnered by Jorge Esquival.*

The Repertoire

Badanesa (Herrera)
Déjame Amar al Pájaro del Amor (Herrera)
Divertimento (Lland)
El Dúo de Siempre (Mendez)
Elogio (Tenorio)
Flower Festival at Genzano Pas de Deux

(Bournonville, staged by Loipa Araujo)
Las Intermitencias del Corazón (Petit)
Paso a Tres (Mendez)
The Firebird (Lefebre)
Time Out of Mind (Macdonald)
Xochiquetzal (Tenorio)

Touring

Venezuela, Puerto Rico, Mexico, Guatemala, El Salvador, Costa Rica, Panama, Colombia, Ecuador, Peru, Chile, Argentina, Uruguay, United States, Brazil, Canada, Republic of Dominica, USSR, German Democrat Republic, Poland, Czechoslovakia, Romania, Hungary, Bulgaria, France, Belgium, Holland, Spain, Luxembourg, Monaco, Italy, Switzerland, Yugoslavia, Portugal, Finland, China, Korea, Vietnam, Mongolia.

AUSTRALIA
The Australian Ballet

Ballet developed permanent foundations in Australia during the 1930s when two dancers from the Ballet Russe de Monte Carlo decided to settle there. The first of these was Hélène Kirsova who made her home in Sydney, in 1937, and opened a school, three years later. She formed a small company from her pupils, taking on the leading roles herself. It gave its first professional performances in July 1941 and, for a short while, flourished. The number of dancers increased and included several former soloists of the Ballet Russe. Tours were made to several major Australian cities and the repertoire included *Swan Lake* and *Les Sylphides* as well as Kirsova's own works. However, World War II depleted the number of male dancers so drastically, that Hélène Kirsova was forced to disband the group and, in 1946, she returned to Europe.

A more lasting influence was that of Edouard Boravansky, who decided to remain in Australia after the 1939 tour of the Ballet Russe. He too established a school in 1940, in Melbourne, with the assistance of his wife Xenia Nikolaeva and the Melbourne Ballet Club. The following year, he founded the Borovansky Company. It presented a typical Ballet Russe repertoire at the Melbourne Princess Theatre, for increasingly longer seasons each year. Furthermore, it was booked by the influential theatrical firm, J. C. Williamson Ltd., when it turned professional in 1944 and embarked on its first tour of the main cities of Australia. This led to many more such tours and also visits to New Zealand. Towns are so scattered in Australia that the Borovansky Company's visits seemed very sporadic and the irregularities were further exacerbated by temporary disbandment of the group. However, Borovansky performed an invaluable service by establishing firm roots for the classic tradition in Australia and by entertaining many audiences with a repertoire which included *Carnaval, Coppélia, Giselle, Les Sylphides* and *Swan Lake*. After his sudden death in 1959 on the eve of another tour, the company came under the leadership of Peggy van Praagh, although, in 1960, it had to be disbanded because of financial difficulties. A British dancer, she had trained with Margaret Craske, Lydia Sokolova, Vera Volkova and Tamara Karsavina. She became a soloist with the Ballet Rambert and was later the principal dancer with Antony Tudor's London Ballet, creating such roles as Episode in His Past in *Jardin aux Lilas* and the Russian Ballerina in *Gala Performance*. After his departure for the United States she continued to lead the company for a short while before joining the Sadler's Wells Ballet. In 1946, she was appointed Ballet Mistress of the newly-formed Sadler's Wells Opera Ballet and later became Assistant Director.

In 1962, the directors of the Australian Elizabethan Theatre Trust and J. C. Williamson Ltd, founded the Australian Ballet and invited Peggy van Praagh to become its first Director. The core of the new company consisted of many dancers from the Borovansky group. Young dancers, trained in Australia and guest artists were also invited.

The company's first season began in Sydney on 2 November, 1962 and guest artists included Sonia Arova, Erik Bruhn, Nikita Dolgushin, Caj Selling, Jonathon Watts and Tatiana Zimina. The repertoire was based on that of the British Royal Ballet and included *Swan Lake, Coppélia, Les Sylphides, Don Quixote, The Lady and the Fool* and *Les Rendezvous*. Also, the new company presented *Melbourne Cup* by the Australian choreographer Rex Reid and the witty, original style of this work brought it considerable success.

The Australian Ballet's The Merry Widow *is the first ballet performance of this popular operetta. The three-act work was created by Ronald Hynd. Here, Lucette Aldous as Valencienne is partnered by John Meehan as Danilo in a pas de deux in the final act.*

Happily, Don Quixote *has enjoyed an increased popularity during the last few years. It is a delightful work full of humour and colour, offering scope for brilliant displays of virtuosity. Here, the crowd tosses Sancho Panza in the air.*

Rex Reid had studied at the Sadler's Wells Ballet School and then gained a broad background of experience with the Original Ballet Russe, International Ballet and the Ballet Rambert before he returned to Australia.

In 1965, when only three years old, the Australian Ballet took the adventurous step of touring abroad. It made its foreign debut at the Baalbek Festival in Lebanon and then visited Europe, including participation in the Commonwealth Arts Festival in London, the International Dance Festival in Paris, and other festivals in France and Britain. This tour proved extremely successful and the company's prima ballerina, Kathleen Gorham, was particularly praised.

At this time, three new and ambitious ballets were commissioned. Rudolf Nureyev staged *Raymonda* and Robert Helpmann created *The Display* and *Yúgen.* This last work was a mixed achievement, because, although it lacked artistic unity, the presentation and spectacular costumes delighted many audiences.

Robert Helpmann was the first of several Australian dancers who became international stars abroad. He was premier danseur with the Sadler's Wells Ballet until 1950 and later a guest artist and choreographer. Other Australian dancers who have achieved recognition abroad include Lucette Aldous,

Elaine Fifield and Kathleen Gorham. The latter returned permanently in 1962 to become prima ballerina of the Australian Ballet and on her retirement from the stage, she acted as guest teacher. Lucette Aldous returned as a principal dancer after a successful career as a soloist with the Ballet Rambert and the London Festival Ballet. Moreover, in 1965, Robert Helpmann was invited to become a co-director with Peggy van Praagh to assist in the development of a national ballet. He became sole director in 1974. Robert Helpmann, Peggy van Praagh and Kathleen Gorham have all received honours for their services to ballet, CBE, DBE and OBE respectively.

The Australian Ballet has striven to present the great classics and maintain their traditions. In 1973, they presented a widely acclaimed version of *The Sleeping Beauty* during their first season at the Sydney Opera House. Much of Petipa's choreography was preserved, faithfully reproduced by Peggy van Praagh and the Prince's Variation in Act II, created by Sir Frederick Ashton, was used. The colourful and spectacular costumes and decor were designed by Kenneth Rowell, famous for his many designs for The Royal Ballet, London.

However, the Australian Ballet does not limit its activities to presenting major classics. Since its inception, it has staged many original one-act works and in 1975, the first full-length production was commissioned. This was the unusual ballet, *The Merry Widow*, based on the operetta by Franz Lehár. The choreography was undertaken by Ronald Hynd, former principal of the Royal Ballet and creator of a number of highly successful works, including *Dvořák Variations*. The light-hearted operetta, *The Merry Widow*, has enjoyed phenomenal success since its première, with numerous revivals all over the world and several film versions. To present it in the form of a ballet was a challenging project, inviting criticism. However, it was considerably less unlikely than the silent film version made by Erich von Stroheim in 1925, which starred Mae Murray and John Gilbert.

The resulting work, which the Australian Ballet has performed both at home and abroad, captured the essence of the original. Lavish and spectacular costumes and décor charmed audiences and the choreography was a delightful romp. *The Merry Widow* will not achieve the stature of such great works as *Swan Lake* or even *Coppélia*, but it has enriched the repertoire of the Australian Ballet and provides a new and refreshing show case for the talents of its many gifted dancers.

The Company

Director:	Sir Robert Helpmann CBE	**Assistant Ballet Master:**	Colin Peasley
Dance Professor:	Leon Kellaway	**Choreologist:**	Barbara Nimmo
Principal Dancers:	Alan Alder	Kelvin Coe	John Meehan
	Lucette Aldous	Marilyn Jones	Marilyn Rowe
	Walter Bourke	Jonathan Kelly	
	Alida Chase	Maria Lang	
Soloists:	Jan Blanch	Joseph Janusaitis	Leigh Rowles
	Sally Collard-Gentle	Michela Kirkaldie	Paul Saliba
	Francis Croese	Rex McNeill	Ross Stretton
	Hilary Debden	Robert Olup	Christine Walsh
	Roma Egan	Anthony Pannell	
	Gail Ferguson	Colin Peasley	
Coryphées:	Dale Barker	Susan Dains	Leigh Matthews
	Mark Brinkley	Chrisa Keramidas	Valmai Roberts

SOUTH AFRICA
The PACT Ballet Company

It is ironic that a country which produced among others, John Cranko, Alexis Rassine, Nadia Nerina, Maryon Lane, Deanne Bergsma and Monica Mason, should have had so many problems establishing its own professional ballet companies.

Perhaps one reason why South Africa is widely recognized as a source for talented dancers and choreographers for companies throughout the world, and in Europe particularly, is because of its high teaching standards. A long history of association with British ballet began with the pioneering teacher Helen Webb, who went to South Africa in 1912 and joined the South African College of Music in Cape Town. From 1916 she staged annual ballet performances with the Cape Town Municipal Orchestra.

Dawn Weller and Malcolm Burn dance the roles of Juliet and Romeo. The sad story of the young 'star-crossed' lovers has inspired many choreographers and is very well suited to the medium of dance.

In 1917 Edouard Espinosa and his sister, Madame Ravodna visited South Africa and did a great deal to encourage systematic training. Madame Ravodna remained in South Africa and did much to develop teaching techniques based on her brother's codification of styles which later became a fundamental part of Britain's Royal Academy of Dancing. Espinosa himself returned regularly to South Africa as an examiner for the Association of Operatic Dancing of Great Britain, the organization from which the Royal Academy of Dancing developed. Examiners and teachers from the Cecchetti Society in London also travelled regularly to South Africa.

In 1923, the South Africa Dancing Teachers Association was formed to establish a uniform standard for training and examinations. In the same year, Helen Webb formed her own company which gave performances in the main cities, travelling as far as Johannesburg and Pietermaritzburg in Natal.

In 1926, Anna Pavlova and a company of 40 dancers, visited Cape Town, Among the works she performed were *The Fairy Doll, Snow Ballet, Amarilla, Dance of the Hours, Bacchanale* and the famous *Dying Swan*. South African audiences went wild and all previous box office records at the Cape Town Opera House were broken. As a result, the number of ballet schools and aspiring dancers increased.

The organization which had been responsible for Pavlova's visit was so encouraged by her reception, it invited Madame Ravodna to stage *The Sleeping Beauty* at Johannesburg. She tackled this project with enthusiasm but petty jealousies and rivalries prevented the performance from taking place. Plans to establish a local company were never realized for the same reason.

Hopes of creating a company were once again revived when Levitikoff's Russian Ballet visited South Africa in 1934. The South African Ballet and Production Club was formed but again quarrels and jealousy disrupted it and the company was disbanded before it achieved anything. A second attempt to form the Ballet Club was made five years later but this failed for the same reasons.

A more successful attempt was made in 1941 by John Connell, director of the Johannesburg City Orchestra. He invited four teachers, Marjorie Sturman, Poppy Frames, Ivy Commee and Lesley Hudson, to present a short ballet divertissement during the opera season. As a result of this Marjorie Sturman formed the Pretoria Ballet Club and this in turn led to the Johannesburg

Festival Ballet Society. High standards were set by both these companies in spite of their amateur status – dancers had to buy their own shoes and pay their travelling expenses. Nevertheless, performances were given, not only in Pretoria and Johannesburg, but in other towns in the Transvaal and in Durban, Natal.

A semi-professional company, called Ballet Theatre, was formed in 1948. It achieved a degree of recognition in 1956 when Margot Fonteyn and Michael Somes appeared as guest artists in *Swan Lake Act II* with a corps of local dancers trained by Marjorie Sturman. Sadly, this triumph was short-lived as financial difficulties caused the company to disband. The same year also saw the end of the Johannesburg Festival Ballet Society, in spite of some financial assistance from the City Council.

In 1960, Yvonne Mounsey, returned to South Africa. Born in Pretoria, she had established an international reputation with the New York City Ballet. On her return to the Transvaal she was horrified to discover the lack of opportunities for young dancers. Together with Denise Schultze and Faith de Villiers she formed the company which eventually became the Johannesburg City Ballet. The Transvaal Education Department subsidised performances in schools. By 1962, the company had become sufficiently professional to stage *Coppélia* with guest artists Maryon Lane and David Blair.

A year later, the Performing Arts Council of the Transvaal was formed. Under the aegis of this council, the PACT Ballet was formed with the Johannesburg City Ballet as its core. Three other performing arts councils were formed at the same time in Cape Province, Natal and the Orange Free State and each of these established a ballet company. Previously, each state had been plagued by the same troubles in establishing a ballet company as the Transvaal. The University of Cape Town Ballet School, founded by Dulcie Howes, has an impressive list of past pupils, including John Cranko, Alfred Rodrigues and Patricia Miller. A company developed from the school which in 1949, gave performances of *Swan Lake* and *Giselle* with guest artists Alicia Markova and Anton Dolin.

The Cape Town Ballet Club, later called the South African National Ballet, merged with the University company and these eventually formed the nucleus of the CAPAB Ballet in 1963. The Cape Town Ballet Club gave the first South African performance of *Les Sylphides* which was, unbelievably, staged as a curtain-raiser to a Boris Karloff film.

The NAPAC Ballet was formed in a similar way in 1965, from the Durban Ballet Club which was founded by Kathleen Rodney. The Orange Free State Group was formed mainly from students but became a full-time professional company in 1965 and changed its name to the PACOFS Ballet.

The establishment of subsidised provincial companies brought about an increase in dance activity in South Africa generally. The companies all gave regular performances of the major classics and mainstream works – *Giselle, The Firebird, Cinderella, Swan Lake, Romeo and Juliet, The Nutcracker, Les Sylphides, The Rake's Progress* and *Les Patineurs*. In addition a series of very popular lunch-hour performances was introduced by the CAPAB and PACT Ballets. These lunch-time performances also gave young South African choreographers an opportunity to present new works.

The PACT company established a considerable reputation with the first major South African ballet, *Raka*, with choreography by Frank Staff and music commissioned specially from Graham Newcater. A number of international figures have been associated with the company including Roland Petit who produced *Carmen*, Yvette Chauviré, Beryl Grey, Eva Evdokimova, Merle Park, Natalia Makarova, Peter Breuer and Anthony Dowell.

It was thought that, once the four principal companies were firmly established, the next development would be a national company. Thus South

Africa would be able to reverse the trend of losing its most talented dancers to foreign companies and not only provide them with opportunities in South Africa, but also attract dancers from other countries. This plan, however, has yet to be realized and has, in fact, suffered major setbacks. In the early 1970s, financial difficulties caused the Orange Free Street company to disband. In 1976 the NAPAC ballet gave its last season. Professional ballet is now centred on the PACT company. There are some signs however, that some of these companies are re-forming for a few performances and CAPAB remains active. It is to be hoped that some time in the future there will be more opportunities to expand professional dance in South Africa.

The Company

Artistic Directors:	Denise Schultze	**Choreologist:**	Carolyn Platau
	Louis Godfrey	**Guest Teachers:**	Marjorie Sturman
Head of Ballet:	Basil Taylor		Audrey King
Ballet Master:	James Riveros		

Principal Dancers:	Faye Daniel	Dawn Weller	James Riveros
	Maxine Denys	Malcolm Burn	Bruce Simpson
	Sianne Strasberg	Edgardo Hartley	

Soloists:	Arlene Juta	Elba Rey	Eugene Christensen
	Nicola Middlemist	Michael Baker	Terence Etheridge
	Gwen Morris	Anthony Bridgman	David Picken

The Repertoire

Giselle 1963
Capriccio 1963
Swan Lake 1963
Sylvia 1964
The Nutcracker 1964
La Giara 1964
Aurora's Wedding 1965
Les Patineurs 1965
Carmen 1965
Cinderella 1966
Czernyana III 1966
Symphonie 29 1967
Divertissements 1967
Le Coq d'Or 1967
Festival in Zaragoza 1967
Raka 1967
The Witchboy 1968
Transfigured Night 1968
Concerto 1968
Symphony for Sylphs 1968
Walpurgisnacht 1968
The Firebird 1968
Five Faces of Euridice 1968
Coppélia 1968
Serenade 1969
Death of a Matador 1969
Les Chats 1969
Les Amants Eternals 1969
La Fille Mal Gardée 1969

Les Sylphides 1970
Polovetsian Dances from Prince Igor 1970
Romeo and Juliet 1970
The Sleeping Beauty 1971
Les Rendezvous 1971
The Dream 1971
Don Quixote Pas de Deux 1971
Capriccio Espagnol 1971
Souvenir 1972
La Bayadère 1973
Graduation Ball 1973
Nongause 1973
Peter and the Wolf 1973
Legend of the Sea 1973
The Seasons 1973
Pas de Fiancées 1974
Suite Romantique 1974
Le Corsair 1974
Scheherazade 1975
La Chamade 1975
Flower Festival Pas de Deux 1975
Dvořák Variations 1975
Vespri 1975
Seven Deadly Sins 1975
Paquita 1975
The Gifts 1975
Afternoon of a Faun 1975
Floristan Pas de Trois 1976

ISRAEL
Bat-Dor Dance Company of Israel

Bat-Dor means 'contemporary' in Hebrew and this very appropriate name epitomizes the company. A young company, the Bat-Dor aims to present a changing repertoire of modern dance which, although firmly rooted in the Graham technique, absorbs new influences from both inside and outside the world of dance.

Moreover the Bat-Dor is an essentially Israeli company with distinctive national characteristics and concerns. The emphasis is on team-work and much of the repertoire is designed for the entire company or for groups of dancers rather than for individual displays of virtuosity. Many of the choreographers and composers who have created work for the Bat-Dor are Israeli and the company has a policy to encourage native talent. Some of the ballets created by the Bat-Dor reflect national concerns. *And After . . .* by Gene Hill Sagan is dedicated to a friend of the choreographer killed in the Yom Kippur War and the ballet is designed against a background of a stylized map of the Golan Heights.

It would be wrong, however, to suggest that the Bat-Dor is isolationist for, although it likes to think of itself as representative of Israel's talent and spirit, it is also open to influences from other parts of the world and is part of that process of cross-pollination which makes dance such an exciting artistic field. Jeanette Ordman, Artistic Director, principal dancer, choreographer and, virtually the founder of the company, was born in South Africa and danced with the Johannesburg Festival Ballet. She has studied in both Britain and the United States and, in fact, her teaching programme is modelled on that of the British Royal Academy of Dancing. The dancers themselves come from a wide variety of backgrounds – Cyprus, USSR, Holland, Germany, Poland, the United States, France, Australia and Brazil. The choreographers whose work features in the repertoire of the Bat-Dor are an equally cosmopolitan selection – Alvin Ailey, Robert Cohan, Charles Czarny, Michel Descombey, Walter Gore, Lar Lubovitch, Gene Hill Sagan, Paul Sanasardo and Paul Taylor.

The Bat-Dor Company grew out of the Bat-Dor Studios which were opened in Tel-Aviv in 1967 under the direction of Jeanette Ordman. She herself studied classical ballet in Britain and when she went to Israel in 1964 she opened her own school where she gave intensive courses in the British Royal Academy of Dancing method to teachers. She arranged for an RAD examiner to come from Britain once a year and this tradition is still carried on in the Bat-Dor Studios.

Later, Jeanette Ordman made an intensive study of modern dance, travelling to the United States to do so. When she returned to Israel, she founded the Bat-Dor Studios. The school now has about 600 pupils who study classical ballet from the age of six, and modern dance, based on the Graham technique, from the age of 10. In 1975 the school extended by opening a branch in Beersheva.

The company itself was created in 1968 with Jeanette Ordman as Artistic Director. Growing out of the school, it has a strong classical basis blended with the fluidity of contemporary dance. It is unique in Israel being the only professional company with its own theatre and a closely linked school.

Bat-Dor tours frequently through Israel, performing in many of the main

Miriam Zamir is partnered by David Dvir in Paul Taylor's Duet. *The large and varied repertoire includes works by many major contemporary choreographers and new works are regularly added.*

cities and rural kibbutzim, which act as centres for the performing arts outside urban areas. The company has also made successful visits to Holland, Italy and Austria and made extended tours of the Far East and Latin America in 1972 and 1973. In 1974, it was invited to appear at the Edinburgh Festival in Scotland. A trip to South Africa in 1976 ensured the company's reputation in yet another part of the world.

The Company	**Artistic Director:**	Jeanette Ordman
	Assistant to the	
	Artistic Director:	Laverne Meyer
	Assistant Rehearsal	
	Directors:	Dafna Rathouse
		Siki Kol
	Principal Dancers:	Igal Berdichevsky
		Yehuda Maor
		Jeanette Ordman
		Miriam Zamir

The Repertoire

Accent Now (Beck)
According to Eve (Butler)
Amazing Grace (Keuter)
And After . . . (Sagan)
Angels and Others (Sanders)
Antiphon (Anthony)
A Time When (Sanders)
Bachinanas Brasileiras (Sanders)
Beach (Gore)
Beyond the Mirror (Perry)
Black Angel (Butler)
Carnival (Sanasardo)
Circles (Descombey)
Concerto (Wright)
Concerto Grosso (Czarny)
Contrasts (Harkarvy)
Couples (van Dantzig)
Cuts (Maor)
Dance Macabre (Wright)
Dance Pictures (Gore)
Dark Elegies (Tudor)
Deadlines (Alum)
Dream, A Little Dream of Me, Sweetheart (Keuter)
Duet (Taylor)
Etudes Chorégraphiques (Descombey)
Fall Gently on thy Head (Keuter)
Fandango (Tudor)
From Hope to Hope (Descombey)
He and She (Sharon)
Horizons in Violet and Blue (Alexandrovitch)
Icarus (Hoving)
Ilanot (Alum)
Images (van Dantzig)
Impressions (Sanders)
In a Clearing (Lubovitch)
In a White Space (Czarny)
I Shall Sing to Thee in the Valley of the Dead, My Beloved (Reiter-Soffer)
Jibe (Redlich)
Juana (Alum)
Judgement of Paris (Tudor)
Kaleidoscope (Hoving)
Likrat (Maor)
Little Improvisations (Tudor)
Little Hell (Sanasardo)

Maya Light (Ordman)
Metallics (Sanasardo)
Mirage (Reiter-Soffer)
Movements in a Rocky Landscape (van Dantzig)
Myth (Sanasardo)
Night Creatures (Ailey)
Night Island (van Dantzig)
Palomas (Alum)
Pearl River (Sanasardo)
Peepshow (Gore)
Phases (Reiter-Soffer)
Place of Change (Cohan)
Poem of Joy (Lubovitch)
Prism (Sharon)
Prologue (Maslow)
Requiem for Sounds (Sagan)
Shakers (Humphrey)
Signalement (Descombey)
Sketches for Nostalgic Children (Sanasardo)
Solitudes (Descombey)
Songs (Anthony)
Stigmata (Redlich)
Streams (Ailey)
Sunny Day (Czarny)
The Bacchae (Maslow)
The Great Peacock (Wright)
The Lovers (Walker)
The Other Us (Carey)
The Serpent (Carey)
The Song of Deborah (Reiter-Soffer)
The Time Before the Time After (Lubovitch)
The Wait (Descombey)
Three Epitaphs (Taylor)
Three Psalms (Walker)
Threshold (Ordman)
Tzaikerk (Cohan)
Us, Them and Everyone (Czarny)
Variations (Wright)
Victim (Gore)
Voices (Sanasardo)
Walls (Sanders)
Whirligogs (Lubovitch)

Touring

Year		Year	
1970	Italy, Malta		France, Holland
1971	Rome, Florence, Vienna, Frankfurt	1973	Brazil, Argentina, Uruguay, Chile, Peru, Venezuela, Mexico
1972	Hongkong, Thailand, Singapore, Korea, Japan, Philippines, Burma, Switzerland,	1974	Great Britain
		1975	South Africa

JAPAN
The Tokyo Ballet Company

As communications and travel grew easier and the world became 'smaller', the essentially non-oriental art of ballet reached Japan and was accepted with enthusiasm and delight. Schools and amateur performing companies of variable standards proliferated. One such school was the Tokyo Ballet School, but Japan had also inherited the problems of the West and financial difficulties forced the school to close in 1964.

The students found themselves without any sense of purpose or direction. A few returned to provincial companies with which they had danced previously and others were invited to join. A relatively unknown young man, Tadatsugu Sasaki, President of Japan Art Staff Incorporated, who had been associated with the technical aspects of the school's performances, suggested that the dancers should form a new Ballet Company. This they did, under his leadership, and in August 1964, Japan's first truly professional ballet company was formed.

Swan Lake and *Marimo* had featured in the school's performing repertoire and the new company wisely decided to begin its activities with these two works. It began by making a national tour with *Swan Lake* and then performing this in Tokyo the following January and February. Later in the same year it performed *Marimo* in the capital. However, Tadatsugu Sasaki was not satisfied by simply re-staging old versions. Instead, A. Varlamov and S. Messerer were invited to act as advisers to the new company and they revised and improved the two works.

In 1966, Olga Tarasova of the Bolshoi Theatre was invited to Tokyo to train the dancers. A brilliant dancer, she was already well-known and greatly admired in Japan. While she was working with the company she staged the Bolshoi Ballet's version of *Giselle* and directed Prokofiev's *Ala and Lolli*. These additions to the repertoire proved very successful and shortly after their introduction, the company made its first tour abroad, visiting the USSR. During this tour it performed *Marimo* and *The Four Seasons of Japan* and these were well received.

In 1967, the company visited the major cities of Japan. Also, in the same year, a new Ballet Master was appointed, Zurab Kikaleishvili. The following year two major guest artists, Maya Plisetskaya and Nicholai Fadeechev, appeared with the Tokyo Ballet in *Swan Lake*. This proved tremendously successful and marked the beginning of a series of many guest appearances from some of the world's leading dancers, including Bessmertnova, Lavrovsky, Alicia Alonso, Heinz Bosl, Denard and Margot Fonteyn, many of whom made repeated visits. The challenge of working with such leading figures has been very stimulating for the Japanese dancers and set them high professional standards.

As well as guest dancers, many guest teachers went to Japan to work with the company. This has given the company the immense advantage of a broad dance background and the opportunity to study a wide variety of different styles from both the European and Soviet traditions. In 1969, Michel Descombey, who had been teaching at the Paris Opera, was invited to create *Mandala* and *Saracenia*. The contrast between Michel Descombey's contemporary approach and the classicism of the company's Russian training proved exciting for both the dancers and their audiences. The success of

Michel Descombey's visit encouraged the Tokyo Ballet to invite other foreign teachers and Ballet Masters. In 1972 Alberto Alonso of the National Ballet of Cuba was invited to direct his famous version of *Carmen* which had been staged at the Bolshoi Theatre, with Maya Plisetskaya in the title role. Working closely with this choreographer and understanding his imaginative approach to such an exciting and passionate story was an immensely fruitful experience for the company. Other ballet masters who have worked with it include Galina Ulanova and Yuri Grigorovich.

As well as the invaluable assistance of foreign teachers, the Tokyo Ballet company has a regular Japanese teacher, Hideteru Kitahara. He is a virile and agile dancer and an exacting teacher. Determined and devoted to his art, he is delighted to co-operate with guest ballet masters and learn from them. The demands he makes on himself are as great as those he makes upon the company and so he has established a relationship of mutual respect essential to development.

The company has been committed to a policy of obtaining the best assistance available since its inception and this attitude extends to ballet orchestras. A Japanese conductor who specializes in ballet music has yet to emerge but Tadatsugu Sasaki tackled this aspect of the company's work with the same enthusiastic and practical approach he applied to dancers and teachers, inviting leading conductors from abroad to take part in guest seasons. The close association with Soviet Ballet extended to Soviet conductors. Vladimir Edelman of the Stanislavsky-Danchenko Theatre and Wahtang Paliashvili of the Tbilisi Opera and Ballet Theatre, Georgia, were guest conductors in 1967 and 1968. In 1970 Michel Queval of the Paris Opera was invited to visit Tokyo and has remained unofficially in charge of major productions since.

The company has formed close associations with this wide range of guest artists mainly through a number of successful overseas tours. Besides several tours in the USSR, in the early 1970s the Tokyo Ballet made an extensive visit to Europe, travelling to 40 cities in eight countries. The appearance of a Japanese company aroused great interest in Western ballet audiences who approached this new phenomenon with some doubts. These misgivings proved quite without foundation and audiences were delighted by the delicate and graceful treatment of the great classics.

1964 was an eventful and memorable year for Japan with major industrial and technological advances, besides the Olympic Games in Tokyo. However, the founding of the Tokyo Ballet was certainly the most creative event of that year. The company has developed and expanded rapidly. New rehearsal rooms have been opened and a school with 130 pupils established. Gala performances with many of the world's leading dancers are regularly presented. The corps de ballet has strengthened and several promising soloists have emerged. Japan has taken to ballet with enormous enthusiasm and its first professional company has quickly achieved major status and looks forward to an exciting future.

The Company

Artistic Director:	Hideteru Kitahara	

Principal Dancers:	Chie Abe	Seiko Sakurai
	Makoto Fukuyama	Hiroko Tomoda
	Kahoru Inoue	Yuko Tomoda
	Hideteru Kitahara	Umeko Wainai
	Mikifumi Nagata	Yukiko Yasuda
	Chikahisa Natsuyama	

The Repertoire

Ala and Lolli	*Les Sylphides*
Carmen	*Mandala*
Cinderella	*Marimo*
Concerto Prokofiev	*Saracenia*
Flower Festival at Genzano	*Swan Lake*
Giselle	*The Nutcracker*
Le Palais de Cristal	*The Sea and the Pearls*

Touring

The company has made several visits to the USSR and extensive tours of Europe and South East Asia.

The Tokyo Ballet is a very recent addition to the dance scene. However, the dancers' polished technique, elegance of line and sheer charm have ensured an international reputation. The company has made successful tours in Europe, Asia and the USSR. The

Picture Credits

Michel Fokine's lyrical and romantic ballet Les Sylphides *is featured in the repertoires of almost every major classical company in the world. At the front, Maris Liepa is shown in the Bolshoi Ballet's superb production. At the back, the Tokyo Ballet is seen in the same work.*